Student Engagement
Identity, Motivation and
Community

Student Engagement
Identity, Motivation and
Community

LIBRI
PUBLISHING

First published in 2013 by Libri Publishing

Copyright © Libri Publishing

Authors retain copyright of individual chapters.

The right of Claus Nygaard, Stuart Brand, Paul Bartholomew and Luke Millard to be identified as the editors of this work has been asserted in accordance with the Copyright, Designs and Patents Act, 1988.

ISBN 978 1 907471 65 0

A CIP catalogue record for this book is available from The British Library

Cover design by Helen Taylor

Design by Carnegie Publishing

Printed in the UK by Short Run Press Ltd

Libri Publishing
Brunel House
Volunteer Way
Faringdon
Oxfordshire
SN7 7YR

Tel: +44 (0)845 873 3837

www.libripublishing.co.uk

Contents

The Glass Ceiling in Student Engagement
Liam Burns   vii

Foreword to Student Engagement: Identity, Motivation
and Community
Professor Craig Mahoney   xi

Chapter 1   Why Student Engagement Matters
Luke Millard, Paul Bartholomew, Stuart Brand & Claus Nygaard   1

Chapter 2   Student Engagement with Learning Resources in
Art & Design: Seeding Possibilities
Sian Everitt Vaughan and Grace Williams   17

Chapter 3   The Effects on Student Engagement of Employing
Students in Professional Roles
Paul Summers, Daisy Pearson, Samuel Gough and Jan Siekierski   35

Chapter 4   Graduate Interns: A Changed Identity as a
Consequence of a Hybrid Role
Mercedes Chambers and Luke Nagle   55

Chapter 5   Social Media and Employability – Creating New
Resources with Students
Mark Ashfield, David Harte and Vanessa Jackson   71

Chapter 6   All Aboard: Using the Student Advisory Board to
Engage Students with University Decision Making
Processes
Sophie Rowe, Emily Cooper and Lynn Fulford   91

Chapter 7   Student Employment and the Impact on Student
Motivations and Attitudes towards University
Ixchelt Acevedo Montesinos, Derek Cassidy and Luke Millard   109

Chapter 8   Differential Student Engagement: Lessons Learned
Caroline Hutchings, Nicola Bartholomew and Oonagh Reilly   125

Chapter 9   Problem-based Learning: Student and Tutor
Perspectives
Kathleen Donnelly and Naomi Francis   145

Chapter 10 Media Industries Beyond the Curriculum: Motivating
Blended Professionalism for Enhanced Student
Engagement and Employability
Kerry Gough, Jamie Morris and Amie Hession   165

Chapter 11 Student Engagement: Enabling Academic Success
through Dynamic Partnerships
Wal Warmington, Trevor Hodge, Sheikh Sela and Anil Kainth 185

Chapter 12 By Appointment to Birmingham City University
Students: Promoting Student Engagement through
Partnership Working
Amanda Andrews, Joanne Jeffries and Bernie St Aubyn 199

Chapter 13 Social Media: An Effective Way to Build a
Community and Develop Partnerships to Promote
Student Engagement?
Emma Flint and James Roden 213

Chapter 14 Beyond the Curriculum: Deepening Reflective
Practice and Widening Student Engagement
David Chapman and Atief Ishaq 235

Chapter 15 Engaging Students as Practitioners through
Experiential Learning
Hannah Phillips, Tom Craig and Christie Phillips 251

Chapter 16 Lightening Up the Dark Side: a Partnership
Approach between a Students' Union and the
University
Paul Chapman, Sarah Blatchford and Elgan Hughes 271

Collected Bibliography 291

The Glass Ceiling in Student Engagement

Liam Burns

President of the National Union of Students in the UK

Student engagement has come a long way in recent history, but sometimes it feels like we've reached a self-imposed glass ceiling. The rhetoric of partnership, student-centred learning and co-creation of learning are not simple concepts and delivering them in reality, and not just in institutional documents, is a real challenge for universities across the globe. *Student Engagement: Identity, Motivation and Community* represents an incredibly powerful attempt to shed light on what partnership could look like in a 21st century institution and goes a long way to teasing out why our goal should be far from simply boosting student numbers on university committees or avoiding students' representatives acting in isolation from where decisions are actually made in the name of autonomy.

Student bodies in the UK are grappling with a shift from centralising representation and services on a few elected officials to empowering students across institutions to make change for themselves. Indeed creating active citizens is one of the most powerful yet under-discussed outcomes of working with students as partners; this document makes a huge contribution to how that benefit can be realised.

For the UK specifically, as the Government tries, and in many regards fails, to create a demand led revolution in quality and standards through ever increasing the individual's contribution to Higher Education, it would be very easy for students to revert to a "consumer" approach to their learning. The status quo is not tenable, so the case studies in these pages represent a response based on partnership and not of transaction;

a timely contribution to our work at the National Union of Students (NUS) in creating a "Manifesto for Partnership" (NUS, 2012) which will grow into how we can revolutionise institutional governance to reflect these principles.

But the challenge is not just to institutions and decision makers in the sector but to the student body itself. We have long cherished the independence of Students' Unions and representative bodies on campus but independence is important only when there are levers to pull. *Student Engagement: Identity, Motivation and Community* confronts us with an important question; what is the point of a Students' Union insisting on acting in isolation to the detriment of being able to create any change for its members? A relationship based on partnership can be flexible. If moments come when students and the institution aren't in agreement then the guiding values and objectives of the partnership can be revisited. Holding independence as sacrosanct will almost certainly mean that no movement is achievable at times of disagreement and is perhaps untenable in an age where the concept of the student body as a homogenous group becomes less and less relevant.

However institutions must also understand that insisting on partnership in the absence of concrete powers for students when there is totemic disagreement becomes disingenuous and vacuous – in an age where students perceive themselves increasingly to be funding the system, such a position is untenable. For that reason in one sense what Birmingham City University has achieved is new, bold and innovative; in another sense, it's exactly what Students' Unions have always sought to do – empower students to shape their own learning on campus and be active citizens everywhere else.

These two roles are not irreconcilable but require honesty in the tensions they create and hard work to resolve them. We must all believe in student leadership and the guiding principle that student representation should be student led. But if you believe in student leadership then you have also to accept that leadership takes compromise, dialogue and partnership working to achieve joint goals. Where Birmingham City University's work is powerful is in its attempt to achieve cultural change throughout the institution rather than rushing to structural, piece meal change on a handful of committees.

For me, it is this relationship where the work described within this book makes a huge contribution. If we are to move beyond student engagement being reduced to the number of students on committees, the response rate of institutional surveys or a "you said, we did" culture of passive focus groups and module evaluation, then institutions and student representative bodies alike have to question some of the long held dogma on how universities and students should interact.

The heartening fact, as other institutions embark on this work, is that students are up for it. Our research continuously shows that whilst students want to be more engaged in the creation of their own learning, they increasingly feel removed from it. Too often we presume that engaging students will result in calls for shiny buildings in response to a "consumer" environment, rather than pedagogical change as part of a learning community. This book gives a robust challenge to that assertion.

Student Engagement: Identity, Motivation and Community is risky and bold. Am I comfortable with all of it? No, but it has always been Students' Unions who have pioneered the student movement and Birmingham City University Students' Union's contribution to this document is no exception. In fact they have been recognised nationally for their work in this area. Their challenge is that we see a step change in how we view students and Students' Unions – as practitioners and change agents, not just in the academic sphere, but in widening access, research and community engagement; only then will "student engagement" break through a rhetorical glass ceiling and reach for far more lofty goals of a genuine learning community. I have no doubt that the seeds planted by this work will result in just that.

Liam Burns
January 2013

Foreword to Student Engagement: Identity, Motivation and Community

Professor Craig Mahoney, Chief Executive,
Higher Education Academy

As international higher education continues to experience considerable growth, with communities across the African nations, India and south-east Asia experiencing huge demand that outstrips supply, the need to constantly review the learning landscapes of mature higher education systems remains a constant challenge. The UK higher education system has undergone considerable metamorphosis in recent years, with the devolution for higher education to the separate nations enabling them to differentiate their offer, most notably in the way the systems are funded, but also in the way they create distinctiveness in research and education. In England this has resulted in fees rising to a maximum of £9,000 per year for students commencing their study from September 2012.

In times of transformation and especially when the financial demands on prospective students change, the relationships between the student and the university, or more crudely between the customer and the provider, will modify and expectations are likely to rise. Accordingly universities with a progressive approach to change have been considering how the resultant impact arising from fee increases might be reconciled as they attempt to more overtly develop the student experience.

The Higher Education Academy (HEA) as the national body with responsibility for enhancing learning and teaching in higher education in the UK, have been working with institutions across the higher education system to help bring about change in learning and teaching, deliberately to improve outcomes for students. The work presented in the excellent publication *Student Engagement: Identity, Motivation and Community* aligns strongly with the work of the HEA and provides a range of stimulating ideas presented by academics and students who are sharing research, knowledge, ideas and solutions in a comprehensive university environment. The case studies, testimonials, research findings and analyses should not be interpreted as a single solution or panacea, but rather opportunities for the reader to review credible action research examples of how changes in student engagement can enable outstanding impact and sometimes unintended positive consequences. Reading the book and engaging with the varied content over 16 chapters, you will find a range of stimulating examples of student–staff working that is making a real difference to achievement, perception, learning and opportunity.

Throughout the book, authors have taken the opportunity to encourage student experiences, gained from many years of learning prior to university, to influence and inform how the learning environment and the way enhancement might be developed in partnership with academic staff, can change. The close working between staff and students remains ever present throughout the book. Readers are encouraged to consider how they have experienced the integration of student knowledge in learning and teaching, or how students have been empowered to influence the learning and teaching processes. The clear and obvious encouragement to share practice, acknowledge cultural difference and improve skills remains a strong theme throughout the book.

The book takes an applied approach to evidence-based change and gives an insight into potential and opportunity from a practitioner perspective. Using a series of compelling case studies, for example the experience of employment of students across the university and the impact this has had on perception, improved relationships, opportunity, skill development and confidence, the reader is encouraged to consider the potential for similar initiatives in other institutions. Working with media studies students, some excellent examples of how social media can be used as an enhancement tool linked to employability, provides a compelling story linked to the changing opportunities our modern world and technology brings, and how this might be better integrated into the wider role of higher education.

Students' Unions across the UK have historically taken a political and advocacy role in the past. Modern students have however, sought a more dynamic interaction between their Students' Unions and the university. Accordingly the rebirth of unions in a new relationship with their university is nicely evidenced in this publication. Close working and learning through partnership strongly presented in the chapter by Chapman, Blatchford and Hughes, where dimensions of student engagement previously defined by the HEA, is brought to life in a compelling story of partnership. Enabling the student voice to have a role across all aspects of the university mission is an increasingly common model in a modern and progressive university system. This chapter provides some excellent insights into an approach taken by this large urban university.

Finally I want to commend this publication as an excellent resource for all higher education institutions as they grapple with the increasingly complex environment they are experiencing, where the spotlight on student experience is becoming increasingly bright, regardless of mission, vision, size, complexity or country of delivery. As CEO of the HEA it is encouraging to see such wonderful examples of a diverse range of approaches taken to support the enhancement of the student experience, recognising that working with students as partners and co-producers of knowledge, can have significant and tangible benefits to not only the student, but to the staff, the institution and the development of future learning landscapes for the next generation of leaders that will enter our esteemed institutions seeking knowledge, learning, development and life-changing experiences.

Craig Mahoney
11th January 2013

Chapter 1

Why Student Engagement Matters

Luke Millard, Paul Bartholomew, Stuart Brand & Claus Nygaard

Student engagement as a driver for institutional and individual development

Student engagement has become a hot topic in universities around the world, much in time with the increasing acknowledgment of student-centred learning practices. Listening to the student voice has long been institutionalised as common practice, be it through student surveys, focus group interviews, or other types of methods for harvesting students' opinions of relevance to the education in question. However, working with ways in which to improve the student experience (Harvey, 2001) requires more than such traditional student surveys. Contextualised evaluation in higher education where goals, practices and results are closely related (Nygaard & Belluigi, 2011) suggests a plausible way forward, where student voice and student role are integrated as important parameters in the development of an engaged student culture. Looking at student culture, there seems to be a benefit for both students and institutions if they succeed in creating a culture where students perceive themselves as partners or employees rather than as pupils or customers (Löfvall & Nygaard, 2012). While pupils wait for the teacher to tell them what to do in the light of the traditional teacher-pupil relation in the classical education institution, and customers expect teachers to fulfil their expectations seeing the university as a (paid for) knowledge provider, it is rather different with partners and employees. Students as partners seek to bridge their own learning process with extracurricular activities as they think of the university as a network for developing learning relations in which they have to invest resources themselves in order to be able to self-develop. Students as employees perceive their own role much along the same lines, as they perceive their study as a full-time study and see their time in university as a full time job. They focus on developing a workplace community among fellow students and faculty also through engagement in curricular and extracurricular activities (Löfvall & Nygaard, 2012). In the light of student culture, it is understandable that universities succeeding in developing a partnership or workplace culture will benefit from highly engaged students.

While student engagement is obviously positive for university culture, maybe the main argument for working with student engagement should be that it leads to improved learning outcomes of students. Arguments have been put forward that engaged students find their learning personally meaningful, they believe the learning tasks are challenging, they find that accomplishing learning tasks is worthy of their time, and they focus on improving their performance and keep on working even when they encounter difficulties (Schlechty, 2011). Published cases of learning and teaching practice have shown a diversity of ways to engage students so that their learning outcomes were enhanced. Waite *et al.* (2009) showed how students were engaged in their own learning processes through outdoor learning fostering unstructured and spontaneous environments for learning. Kumar (2009) showed how students were engaged in their own learning processes through modelling professional assessment centres in their curriculum. Papadimitriou (2009) showed how students were engaged in their own learning processes through teamwork and portfolios in a physical classroom setting. Lange (2010) showed how students were engaged in their own learning processes through creative conversations and critical reviews of their own work. All cases show remarkably positive signs of student engagement and improvement in student learning outcomes.

Engaging students as academic writers

As can be seen above, there are multiple sources pointing towards the advantage of developing both institutional practices and teaching and learning practices for student engagement and subsequent learning outcomes. This book itself, with its multiple chapters reporting on student engagement is a prime and current example of this.

One major aspect of this book distinguishes it remarkably from any other published work on student engagement. Not only is this book dealing in depth with cases of student engagement, more importantly it is itself a product of true student engagement, as all chapters are written in close collaboration between students and staff at Birmingham City University (BCU) in the UK.

The idea for this collaborative writing project was fostered at the beginning of 2012 in dialogues between LIHE (The International Academic Association for the Enhancement of Learning-Centred Higher Education) and CELT (the Centre for Enhancement of Learning and Teaching at BCU), the Students' Union at Birmingham City University and Libri Publishing Ltd.

February 2012: circulation of symposium call

March 26-27, 2012: launch meetings at BCU. Hear about the project!

May 7, 2012: submission of three-page chapter proposal for double-blind review

May 14, 2012: notification to authors of accepted chapter proposals

May 21, 2012: editorial meeting with all authors of accepted chapters

September 1, 2012: submission of full chapters

October 16-18, 2012: residential writing symposium at Wroxall Abbey

November 1, 2012: submission of finalised chapter for editorial reviews

January 11, 2013: manuscript finalised for printing

April 2013: anthology published worldwide

April 2013: anthology presented at book launch at BCU

Table 1: Important deadlines of the collaborative writing project at BCU.

A symposium call with the title: "Student Engagement through Partnership" was distributed throughout BCU during February 2012 in which it stated:

> *"Students and staff at BCU are invited to contribute to the writing of the anthology 'Student engagement through partnership' showcasing the good collaborative practices taking place between students and staff at BCU. The anthology will be published worldwide by Libri Publishing Ltd. Join*

fellow authors for an inspiring and productive project that culminates with a residential symposium at the magnificent Wroxall Abbey where all participating authors will meet from October 16-18, 2012 to review, edit and finalise their chapters for publication." (LIHE/BCU symposium call, 2012:2).

Further, students and staff were motivated to participate in the writing project with the following one-liners:

"Why participate?

* as a student you will:

- *share your ideas and approaches to teaching and learning at BCU*

- *influence how teaching and learning is developed and carried out at BCU in the future*

- *share your student culture with students and staff across faculties*

- *work closely together with members of staff who are interested in student and staff partnerships*

- *participate in an inspiring and much rewarding process of writing a chapter for an international anthology to be published worldwide by a recognised publishing house*

- *boost your academic skills and your writing skills*

- *be enriched by participating in a collaborative residential symposium*

* as a member of staff you will:

- *work closely together with students and other members of staff who are interested in student and staff partnerships*

- *get direct feedback from students about their engagement in teaching and learning activities at BCU*

- *share your own ideas and approaches to teaching and learning at BCU*

- *influence how teaching and learning is developed and carried out at BCU in the future*

- *participate in an inspiring and rewarding process of writing a chapter for an international anthology to be published worldwide by a recognised publishing house*

- be enriched by participating in a collaborative residential symposium"
(LIHE/BCU symposium call, 2012:3).

Two launch meetings were arranged during lunch breaks on March 26 and 27, 2012 where a total of almost 100 people showed up to hear more about the writing project. Some students came alone, some staff members came alone, and some potential writing groups of staff and students had already formed on the basis of the symposium call and they arrived together. Director of CELT at BCU, Professor Stuart Brand introduced the project and his visions for the project as a driver for further developing a culture of partnership at BCU. Director of LIHE, Professor Claus Nygaard introduced the LIHE symposium model which would drive the project towards the finalising of the manuscript for publication, and Managing Director of Libri Publishing Ltd. Paul Jervis talked about the review process and quality benchmarks of the publishing house.

May 7, 2012 saw the submission of 23 chapter proposals written in collaboration between 52 authors (29 students and 23 faculty members). After a double-blind review process involving international members of the LIHE review panel had taken place 15 chapter proposals were accepted and 8 were rejected. All accepted authors were invited to an editorial meeting on May 21, 2012. Here Professor Claus Nygaard shared the project status and focused on his editorial interpretation of the reviewers' comments, while Professor Paul Bartholomew from CELT at BCU announced a potential clustering of chapters for the manuscript and formed collegial groups within each cluster, so authors of similar chapters could start sharing ideas and practices early in their writing phase. Writing teams were then seated together with the other writing teams within their cluster to discuss their various approaches to student engagement. Following this meeting staff and students had a little more than three months to write their full chapter for submission, during which they benefited from writing support at CELT at BCU.

Come September 1, 2012 the authors submitted 15 full chapters for the manuscript. Collegial review groups were formed, and all chapters were circulated to the participants for collegial reviews. During this period all four editors of the book made thorough reviews of the entire manuscript.

October 16–18, 2012 saw 33 authors participate in a very productive writing symposium at the secluded country estate Wroxall Abbey outside Birmingham. 15 students and 18 faculty members worked closely together, both within each writing team and across writing teams to help each other finalise all chapters for publication. Collegial reviews were shared, writing sessions were facilitated, and each writing team received four editorial reviews. Not only was the residential symposium a success in terms of academic writing (which can be seen from the following chapters), but it served to further create a unique sense of belonging, community and achievement within the wider group of faculty and students. Video testimonials from the participants are to be found online at www.lihe.info, and they clearly show how this symposium brought a further sense of belonging to BCU, and a certain proudness to be a part of the project and to show one's best practice to an outside community.

The period from December 1, 2012 to January 11, 2013 was used for intensive editorial work on the manuscript, which was then handed over to Libri Publishing Ltd. for publication and distribution.

April 2013 will see the book in bookstores worldwide, and a book launch at BCU inviting both students and faculty members to share the product of this unique and remarkable example of student engagement in a university setting. CELT at BCU has pre-ordered 500 copies of the book to hand out to students and faculty members to share not only the good story about the writing process and symposium itself, but more importantly the 15 cases of inspiring first-hand accounts from student and staff of pioneering student engagement practices at BCU.

Having talked intensively about the LIHE/BCU symposium above, let us broaden out the discussion of student engagement by contextualising it on a larger level. Although writing this book had the positive side effect of creating a learning community at BCU between students and staff from different faculties, we also believe that working with student engagement in a university setting has the potential to develop a learning community in many different ways.

This book's institutional context

Each of the chapters in this book is co-authored by students and staff; indeed, it was a requirement for being considered for inclusion that chapters went beyond descriptions of student/staff collaborations and actually emerged from student/staff co-authorship. This requirement emerges from, and is reflective of, our whole institutional approach to student engage-ment; an approach that places the notion of students working with staff, as partners in the improvement of the learning experience, at the centre of our institutional enhancement agenda. We acknowledge that as an institution we are not unique in working with students as partners, but we contend that few institutions have taken the strategic approach to student engage-ment that is a characteristic of Birmingham City University.

The initial aim of the student engagement activities at the University was to create a greater sense of learning community within the institu-tion. The institution, a large metropolitan university of 24,000 students, was a large university, spread across eight campuses with limited student or institutional aspiration for student engagement with a university-wide community. This context would typically translate into students attending a lecture and then returning to their extra-curricular lives off campus, with few becoming engaged with any other form of university activity. This was a concern for those at the University who wished to see students gain from a whole university experience and develop the skills and experiences that wider engagement might offer.

As a response to a consideration of this context, in 2008 the Univer-sity embarked upon a student engagement programme, led through the CELT with a new, strong partnership with Birmingham City Students' Union. This partnership was both pragmatically and symbolically effec-tive, offering new opportunities to reach students while demonstrating to all stakeholders a tangible commitment to new ways of working. The first output of this relationship with the Students' Union resulted in the crea-tion of the Student Academic Partners (SAP) scheme; an initiative that enabled students to be paid to work alongside staff on projects intended to enhance the learning experience of students, and often, the working lives of staff. At the time of writing, the SAP scheme has been operating for four years and supports over fifty projects every year – each with the potential to reinvigorate curriculum and improve students' learning experiences. Many of the projects identified in this book emerge from SAP projects and the success of the overall scheme has had an impact upon the University's approach to engaging with students, enabling other initiatives to be developed. Examples of follow-on initiatives include: a student academic mentoring programme and a collaborative projects scheme characterised by a multidisciplinary cross-faculty focus. Perhaps most significant though, is the opportunity the institution has had to become more aware of the value and ability of its own students.

An institutional partnership with Northwest Missouri State University (NWMSU) in the United States demonstrated to us a model for working with students that reveals, and capitalises upon, the broader value of students as a valuable (and valued) human resource. NWMSU's model of employing students across all university services demonstrated enormous potential for enhancing a sense of belonging and community through the creation of co-delivered services and shared vested interests. We too are embarked on a programme of widespread employment of our students and, like NWMSU are motivated by the enhanced levels of student engagement that cascade from such initiatives. Student employment is also discussed in chapters within this volume and such inclusion reflects the evolving journey that students and staff at the University are undertaking.

Developing the learning community through student engagement

In recent years student engagement seems to have become identified and accepted as a universal good across the university sector. It has reached the status of one of Foucault's regimes of truth (2000), being viewed as a panacea to solve a myriad of problems that students and the HE sector encounter. Kuh (2009:683) defined student engagement as *"the time and effort students devote to activities that are empirically linked to desired outcomes of college and what institutions do to induce students to participate in these activities"*. Although there are many definitions of student engagement in the literature, this one is particularly useful in our context as it reflects elements of the partnership nature of the relationship between the student and the university. For both to achieve the outcomes they seek, they need to work together and input their own time and resource.

In the UK, the introduction of higher student fees has engendered a debate around the perception of students in relation to higher education as a market; discussions about whether students should be viewed as consumers or partners abound. Our University has a clear position in relation to these discussions and this book could be seen as a testament to our institutional commitment to the 'students-as-partners' cause.

The policy background – partnership or consumerism

These developments are set against a rapidly evolving policy landscape. One of the first significant instances of a new consideration of the debate around the perception of the role of students in the new fee-paying UK higher education sector came in a report by the Quality Assurance Agency (2009). This was one of the first governance-based instances of the recognition that *"co-production could bring numerous benefits"*. It suggested that there may be a myriad of benefits from this approach which *"could lead to increased learner satisfaction, reduced student anxiety and greater understanding of learner needs, increased satisfaction amongst academic staff, and improved educational outcomes"*. The report also identified a number of reasons as to why the discourse of students as consumers had weaknesses and would in fact *"throw the system off balance"*. It drew upon the work of McCulloch (2009), which argued there were at least eight difficulties from such a consumer-based approach, which included increased student passivity, failure to encourage deep learning and the compartmentalisation of education as a product not a process. From an engagement perspective McCulloch also felt that consumerism would lead to students seeing themselves as individuals and increase competitiveness at the expense of generating the community.

More recently Gibbs (2012: 11) has explored the notion of students as consumers through a series of interviews with leaders in the sector and noted that:

> *"While there is a sense in which students are being treated as consumers of a product, institutions with good and improving NSS scores often have initiatives that engage students as co-producers of knowledge, or partners in an educational enterprise."*

The status of student engagement has been formally recognised within the governance of the UK Higher Education sector through the introduction by the Quality Assurance Agency (QAA) of a new UK Quality Code for Higher Education on Student Engagement (2012). This code, against which all universities will be judged during their institutional inspections, states that student engagement:

"covers two domains relating to:

• *Improving the motivation of students to engage in learning and to learn independently;*

• *The participations of students in quality enhancement and quality assurance processes, resulting in the improvement of their educational experience."*

The Quality Code actually goes further and explicitly identifies an expectation of Higher Education providers that they are required to meet, namely that: *"Higher Education providers take deliberate steps to engage all students, individually and collectively, as partners in the assurance and enhancement of their educational experience"*. Many of the chapters in this book demonstrate this partnership approach to quality enhancement.

As Trowler's (2010) review of student engagement literature identified *"policy levers such as funding frameworks, systemic assessment schemes and quality frameworks could have a significant impact on encouraging, or discouraging, an emphasis on student engagement at an institutional level"*. She asserted that if quality mechanisms queried learning rather than teaching, it *"would require institutions to focus on what students are actually doing, rather than on what the institutions are providing for them to do or not to do"*.

The position of the National Union of Students (NUS) in this developing paradigm is of great interest as it, like students, staff and universities, has been on a journey to understand the new financial imperatives and the resulting relationship between government, students and the HE sector. The NUS has moved significantly from its traditional approach of holding universities to account to one of seeking to work in partnership with universities to benefit its members.

The new NUS Manifesto for Partnership (2012) is a significant step in this development of position and acknowledges that *"student engagement as a policy priority is relatively recent"*. It has significant implications for the NUS: *"we are moving beyond a narrow focus on the validity of various systems of student representation and instead describing concepts linked to student identities and the potential of individuals to influence their environment"*. The role of identity within the student voice is a common theme amongst the chapters in this book and is explored in greater detail herein.

Perhaps it is not surprising that the NUS (2012) manifesto rejects the notion of student consumerism. "*The students as consumers model assumes that the experience of attending higher education is something that can be packaged and sold*" and negates the ability of students to influence their environment and learning. Further, it states that "*conceiving of students as consumers is a thoroughly impoverished way of describing the relationship between students and their institutions, which ought to be one of mutual trust, care and respect*". The value of engagement is highlighted in many chapters in this volume as students and staff recognise the changing relationship and students recognise particularly the value and trust placed with them.

The NUS also acknowledges the power implications of the consumer model, which in one light it may welcome as it should strengthen the power of students but in another is recognised as a potential risk: "*If we seek to engage students merely in order to find out what they want and give it to them, we reproduce this dangerous narrative of consumerism and lose sight of the responsibility of educators to challenge and stretch students*".

A new term has also entered the language of student engagement through the "*What works? Student retention and success*" programme co-ordinated through the Higher Education Academy. The resultant publication (Thomas, 2012) considered the evidence of seven national research projects into student retention and success and concluded that "*belonging is critical to student retention and success*". The evidence from the projects "*firmly points to the importance of students having a strong sense of belonging in HE, which is the result of engagement*".

Belonging is not something that a consumer of a service naturally feels when they purchase a good or a service, but it is something that can be generated through a shared partnership activity. Thomas believes that belonging is closely aligned to academic and social student engagement and defines belonging as "*students' subjective feelings of relatedness or connectedness to the institution*". Thomas highlights the work of Goodenow (1993) which described belonging in an educational environment as "*Students' sense of being accepted, valued, included and encouraged by others (teachers and peers) in the academic classroom setting and of feeling oneself to be an important part of the life and activity of the class*".

Gibbs (2012) states that "*students do not consume knowledge but* construct it in a personal way in the context of learning environments that include teaching: they are co-producers and collaborators". Through working with students as partners we believe we make them more effective and motivated learners. The chapters in this volume will reflect this belief. However, we also need to recognise that institutions may be being persuaded of the need to initiate student engagement at their institutions for reasons that are not about just benefitting students. As Gibbs (2012) states "improving students' effectiveness as learners has more impact on performance and learning gains than does improving teaching or improving curricula". If institutions see engagement as a mechanism to improve their own standings through improved student retention and success then, from one perspective, they could be said to be making the right move, if not perhaps for entirely altruistic reasons.

The next stage for the development of this area of work is that of scalability of engagement activities to cement the vision of students as partners as being applicable to the majority of students at the University, not just a minority. The NUS recognises that not all students will want to engage with the partnership model and that some students will take a more passive, consumer based approach. As Rachel Wenstone, Vice President (HE) at the NUS states in the introduction to the NUS report (2012):

> "We have spent enough time condemning consumerism in education, and now we need to articulate the alternative. Student engagement is a great concept but it needs to be deployed to radical ends. Students as partners is not just a nice to have, I believe it has the potential to help bring about social and educational transformation."

The narrative of student engagement within this book

Freire's Pedagogy of the Oppressed (1972:66) in a discussion around the dialogue that takes place between educator and student states that "Authentic education is not carried out by A for B or by A about B, but rather by A with B, mediated by the world – a world which impresses and challenges both parties, giving rise to views or opinions about it". The act of working with students as partners is reflected within this assertion.

Identity

6
2 4
5 7
3

13 16

12 14   10
15   8 9

11

Community   Motivation

Figure 1: Chapters (by order number) clustered by theme

In addition Freire, in considering the way in which man decodes and understands the world around himself, suggests that the methodology required to establish sense *"requires the investigators and the people (who would normally be considered objects of that investigation) to act as co-investigators"*. This term of co-investigators echoes nicely with that of co-producers or co-creators as part of a partnership-based approach to quality enhancement.

The chapters you will encounter in this volume are co-written by students and staff and therefore reflect a mix of styles, approaches and previous experience of writing for publication. They are clustered into three themes: identity, motivation and community (Figure 1).

A section on 'Identity' reflects the changing nature of student, staff and organisational identities. Chapters two to seven will offer insights into how students are viewed as an asset or resource by staff through to the changing nature of that relationship and the motivations for all those involved in engagement activities. Vaughan and Williams open this section with a consideration of the student as a practitioner partner, an asset that can support innovation and development. The chapters by Summers *et al.* and Chambers and Nagle consider the role of students in the organisation and the impact this has on their own perceptions and those of students and staff. This is further explored within work of

Ashfield *et al.* and Rowe *et al.* who consider the new relationships that have been developed. The Identity section is completed with a chapter by Montesinos *et al.* who consider the conflated identity of students as staff and the impact this has upon them and the community.

The second book section, on motivation, contains four chapters which discuss the motivation for students and staff to engage in these activities. It is led by Hutchings *et al.* who offer an in-depth exploration of the motivations for students to be engaged as student practitioners and partners. The theme is then taken on by Donnelly and Francis, who demonstrate the value of the student voice within a module to discover the motivations for student success. Gough *et al.* consider professional motivations for engagement while a chapter by Warmington *et al.* completes the section with a consideration of the new conversations and understandings that can be generated through partnership.

The volume finishes with five chapters that discuss student engagement as a vehicle for creating the learning community. Andrews *et al.* offer a chapter that considers the creation of a community of learning at the modular level. A chapter follows from Flint and Roden who consider the role of students in the wider community and the opportunities for social media to support this work. In their chapter, Chapman and Ishaq also consider the lessons the wider community can relay to student engagement while Philips *et al.* showcase the role of students as practitioners in community projects and the benefits this has upon student learning. The section and the book are concluded with a chapter from Chapman *et al.* with a macro-reflection on the role of students, Students' Unions and the institution in the new student engagement conversations.

About the authors

Luke Millard is Head of Learning Partnerships at Birmingham City University. He can be contacted at **luke.millard@bcu.ac.uk**

Paul Bartholomew is Head of Curriculum Design and Academic Staff Development at Birmingham City University. He can be contacted at **paul.bartholomew@bcu.ac.uk**

Stuart Brand is Director of Learning Experience at Birmingham City University. He can be contacted at **stuart.brand@bcu.ac.uk**

Claus Nygaard is Professor in Management Education at Copenhagen Business School, Denmark and Director of LiHE. He can be contacted at **lihesupport@gmail.com**

Chapter 2

Student Engagement with Learning Resources in Art & Design: Seeding Possibilities

Sian Everitt Vaughan and Grace Williams

Introduction

This chapter reflects upon the potential of applying the methodologies and conceptual frameworks of a creative practice-led research approach to student engagement with learning resources. It follows the learning journey undertaken by staff and students on a project to enhance to students the visibility and potential of Birmingham City University (BCU) Art and Design Archives. This was a project where the outcomes intentionally were not prescribed, allowing an organic emergent approach to engagement, process and reflection. The chapter discusses the attitudinal changes required from staff to facilitate student-led and practice-led research partnership approaches to the exploitation of learning resources. It reveals how reflection, emotional intelligence and a fluid repositioning of identities nurture amongst staff and students a fertile sense of community. It also demonstrates the nature of engagement in practice-led research in art and design to educators in other disciplines.

Sowing the seeds

The staff responsible for the Art and Design Archives recognised as problematic that, whilst used by research students and academics for historical research, the Archives are rarely used by the practice-based students. So, although housed in the School of Art, the Archives are not exploited by art students as a resource for their creative work in the studios. This is particularly problematic given that there has been recognition of "an archival impulse" in recent contemporary art in which artists have engaged actively with archive and museum collections and with concepts of the archival and historical (Foster, 2004; Merewether, 2005). We decided to engage with students in a creative partnership to address this perceived disjuncture between university and professional art practice.

Central to the nature of the engagement in this project was the fertile ground of the Art and Design Archives, both in terms of the richness of the resources they contain and their position, and that of their staff, outside and alongside the curriculums in the School of Art. The Art and Design Archives contain both art and archival collections. As well as institutional records reflecting changes in art and design education from the mid-nineteenth century until c.1970, there are collections relating to public art commissioning in the late twentieth century, child art, and handwriting. Surely such a diverse richness of written documents, photographs, slides, drawings, paintings, designs, plans and objects is a treasure trove of source material and inspiration for students in art and design? As well as aiming to encourage art students to use the Archives as a learning resource for their creative practice, staff were keen to reflect on the management of the resource and the degree of organisational creativity the policies and procedures embodied or constrained. In this way our project can be situated in relation to wider discourse around creativity in higher education and creativity in teaching (Nygaard *et al.*, 2010). Although housed in the School of Art building, the Archives are funded and managed as part of the central research infrastructure of Birmingham Institute of Art and Design (BIAD), a faculty of BCU. Sitting outside BIAD's discipline-specific School structure gives a degree of independence and flexibility rather than being constrained by the requirements and timetables of programme specifications and module descriptors. However, it does carry also an inherent risk of isolation. The challenge at the forefront of our minds as staff was how to embed in the staff and student body a consciousness of the possibilities of the Archives as a learning resource, without prescribing how that resource should be used.

Staff had tried to raise the Archives' profile through inclusion in

Student Handbooks and presentations both as part of student induction and to groups of teaching staff, but with little discernible impact:

> *"It felt a little disingenuous for me as an historian and researcher to be telling practitioners how to use the Archives to develop their artistic practice. It was too didactic when what I wanted was dialogue, multiple conversations in which to create and negotiate possibilities."* (Staff Partner 1)

So it was intuitive for the staff to create a project in which they would learn from the practitioners. Spurred by the opportunity presented by the University's Student Academic Partners (SAP) scheme, it was decided to engage with the student practitioners rather than the Fine Art staff, as this would retain the independence and widest possible potential afforded by sitting outside the strictures of course requirements. Through discussions with Course Directors, two postgraduate students who had already shown an interest in the archival impulse in contemporary art were suggested as potential partners. It was hoped that their pre-existing knowledge and interest would ensure intrinsic as well as extrinsic motivation, resulting in increased levels of engagement, as discussed in Hutchings *et al.*, in this volume. They would work alongside the two members of staff responsible for the Archives, one a lecturer/researcher and the other an Archive assistant. Immediately it became obvious that the student partners shared the enthusiasm of the staff partners for the creative potential of the resource, and an atmosphere of excitement and the sense of a shared endeavour soon permeated the new project team as together we prepared an application for funding through SAP.

This could be seen to be the application of a problem-based learning (PBL) approach (Biggs & Tang, 2007; Dineen *et al.*, 2005). Despite the synergies, our project differed in significant aspects to PBL. The project was based around a real issue; it was neither a simulation, nor a designed problem. Sitting outside the curriculum, there were no specified learning outcomes for the students, although the staff were interested in learning more about the problem and hoped that the students would aid and join in a mutual learning journey. Obviously the SAP scheme would be beneficial to the student partners and could aid their employability as discussed in Montesinos *et al.*, in this volume; however this was implicit rather than an expressed aim for the project. The interpersonal dynamic of the project team also differed from the norm of PBL in that staff were not outside as advisors or facilitators. It was envisaged initially and then operated as a true partnership between staff and students with differing areas of expertise and experience, working as we shall describe as equals in flexible and varying roles as the project emerged.

The staff chose intuitively to create a project in which they would learn from the students and in which the outcomes were intentionally not prescribed, allowing an organic emergent approach. This approach echoed and suggested the methodologies and conceptual frameworks of creative practice-led research in art and design (Gray & Marlins, 2004; Sullivan, 2009). Through the use of an art and design-led perspective of playful experimentation, the Archives emerged as a site of untapped creative inspiration, and the experiential nature of learning through doing became central to the exploitation of this hidden resource. Experiential learning is central to art and design research and it feeds from the three principles of constructive learning (Gray & Marlins, 2004:2), thus, in the terms of our project learning should be:

+ *A response to previous individual knowledge,* so student partners with an allied interest were sought actively;

+ *An active exploration,* the onus of the project was on a creative response towards the Archives as a site for inspiration, but with no targeted outcome allowing for self-directed progression;

+ *A response to interaction within a social context,* the hierarchy of the staff and student relationship consciously was removed to create a dynamic space for engagement.

Art and design seeks to make research and resources more usable through visualisation and so the ability to implement a practice-led research approach, with the freedom to tailor directly to student interaction, propelled the momentum of the entire project.

Germinating

The preliminary steps towards formulating our working relationships within the context of the project began with an informal and open conversation that initiated the breakdown of any possible boundaries between the position of staff and student. Acknowledging the need for an equal partnership in which self-directed engagement took a central focus was implicit in the discussion. In practice-led research, as with much higher level research, *"the relationship shifts from student and supervisor to peer and peer...the gradual development of confidence and capacity for autonomous working is an essential part of the learning process"* (Gray & Marlins, 2004:160). Adopting a higher research approach that placed the onus on personal practice-led learning journeys within this project allowed for peer to peer dialogues:

> *"A key motivation for my involvement as a student partner was the ability to work equally alongside staff and actively implement changes that perhaps would otherwise have been overlooked. Opportunities for students to do this are often scarce or limited by structures such as open forums. The initiation of this new collaborative approach with an open debate provided a clearer definition of roles and a platform for a dynamic working relationship devoid of hierarchy."* (Student Partner 1)

It was unanimously accepted that the problem of under-usage of the Archives as a resource for creative interaction required a direct student perspective to develop successful avenues of resolution. Student partners gained an acute consciousness of the potential impact on the wider student body and how the perceptions and experiences of current students could inform and improve future student engagement with the Archives as a resource. Using this as a central focus, we initiated the project by adopting a double-stranded approach spanning differing aspects of art and design disciplines so as to impact on the widest student community. The project benefited from a broad student skill set hailing from MA Contemporary Curatorial Practice and MA Fine Art which provided the opportunity for many possible outcomes. As the project was located within the creative arts it seemed completely natural to expect a non-outcome based approach, instead placing the onus on the natural developments that occurred during a period of personal creative research.

> *"The opportunity to spend many hours in the archives undertaking research that was totally unrestricted in regards to what I was looking*

for provided a very valuable extension into my own professional practice and development. As an aspiring curator I viewed this opportunity as a starting point for the development of many new ideas for possible future projects and exhibitions." (Student Partner 2)

Discussions in project meetings revealed that removing the drive of an outcome based approach was never viewed by either student partner as a lack of structure or a method by which standards would be drastically reduced. It is common practice within Art and Design education for students to undertake independent creative thinking and ownership (Belluigi, 2010) which is continuously supported through tutorials and relationships with other collaborators as professionals, similar to the characteristics of media education as discussed in Ashfield *et al.*, in this volume. It was in using this Art and Design approach and the continuation of dialogues amongst the project team that more evolved outcomes began to emerge. The momentum of the project also grew as personal research journeys highlighted more defined areas of interest; this was reflected in the independent roles taken on by student partners.

"The creative freedom provided through a period of experimental research propelled a higher level of professional development; I became more aware of my ability to acknowledge strengths, not only as a creative practitioner but also in acquired peer teaching skills through the collaborative presentation of student seminars and the organisation of staff and student workshops." (Student Partner 1)

The project took a positive student-focused dynamic which enabled a problem which required a direct student perspective to be tackled in the most appropriate way. Staff members actively supported and participated in the discussion and development of ideas but remained conscious of the non hierarchal nature of our collaboration maintaining the equality of discussion. Central to this was the recognition by all involved of the fluidity in power relationships between staff and students in contrast to a more traditional paternalistic power relationship in academia as outlined in Hutchings *et al.*, in this volume.

Blossoming

The project blossomed and here we describe the processes, events and activities generated and undertaken. Initially using a private blog as a project tool for communication and sharing research, we soon recognised the potential and usefulness of the material we were gathering and sharing. Thus we decided to cultivate this material and form it into a new public website which became a key project outcome. We were keen not to duplicate the Archives' presence on the BIAD website both in terms of content and the institutional look and feel. So the new website (archivesandcreativepractice. posterous.com later changed to www.archivesandcreativepractice.com) was created using Posterous enabling the relatively easy incorporation of images and video. As well as a *case study* section on the website documenting creative interactions with the Art and Design Archives, an *inspiration* section gives detailed examples of the 'archival turn' in contemporary art practice. *Resources* contains annotated lists of relevant books, articles, exhibition catalogues and websites. The student partners, although already interested in art practice and archives, drew the staff's attention to the fact that they themselves and many students were unsure of how to behave in the Archives and were thus reluctant to visit. So a *How To* section provides guidance on copyright, research ethics and also on the basics of what to expect when visiting the archives reframed from the normal printed handout of Rules for Researchers as a light-hearted silent movie which provided a base of knowledge making students feel more comfortable when visiting the Archives (Figure 1). A *Blog* section enables us to post announcements, images and reflections about project events. Crucially each section of the new website has been co-researched and co-written by us as staff and students.

The student partners became acutely aware that generating interest amongst the wider student population required a central element of student participation. Conscious of this we initiated an early link with peer groups by co-presenting a seminar as part of the taught course for the Art-based Masters programme. We openly welcomed critique and suggestions as to useful ways of making the Archive more accessible. Promotion of the Archives as an active resource which could be utilised by everyone was vital and this was reflected in the responses we received. In direct response, we established a Facebook page for the project and

Figure 1: 'How to use the Archives: A short guide'

generated a QR code linking to the new website which we used on all flyers and posters for project events.

At the seminar the Masters students expressed a lack of knowledge as to the location and contents of the Archives as well as how it could be relevant to their studies as art practitioners. Processing this feedback we felt the best way to move forward was to echo the process of learning through doing that we had taken as a methodology for the project to begin our own journeys and apply it to the wider student population. A series of events in the form of exhibitions of student partner artistic engagements as working examples of how creative projects could develop began to create a buzz around the project and this was followed by a number of peer-led workshops that introduced staff and students at all stages to good practice within the Archives (Figure 2).

> "I think it should be given to all students when they first start as it is a great place to get inspiration. The session was very informative and I feel confident that I would know how to find things if I wanted to." (Student A)

The Archives' location within the School of Art building but outside the taught curriculum also provided an opportunity to create a different type of community that crossed all levels and actively encouraged learning through shared experience. The formation of a Craftswoman's Club, inspired by the discovery of a 1902 minute book of the original Craftsman's Club which formed in Birmingham during the Arts and Crafts movement and excluded women members, inspired a twice monthly crafts

Figure 2: Thematic introductions to the Archive: Futuristic visions of Yesterday

workshop. Formed as a Craftswoman's Club to highlight the historical sexism in historical education, in reality it is not gender specific and male students do attend. Each session was based on a skill once taught within the School of Art and a short discussion of the archival objects or photographs that acted as inspiration started each session so students slowly began to learn about the collections in a more informal way. This is also where we began to see the web resource as a major outcome as after each session images and details of the workshops would be uploaded to the blog. This encouraged participating students to access the wealth of collected resources which directly cited notions of the archival within contemporary art, crossing back into taught theory modules on the undergraduate and post-graduate programs.

Each workshop had a different invited host from amongst staff, students and technicians which consciously removed the hierarchy of teaching within the university environment. This created a social atmosphere alongside an ever expanding knowledge base which made all participants feel part of a wider community of learning. Feedback from the workshops showed that a sense of community is often hard to find particularly within Art and Design where much of the learning is self-directed. The Craftswoman's Club resulted in an extended dialogue that created a strong sense of support between students that had perhaps previously appeared absent.

> "I met a lot of interesting women through doing the sessions. It also acted as a forum to discuss important issues such as mental health and provided a great support network that is not found in the university."
> (Student B)

> "I saw a big potential in its development due to it giving us the opportunity to meet, be engaged in an artistic orientated process of learning and working together. In the same way it kept the informal, more home orientated atmosphere of afternoon tea, friend's gossips, news etc." (Student C)

> "Being an older student you feel that the uni has many nights out but not aimed at people who work! So this was great." (Student D)

Figure 3: The Craftswoman's Club

The importance of a learning space which utilises an atmosphere of collaboration and community in which staff and students are equal partners allowed dialogues to flourish and students who previously had felt isolated from the university became part of an informal network which remained outside of the taught curriculum. This strengthened engagement through student-to-student interaction and in turn building the skills required for more successful learning away from the structure of the university. In fact in two cases this directly translated into employment.

> "As a direct result of the Craftswoman's club I have been introduced to two artists/makers who I have employed through Arts on our Doorstep to host workshops at the Community Craft Club that I successfully acquired funding for. This employment and growing network is a direct result of the Craftswoman's Club." (Student E)

This open approach to involving the wider student body in activities outside the curriculum, positively contributed to the social community

27

which in turn encouraged a heightened level of engagement. Students who had previously preferred to work away from the university environment began to become more dynamic members of the student population.

Harvesting

We have harvested many fruits from our project. The flexibility of a project which retained no preconceived outcomes perhaps unsurprisingly produced 'unexpected' results. It may perhaps appear paradoxical to describe results as unexpected in relation to our project's purposeful lack of prescribed outcomes but it is the nature of these outcomes which illustrates the success of implementing a reflexive creative practice-led approach. Practice-led research has often been likened to falling down an Alice-in-Wonderland-style rabbit hole (Gray & Marlins, 2004) producing lateral thinking with engaging and interdisciplinary results. The creative thinking that naturally generated outcomes within this project could have been completely overlooked and with it the period of self development that creates independence had a closed outcome based approach been employed.

The variety of outcomes that took form throughout the course of the project truly reflected this interdisciplinary engagement. Student partners had not anticipated the influence that involvement with the Archives would have on their experience of the curriculum and learning outcomes in taught programmes.

> "The theoretical and contextual knowledge gathered during my time researching and creating project related events became strongly aligned with interests within my own creative practice. Many of the resources collectively collated for the project website became invaluable to my own research in practice and my final written submission reflected this with a focus on the role of the personal archive within contemporary art practice." (Student Partner 1)

Obviously through the creation of an online resource, the project has a legacy beyond pilot and demonstrator interactions with the Archives. Through the Craftswoman's Club a learning community has been formed that whilst sharing skills encourages discussion and reflection on the collections in the Archives, the changes in pedagogy art education over the past hundred and fifty years and the archival turn in contemporary art practice. This will be continued with a new series of programmed events at the start of each term, building on previous success new students will be encouraged to attend alongside alumni and current members creating an ever-expanding support network as well as a strong link with the Archives as a site for creative engagement. Further to this, applications for funding have been investigated in order to make The Craftswoman's Club a more permanent fixture ensuring future students benefit from a community of learning outside the academic curriculum.

> "Knowing that an idea as simple as appropriating a historical group so entrenched with the lineage of the university as well as the local area could benefit the experience of future students increasing confidence in skills and future prospects, as it has done for me, is an unbelievable thought. Knowing that I helped to implement and sustain that is even more remarkable." (Student Partner 1)

The extension of outcomes such as The Craftswoman's Club into fledgling projects outside of the umbrella project perfectly illustrates the ability of students to propel ideas into workable and sustainable results when given the freedom to create responses to problems without fixed structures which in turn produce limitations. It also highlights the fruits that can be gained when fluidity is adopted in the repositioning of staff and student identities, facilitating a truly dynamic co-creative partnership and enabling the continuation of personal journeys. The project has also provoked thinking about the benefits of a more holistic approach to both the Archives as a resource and the Fine Art students as practitioners that could encompass course requirements and student assessment but also facilitate extracurricular and Continuing Professional Development (CPD) activities.

The legacy of the project was always a central issue that continued to be debated and we remained adamant that the best way to keep the Archive in the student consciousness was through the networks and dialogues of peer to peer and staff to student interaction. Thus, the Archive will continue to be actively promoted through theoretical modules and lectures, with staff members directing students to the wealth of resources located on the project website, alongside activities organised through The Craftswoman's Club.

It is also worth considering the seeds for the future that have resulted from our individual experiences. This has been a transformative learning experience for both staff and students involved as a result of critical reflection and awareness of changing identities (Mezirow, 2009). For student partners the journey from a state of independent self-directed learning, characteristic of fine art education, to a consideration of enhancing the experience of peers was central to the development of personal confidence. A confidence in the application of skills highly relevant to personal future career plans.

> "The skills gained throughout the project and the attitudinal change towards my position from a student to more equal peer to peer style learning boosted the confidence I had in implementing ideas and change to the benefit of fellow student peers. On a more personal note it provided the opportunity to command situations that are highly relevant to my chosen career path. Through the hosting of student seminars and workshops I have a heightened confidence in addressing varied audiences including peers and professionals, a vital skill to have experience in as an emerging artist and aspirant lecturer. I have also formed solid working relationships with involved staff members, a relationship which has successfully helped nurture the development and acquirement of a funded research placement for doctoral study." (Student Partner 1)

Student partners made links with the curriculum and learning outcomes in taught programmes and project experiences informed both assignments and career aspirations. Löfvall & Nygaard (2013) argue: "While learning is contextually bound, it is not solely a social endeavour. Learning is also inspired and driven by individual processes which are closely linked to the identity of the learner." Engagement through this project encouraged the student partners to question, re-define and broaden their sense of identity. This reflection and ability to flexibly re-position their identity enhanced their confidence and consequently their learning.

Staff partners had not been conscious at times of the significance of the desire to learn from students. This decision was intuitive and immensely rewarding.

"Seeing the students' enthusiasm for the project and the Archives reignited my own enthusiasm and has inspired me." (Staff Partner 1)

It has however, required attitudinal changes in the self-perception of staff to facilitate such a degree of student agency. The dynamics of the partnership were fluid responding to the organic growth of the project. Undoubtedly there has been co-creation of knowledge between staff and students, but there have also been periods when it has been appropriate for staff to take a back seat, being available as a critical friend as needed, as defined by Costa and Kallick (1993). It may have been a natural step to wish to learn from student partners as *experts in being artists and art-students* but concomitant with this was a personal repositioning as *non-experts* and as *learners*. This is a very different role to the more traditional concept of the academic as expert and the archivist as gatekeeper to authoritative and legitimising sources.

The staff have had to be prepared to accept criticism from student partners, the recognition that practices might be perceived in ways not anticipated. It had been assumed that the Archives were an open and available learning resource, yet the student partners informed staff that there was a reluctance to cross the threshold as most students did not feel that the Archives were for them, they did not perceive the relevance of the Archives to their activities in the School of Art.

"It was a surprise to learn that some of them didn't realise they could use them despite the notice on the door." (Staff Partner 2)

This is one of the dangers of independence from BIAD's discipline specific School structure and also a consequence of being an open resource instead of being an assessable element of course programmes. It also demonstrated that staff had overlooked the many common cultural and social barriers to museum and archives visiting that are widely recognised in the cultural sector (Black, 2005). Just because the art students are already within a cultural institution (an art school), it should not have been assumed that they had therefore overcome these barriers in all instances.

The student partners also personally demonstrated that once braving the threshold, the wealth of material and staff openness to the myriad ways and things in which practice-based students might find inspiration in the fertile ground of the Archives could be too daunting. This project has revealed that the balance is wrong.

> "I also learnt about the psychological barriers to practice-based students visiting us posed by the format of our website and in particular the lengthy statement of the rules on it." (Staff Partner 2)

Our official website is aimed at historians and family historians. Staff are used to providing guidance and orientation for traditional historical research in the Archives by answering queries, providing access to a catalogue database, assisting with the interpretation and contextualisation of documents and signposting secondary literature. In simply discounting this as inappropriate for practice-led research staff had inadvertently created a void. Believing that being flexible and non-prescriptive would facilitate engagement, as staff we had failed to recognise that the students still needed some guidance and support to establish the knowledge base and confidence from which to then explore and innovate. The silent-movie adaption of the Rules and the development of a template for thematic workshops and research guides both highlighted these issues and began to address them.

There was also a paradoxical disjuncture between the 'hands off' approach to not prescribing what practice-based students might find of interest in the collections and then the 'hands off' policies and procedures in terms of preservation, copyright and data protection which of necessity do constrain how the collections might be used. This is a contradiction that cannot be overcome if the learning resource is to be managed to professional archival standards. The project has demonstrated a need to be more explicit in how this is communicated to practice-led students as part of a conversation, as part of an adult with adult dialogue rather a parent to child dictat, to appropriate the terms of Transactional Analysis (Hay, 2009).

The significance of the emotional basis of interactions with the Archives has been a revelation. The emotional experience for all involved is something perhaps not recognised enough in the management of learning resources although identified and encouraged in the concept of "teaching with emotional intelligence" for lecturers (Mortiboys, 2011). The experience and learning journey undertaken through this project has highlighted a need to be aware not only of the potential of the collections as a resource for practice-based students but also to recognise and manage the Archives as both a physical and emotional environment with which they engage. Staff roles have to be flexible moving between positions as informed guides, facilitators, trainers, teachers and co-researchers and yet at times it is still necessary to act as gatekeepers to protect the Archives for future generations of students. This is a complex balancing act and requires emotional intelligence in relation to identifying student needs and in relation to recognising and switching staff roles positions. Staff emotional responses to participating in the project varied, from excitement to frustration. Frustration in the inability to fully participate in workshops and project events due to other meeting and teaching commitments and at times with being pushed beyond comfort zones with technology.

> "I never felt comfortable about using the blog... [and] hated being filmed and seeing myself in the photos of the workshops that appeared on the website though I recognised the benefits brought by the more interactive and visual approach." (Staff Partner 2)

As staff and student partners we realised early in the project that it was our enthusiasm for the possibilities of the learning resource that we most wanted to share and engender in others. However, with enthusiasm comes expectations and we have all learnt that we need to be more aware of these so that we can manage and respond to expectations with emotional intelligence. The opening up of the Archives to different types of enquiry and use through practice-led approaches is a further layer of complexity as it inevitably brings additional nuances to the balancing act of staff roles. It is a rewarding challenge to face and through student engagement the harvest has been fruitful.

> "It has been enjoyable, rewarding and at times challenging to keep up with the students' ideas. I wish we had done this a long time ago!" (Staff Partner 1)

About the authors

Dr. Sian Everitt Vaughan is a lecturer, researcher and keeper of Archives at Birmingham Institute of Art and Design (BIAD), Birmingham City University. She can be contacted at **sian.vaughan@bcu.ac.uk**

Grace Williams having completed her MA Fine Art is now studying for a practice-led PhD at Birmingham Institute of Art and Design (BIAD), Birmingham City University. She can be contacted at **grace.williams2@ mail.bcu.ac.uk**

Chapter 3

The Effects on Student Engagement of Employing Students in Professional Roles

Paul Summers, Daisy Pearson, Samuel Gough and Jan Siekierski

Introduction

This chapter sets out to explore the effect on learning and teaching of the Studio Manager and Laboratory Manager placement positions at Birmingham City University's (BCU) School of Digital Media Technologies (DMT). It was a predecessor of the University's Student Academic Partnership (SAP) scheme, which aims to enhance the learning experience of the student at the same time as benefiting the course and faculty to which the student belongs. They are two full time paid positions, for which two students are selected after they have completed their second year. Once they have finished their placement, they return into the third year of undergraduate study.

The posts are open to students from three different courses within the School of Digital Media Technology. This year long placement is a role in which the student works closely with all the staff who use the audio studios at BCU's Millennium Point campus. They are well established and predate the University's SAP schemes, as they have been running since 2008. Unlike the SAP scheme, whereby remuneration of the Student Partner is facilitated through the scheme's own funding, the two positions offered at DMT are funded by the school itself. This provides some indication of the importance that the University places on these roles.

To be awarded one of these positions, the student must apply externally through official means, just as any other staff member would. They have to participate in an official interview and the panel consists of members of academic staff from within the School. The role strengthens the students' professional knowledge and experience as it provides a real-life situation they would be exposed to when finding a job.

The roles align well to the University's aims for student participation and engagement, by integrating students into the teaching and pedagogic research communities of faculties. This is intended to challenge traditional hierarchical relationships that are normally present (Robinson, 2012) and the lack of equality in decision-making that follows (Chambers and Nagle, in this volume). This provides a way to develop collaboration between students and staff and generates a sense of ownership and pride in the institution and its programmes. The Studio Manager role includes daily jobs such as running the studio booking system, preparing the studio rooms for classes, delivery and helping out with studio tutorials, liaising with other areas of staff such as security, reception and connecting the staff and students across the school and other schools as necessary. Alongside these largely administrative roles the Studio Manager is required to offer technical help and act as supervisor to all the students using the studios, as well as being required to repair any damaged equipment and prepare any equipment for external use.

The Laboratory Manager is required to maintain the laboratories and prepare them for classes. Duties include the support of learning and teaching activities and the development of materials or ideas for use in the classroom. As the Student Partners are not only students but also members of staff, they naturally become mediators between the two parties.

The facilities themselves are used in tutorials by three different degree courses, which are Sound Engineering and Production (200 students), Sound and Multimedia Technology (60 students) and Television Technology and Production (40 students). The studios are also borrowed and shared between other courses at times, such as Music Technology (90 students), Multimedia Technology (60 students), Film Production and Technology (110 students), and Film Technology and Special Effects (30 students). [N.B. all estimates of student numbers for the coming academic year].

Methodology

This chapter will use Kirkpatrick's (1983) four-level model for assessing training effectiveness, in order to evaluate this scheme. It provides a well-recognised, established and understood approach to structuring considerations of the roles.

Level 1 – Reaction: the reaction evaluation is how the delegates felt about the training or learning experience, in this case, what they thought about the feedback method.

Level 2 – Learning: the learning evaluation looks at the extent to which participants improved and increased knowledge and skills and changed attitudes as a result of the feedback given.

Level 3 – Behaviour: the behaviour evaluation is the extent of applied learning back on the job; its implementation. Will the feedback change their behaviour for future work?

Level 4 – Results: the results evaluation is the effect on the business or environment by the trainee.

Data was collected from three separate groups of individuals involved with this scheme. This data was collected in differing methods according to the nature and number of the participants from whom it was being collected. Details of these methods are identified below.

In addition, in order to structure our consideration of student engagement, we developed a list of criteria, based upon the works of both Chickering and Gamson (1987) and the National Survey of Student Engagement (2009). We see engagement that:

+ Encourages student-academic contact;

+ Encourages cooperation among students;

+ Encourages active and collaborative learning;

+ Emphasises time spent on enriching educational experiences;

+ Communicates high expectations & high level of challenge;

+ Respects diverse talents and ways of learning;

+ Provides a supportive environment.

Approaches to data collection

Data was gathered from academic staff, who had varying degrees of contact with the Student Partners, during a series of structured interviews. Due to the small number of staff involved in working with the Student Partners, limitations on numbers favoured this approach.

Additionally, a number of structured interviews were conducted with current and previous Student Partners, who had undertaken a sandwich year employment position within the faculty. These were largely reflective in nature. The low number of potential respondents favoured this approach as it provided a more detailed insight into the learning opportunities, aspirations, intentions and lived experience of being a Student Partner.

Two questionnaires were sent out to the wider student group in the faculty. The first sent to students who had completed the second year. This is the year that largely works with the Student Partners in their positions in the faculty and the year from which the new Student Partner will be selected. The second questionnaire was sent to students in their final year, into which the Student Partner returns. The two years will naturally have differing experiences of engaging with both the current and previous partners and so information was collected from them separately. The questionnaires were returned by 33 of the 123 students across both years (27% response rate).

The aim of the questionnaire was to determine how the wider student group had engaged with the Student Partners and how these interactions had affected their learning and their experience of learning, whilst studying within the faculty.

Expectations of the roles

Each of the individuals or groups involved will naturally have different expectations of the project. The initial expectations of each of the stakeholders were anticipated as being the following, separated by perspective.

Academic perspective

The intended outcomes for this partnership, from the academic perspective can be summarised as:

  + Effective studio management;

  + To provide a learning opportunity for an individual;

  + To provide graduate level experience;

  + To provide a better learning experience for the wider student group;

  + To increase student participation and engagement.

Having been a user of the studios, the Student Partner is expected to bring a degree of familiarity and contextual understanding to the role that is very valuable. Perhaps the most clearly intended outcome of the partnership, beyond the simple management of the studios is the Student Partner's experience of a realistic, vocational environment, providing useful graduate level experience to aid the student in their future career. As the role is equivalent to others found in professional and non-academic contexts, it provides a clear opportunity for the student to learn as he or she works. Whilst it is clear to see how both the student and academic partners benefit from such an arrangement, it is perhaps easy to miss the indirect benefits to the wider student community. Students are able to work with a Studio Manager with whom they are already acquainted, with the intention that this would not only make them easier to approach but, as a peer they also have more understanding of the student perspective. It is intended that students would more readily engage with a Studio Manager with whom they feel less of a power relationship with and would therefore be more able to collaborate on issues as equals. It is also true that, once the placement is over, the Studio Manager will be seen by the student community to be an individual capable and willing to give advice and support.

Student partner perspective

Though there are clearly a number of shared objectives between the Student and the Academic Partners, the partners have individual perspectives and differing focuses. The key outcomes of the partnership, observed by the current and previous Student Partners are:

+ Learning;

+ Career experience;

+ Development of a professional identity;

+ Development of relationships with the year group into which they will be joining when they return from placement.

During the interviews, the Student Partners have noted their individual approach to the role, the objectives that they set themselves and the identity that they consequently developed.

Though it was not part of the intended outcomes of the scheme from the perspective of the academic, the Student Partners have noted an expectation that returning to study after completing a placement year might be easier when compared to those students who took external placements. This expectation resulted from the perceived bond they had built with the year they had supported, into which they would return.

Observations

As stated, the first three levels of Kirkpatrick's (1983) model are used to structure considerations here: reaction, learning, behaviour. Each level is broken down into perspective of academic staff, Student Partners and the wider student group.

Level I: Reaction (the Academic Partner perspective)

When asked whether the role was important to the department, all staff members agreed that the roles are essential. The following quote typifies this:

"These schemes are essential to the running of DMT sound technology related courses. They have been used (in particular the Studio Manager position) to provide desperately needed support of physical resources such as equipment, rooms and teaching materials. Effectively these placements have provided the Faculty with much needed staff without needing to recruit full-time contractual positions." (Academic Staff Member)

Level 1: Reaction (the Student Partner perspective)

Naturally some students noted frustrations of working in a HE environment such as dealing with bureaucracy, though all the students that participated in the scheme said they learned a lot from doing it. Each had a good deal of experience, both in life and in their chosen topic, by the end of their placement year, though as is described below by one of the Student Partners, most said that they would not want to do the same role again:

"I feel that the nature of the position is that it gives you the encouragement to thrive at what you do best and then use these skills to move on to bigger and better things." (Student Partner)

Level 1: Reaction (wider student body perspective)

The student body was questioned as to its opinion on how the roles were performed and fulfilled during the year by the Student Partners. When asked, 58% of second year students gave the Student Partners 5/5 when asked if they met up to their expectations of what a Studio Manager should be whilst 37% gave 4/5 leaving some suggestion of improvement. When asked the same, third year students were equally positive in their response with 50% giving a 5/5 rating. All respondents across both year groups answered in the positive (above 3/5).

These ratings suggest that the student body was satisfied with the performance of the Student Partners within the roles and the roles themselves.

Level 2: Learning (Academic Partner perspective)

The tutors were asked what they thought of the teaching and learning opportunities provided by the use of Student Partners. The responses were varied with some tutors pointing to people skills and functional, discipline related aspects, and others identifying activities that would contribute to a Student Partners academic development, such as the development of 'new practical elements' for in class work. This statement on the Lab Manager role, is perhaps the most descriptive in this respect:

> "Students undertaking this role will learn via vocational experiences and improve their management skills, people skills and organisational time management." (Tutor)

While the objectives are set for the students, the staff may also benefit from their own experience concerning working with the Student Partners. Tutors were noted as not only benefiting from gaining insight in to student attitudes and behaviour, but also in how they managed the practical application of discipline related knowledge.

Level 2: Learning (Student Partner perspective)

The main aim of the scheme is to provide an excellent learning experience for the Student Partner. Here, the students were asked how they believe they had been most changed by the placement. One Student Partner explains how the placement had helped him to realise that the career he had previously dreamed of was not for him, and that through doing the placement, he realised his professional strengths allowed for different career paths to investigate. He went to say that he had achieved "clearer career objectives, increased professional confidence, realisation of personal strengths and weaknesses". Other accounts are provided by the following two Student Partners:

> "The placement has changed me most in terms of my approach to work and my people skills. I have learnt not to shy away from confrontation when it is necessary, and I have learnt about when confrontation is necessary. I have learnt a lot about my own beliefs and morals during the placement, and about other peoples expectations of course, staff, students

etc. I have learnt many life skills and expect to use these in the future. I believe I am largely a changed person, and although I feel that a lot of my own naivety has been eradicated." (Student Partner)

"I grew up a bit and started taking responsibility for things a bit more. I developed better inter-personal skills as I was forced to interact with other people." (Student Partner)

Level 2: Learning (wider student body perspective)

One of the benefits of these roles being filled by students is that the students engage more easily and fully with the facilities around them and gain a broader experience. When asked if they were at ease asking the Student Partner for help, 64% of third years said they were. When asked if it was easier to engage with a Student Partner than a staff member, 84% of second years said yes it was and 74% said they believe a Student Partner would more easily relate to their issues than a staff member. This suggests that having a student in the managerial roles is a good way to build a trusting and respectful relationship between students and the University. The easier the student feels about asking for help, the more engaged they become and the further they can develop.

Issues are likely to occur in communication between student and staff. This is inevitable, but by having a Student Partner present within the learning community, the communications can be smoothed out and vital messages received more clearly by both parties at the same time as nurturing personal skills for the Student Partner. This results in student engagement being promoted and the learning experience improving.

Level 3: Behaviour (Academic Partner perspective)

Academic staff were asked their opinion on the development and experience of the Student Partner. They were asked if the student fulfilled the role and whether they fully engaged. Most agreed that the students definitely fulfilled their roles, but all stated that there were some actions that could take place to help the Student Partners develop more fully and to define the roles themselves better, as shown below:

"Yes [the role was] satisfied. But more can be done in supporting staff and students particularly for Media Technology/Moving Image Technology Modules. I think more (and better) involvement and briefing from module teams across all course would facilitate this." (Academic Staff Member)

Level 3: Behaviour (wider student body perspective)

We asked the student body how they felt about working with a Student Partner rather than a staff member. 89% of second years said they would rather work with a Student Partner and 63% said they felt more at ease with a Student Partner. A comparable 64% of third years agreed with this sentiment, saying they were more at ease with Student Partners.

It seems that behaviour was modified in terms of how they engage with the Student Partners, which was something that continued after their return to study with 57% of students continuing to take advice from the returning Student Partners.

Level 4: Results (Student Partner perspective)

The experience of being a Student Partner has resulted in positive effects in the present studio manager's approach to learning, stating that she is more dedicated due to her time in the role. She also notes that her confidence and her approach to her life have received similar positive results.

The role has resulted in a similar reappraisal in the previous Studio Manager as he describes in the following statement:

"It made me realise, however, that my greatest strengths, and what gave me the most satisfaction was in helping others in becoming successful in their areas of strength, and to in many ways be the unsung hero behind the scenes that allows for creative minds to do their thing uninhibited." (Previous Studio Manager)

These statements are supported by data gathered from the SAP scheme by Montesinos, Cassidy and Millard (in this volume) which identifies similar positive effects in confidence, motivation, enthusiasm and skills.

Level 4: Results (Academic Partner perspective)

The scheme has been successful in achieving many of its intended outcomes. It has resulted in the successful running of the labs and studio. One lecturer described them as *"Invaluable to the support of the lab"* and another stated that *"These schemes are essential to the running of DMT sound technology related courses".*

Observed engagement

As stated previously we have employed a modified and combined version of both Chickering & Gamson (1987) and NSSE (2009) criteria to structure our considerations around engagement. These criteria are discussed below with reference to the reflective accounts and questionnaires collected from the academics, students and Student Partners.

Encourages student–academic contact

There are many aspects of engagement and perhaps one of the more apparent is the direct engagement of academic staff with students. Skinner & Belmont (1993) state that it is this interaction that defines engagement on a behavioural and emotional level in the classroom. One of the lecturers noted that the Laboratory Manager had *"engaged with his role and provided active support for students and teaching staff the whole year"*. Another added that he was a *"very valuable member of the team. Really a key player we couldn't have done without"*. There is an expectation and a requirement for the Student Partners to become part of the team and therefore engagement with faculty staff is not an optional aspect of the role.

Encourages cooperation among students

The selection of a Student Partner as opposed to any other employee was not only to enhance learning and to offer discipline relevant experience. It was expected that the student would relate to and be able to work better with their fellow students. One lecturer's comments on the Studio Manager suggest that this has been achieved, stating that she *"…was a valued member of the team in the eyes of students, changing the dynamic amongst students and the studio management system for the better".*

When the Student Partners assume their roles, they are already known to the wider student community. This presents them with fewer social barriers to overcome than if the position were filled by a non-student. Historically, Student Partners have become role-models and advisors to their cohort, supporting those who expressed interest in taking over the responsibility themselves, as the current Studio Manager explains:

> *"During my second year, I spent a lot of time with the Studio Manager before discussing in detail the pros and cons of the position. Being that he was the only person to have been in the same situation, the only support that truly helped was that of the previous Studio Manager who mentored me as I went."* (Current Studio Manager)

Both the current and previous Studio Manager, note that doing a placement affects how they re-integrate with, or expect to reintegrate with the students after this time.

> *"I believe I have built friendships with students in the current second year, which will become my peers. So socially, I do not believe there will be an issue, although of course the experience will be very different, and I will miss my old peers."* (Current Studio Manager)

> *"I believe that I built up an excellent rapport with a majority of the students across the faculty, so I didn't feel I had an issue re-integrating in that respect - I knew my new cohort very well having working closely with many of them the previous year."* (Previous Studio Manager)

Of course, the views above only affect the Student Partners and while this is important, the greatest effect on student engagement comes through influencing the engagement of the wider student cohort. In order to measure this, we asked questions and collected information below about this engagement.

	Yes it was easier to engage with them	It made no difference
Did you find it easier to engage with a student employed Studio Manager than if the manager were a non-student employee? (Respondents from 3rd year)	64%	36%
Would you feel more at ease asking for advice from a student employee than you would an academic member of staff? (Respondents from 2nd year)	Yes 63%	No 37%
Do you feel that the student employees were more able to relate to you and your situation, than academic staff? (Respondents from 2nd year)	Yes 74%	No 26%
Did you prefer working with a student Studio Manager than if the manager were a non-student employee? (Respondents from 2nd year)	Yes 89%	No 11%
Did you find it easier to engage with a student Studio Manager than if the manager were a non-student employee? (Respondents from 2nd year)	Yes 84%	No 16%

These results suggest that engagement was positively affected by the use of Student Partners. Although one might have anticipated that the wider student community would prefer work with an experienced manager, their preference seems to be for a Student Partner. It could be reasonably argued that this is related to the ease with which they are able to approach them for advice. This wider concept of the changing perceptions of the relationship between students and staff through partnership working is discussed further by Andrews, Jeffries and St Aubyn (in this volume).

Encourages active and collaborative learning

One of the current Student Partners spoke about her collaborative experiences:

> "I simply loved our audio studios at university and the opportunity to be part of their maintenance and development, to give back to the community that used them and to attempt inspire to the users (like the previous placement student) really lit my fire…Vital roles for me this year have been peacekeeper and communications officer. By this I mean I have acted as mediator between staff and student, between fellow students and even fellow staff." (Current Student Partner)

Her account above gives some indication of the level of contact and engagement that is required of the role. Interestingly, the positive effect on engagement extends beyond the partnership as the partners return to their studies in the following year. This is indicated by responses below.

- Once the student had returned to study, did you ever ask them for advice in the same way that you might have done while they were in their paid employment with BCU? (Respondents from 3rd year)

  o Yes (57%)

  o No (43%)

- If you had a studio related question, would you be more inclined to ask the new Studio Manager, or the ex-Studio Manager who had re-joined the students in the final year? (Respondents from 3rd year)

  o I might ask either of them (43%)

  o I would probably ask the ex-Studio Manager (14%)

  o I would probably ask the new Studio Manager (43%)

Emphasises time spent on enriching educational experiences

The expectation of the academic staff is that there is an educational benefit to employing a Student Partner, as discussed by this lecturer:

> "The Lab Manager position [for the past years] requires the students to have a high level of scientific background and the role provides plenty of opportunity for the students to become engaged in class development, teaching and learning support and research based activities." (Lecturer)

The following sections are selected from one of the interviews, to give a flavour of the types of responsibilities and associated learning opportunities that the Student Partners had. The duties below are often discipline specific and are considered to be approximately of graduate level. As the current Studio Manager states:

"I was required primarily to maintain and look after the University's audio studios, all the audio equipment (such as microphones, outboard, mixing desks, speakers etc.), offer technical and creative advice to students during their recording or mixing sessions, manage the studio booking system, help set up for lectures and tutorials as well as providing cover when needed." … "It has taught me to read people and situations in ways I wouldn't have considered before." (Current Studio Manager)

The following question measures the wider student appreciation of this knowledge. It can be seen that one respondent here has said that they would have less respect. Given the respondents other answers, this could have been entered by mistake. Overall, there is a strong majority that recognise and respect the knowledge gained by the Student Partners.

+ If you had reason to talk to the student who had returned to your year after doing a placement with BCU, would you have increased respect for their opinions based on the knowledge gained? (Respondents from 3rd year)

  o Yes (79%)

  o No, no change in opinion (14%)

  o No, I would have less respect for their opinion (7%)

Communicates high expectations & high level of challenge

As this lecturer identifies "The Lab Manager position … requires the students to have a high level of scientific background", which was something that the Student Partners were aware of even before they applied. The current Studio Manager's account of her interview is quite revealing here:

"I think the interview and preparation process was absolutely invaluable. I approached it as I would anything else- thoroughly and whole spiritedly- but it was being able to perform under scrutiny that really tested me. The added pressure was that, being a 70-80%+ student for two years, there are certain things that tutors may have come to expect and I set my own standard bar very high." (Current Studio Manager)

You will see from the responses below that, with the high expectations for the role, this has translated well into satisfaction from the wider student group who interact with them.

How would you say that the Student Partner was able to meet your expectations for their role? (Respondents from 3rd year)

- Five [Very well] (50%)

- Four 43%

- Three 7%

- Two 0%

- One (Not at all) 0%

These high standards of practice adopted have been noted as extending past the employment of the Student Partner. The previous Studio Manager expressed his delight at his development early in the year when he realised he had handed in work early for the first time in his life.

Respects diverse talents and ways of learning

The various Student Partners are afforded a good deal of freedom, to modify and enhance processes to benefit themselves as well as the student groups that they are supporting. In this sense, the diversity of the methods of learning employed is largely open.

Provides a supportive environment

Academic staff have always worked to develop a supportive environment for the Student Partners which, as this account from the previous Studio Manager illustrates, has largely been effective:

> "I also feel that the nature of the position is that it gives you the encouragement to thrive at what you do best, whatever that is - for Tim it was editing when the studios were empty, the skills he gained doing so allowing him to gain an assistant's position at a studio in London - for me, it was being a manager - doing all the mundane [things] that kept things tidy and smooth and working, but without people ever really noticing and then use these skills to move on to bigger and better things." (Previous Studio Manager)

There is perhaps more that could be done to support the Student Partners who will be entering unfamiliar territory, which is noted by one Student Partner and echoed by one lecturer who recommends *"more (and better) involvement and briefing from module teams across all course would facilitate this"*.

How would you say that the Student Partners were able to meet your expectations for their role?	Not at all			Very well	
	1	2	3	4	5
Respondents from 2nd year	0%	0%	5%	37%	58%
Respondents from 3rd year	0%	0%	7%	43%	50%

Following on from the support of the Student Partners, the above responses provide some indication that the Student Partners have been able to provide a good level of support to the wider student groups.

Conclusion

The use of Student Partners to fill roles inside the faculty such as Studio Manager and Laboratory Manager has been shown to have several important and positive effects on the academic staff, Student Partners and the wider student group. These effects are varied and cover aspects of engagement, learning and experience of learning in the school.

From the arguments previously discussed, we would suggest that the key benefits of employing a Student Partner to fill positions such as these, can be summarised as follows:

+ Student engagement is benefited through the mediating effect of having a Student Partner bridge the gap between staff and students;

+ Students can have a more inspiring and engaging learning experience through having a positive role model with whom they can easily relate;

+ New learning opportunities are created for students and Student Partners alike, especially in terms of real world vocational experience, which become invaluable in a graduate employment situation.

In order to replicate the successes that we have enjoyed with this partnership scheme, there are several key suggestions that we would offer:

- Allow the SAP enough freedom to make their own mark, otherwise the student would merely be using the academic's methods and preferences, and would not benefit from the insight that the student will have;

- Encourage communication and building of a relationship between predecessor and successor. This encourages the development of a student learning community and support network;

- Identify unique skills and interests of incoming Student Partners so that they can be effectively used;

- Ensure SAPs feel well supported by academic staff. This is perhaps contradictory to the freedom to do things their own way and can perhaps lead to the need to walk a fine line.

This closing statement from this year's studio manager, provides a good point on which to end, as she sums up her experience of participating in the scheme:

> "As a student next year, I will be more dedicated because this year has proven to me how much I care about the people here, about the studios here and about my ability to fly somewhere else afterwards. It has changed the way I view the course content, the way I approach things personally and, in honesty, my whole approach to life. My employability has risen in so many aspects as a person, and professionally my CV looks great. What I personally made of the placement makes me feel worth the positions I can now apply for (with an element of confidence in success) if they are technically based. Emotionally, I feel like I can face anything!" (Current Studio Manager)

About the authors

Paul Summers is a Senior Lecturer in Digital Media Technologies at the faculty of Technology Engineering and the Environment, at Birmingham City University. He can be contacted at **paul.summers@bcu.ac.uk**

Daisy Pearson is a Student Partner in the Faculty of Technology, Engineering and the Environment and a student on the Sound Engineering and Production course at Birmingham City University. She can be contacted at **Daisy.Pearson@mail.bcu.ac.uk**

Samuel Gough was a Student Partner in the Faculty of Technology, Engineering and the Environment and a student on the Sound Engineering and Production course at Birmingham City University. He can be contacted at **samuel.gough@me.com**

Jan Siekierski is a Senior Lecturer in Digital Media Technologies at the faculty of Technology Engineering and the Environment, at Birmingham City University. He can be contacted at **jan.siekierski@bcu.ac.uk**

Chapter 4

Graduate Interns: A Changed Identity as a Consequence of a Hybrid Role

Mercedes Chambers and Luke Nagle

Introduction and definition of terminology

The call for this chapter specified that the team comprise staff and students. This chapter has been written by two graduate interns who are studying courses at Birmingham City University (the University) and as such has been written by people who are in dual roles as both staff and student. This unique situation enables both of us to view the University from two perspectives.

This chapter will look at how graduates employed within the University are individually placed, due to this dual perspective, to impact upon the working methods of the University and the effect on graduates' identity, as they move from student to employee, of working at the University.

What is meant by internships in this context is the employment of recent graduates of the University at a fair but affordable rate. As well as employment, the interns gain experience, training and networking opportunities which aid their personal professional development.

Within this chapter we discuss our own experiences as graduate interns and also offer a generalised view other graduate interns might encounter within other areas of the University or the wider UK Higher Education Sector. We were employed as graduate interns by the Centre for Enhancement of Learning and Teaching (CELT). To distinguish between ourselves and the more generalised view, which we term simply graduate interns, we refer to ourselves as CELT graduate interns (CGIs).

As CGIs we were employed to conduct an analysis of the existing student engagement initiatives, develop new initiatives and pilot the possibility of employing more graduate interns within our University.

As the first CGIs we have been involved in a diverse range of jobs largely facilitating the area of student engagement which will be discussed shortly within the chapter. This has included but is not limited to:

+ Analysis and evaluation of existing student engagement initiatives within the University;

+ Recommending ways to improve and expand these initiatives;

+ The development of new university-wide initiatives to engage a greater number of students;

+ The coordination, administration and project management of student engagement initiatives.

It is not our aim in this chapter to describe at length the type of work that was completed. This chapter will instead look at how graduate interns are well placed to undertake the work in which they have been involved; the impact employing graduates as interns can have on the working methods of their colleagues and the impact on the wider University. It will also consider why graduates may want to apply for internship positions at their university and what benefits they gain. Finally we will offer suggestions for how graduate interns could be introduced into other institutions.

The role of graduate interns in student engagement

Graduate interns' closer association to students and ability to convey legitimacy in the student voice, in comparison to more established staff, enables them to carry out this role effectively. Increased student participation numbers in different student engagement initiatives at BCU indicates that students care about improving the 'learning community'. However, as discussed within the literature (Robinson, 2012), students can be constrained by hierarchical relationships present between staff and students. This suggests students are not equal decision-makers, which juxtaposes the notion of what the University is trying to achieve; namely improving students learning experience and involving the 'student voice' through engagement and equal partnership with staff.

The argument endorsed by BCU is that student participation can have a positive effect on students accessing learning opportunities and improve their future development (Brennan & Shah, 2011). However, without access to the 'student voice' staff cannot be responsive to the needs of students and cannot ensure that the student perspective is truly reflected in all of the BCU activities. In order to counteract this problem the placement of graduate interns can improve the relationship between staff and students and also between students and students. As CGIs we were involved directly with different BCU initiatives prior to being employed by the university and we have first-hand experience that has helped us to develop skills to better our understanding of what is expected from us within our internships.

Within the literature around student engagement and graduate internships there are many varied definitions with subtle nuances and specific attributes. In the context of this chapter student engagement refers to: *"the amount of time and effort students put into their studies and educationally purposeful activities and how the institution deploys its resources... other learning opportunities, and supports services to induce students to participate in activities that lead to the experiences and desired outcomes such as persistence, satisfaction, learning, and graduation"* (Kuh et al.,2007 cited in Harper & Quaye, 2009: 3). Students and graduate interns may offer a different insight into developing services across the University, creating a student friendly and fun environment, ulti-mately creating a better learning experience for students. Thus, student engagement not only encourages students to be involved and part of the process but also values their perspectives.

Similarly, researchers (Lowden *et al.*, 2011) acknowledge that grad-uate interns offer organisations a practical and professional competence acquired from their degrees; possess great people skills; and, use their initiative, leadership abilities and maturity to bring additional value to those organisations. Therefore, within the UK Higher Education Sector we consider graduate interns to be a catalyst for change; they are well placed within an institution to appeal to students at an appropriate level because they have recent student insight and can influence how the institution works in partnership with students. In this chapter we refer specifically to graduates in this role as interns but we recognise that others could potentially fulfil this role including third year students, year out sandwich students, postgraduate students as well as graduates.

How is the graduate internship programme received by our department?

We undertook a qualitative evaluation of: impact we (as CGIs) had on our department and our colleagues; whether we were well placed to conduct work in the student engagement realm; and how we had benefitted. This is largely because the work we have undertaken has been part of larger university-wide initiatives and, as such, it is hard to attribute definitive value to the impact we have had individually. However, we would suggest that employing CGIs has effected transformations in attitudes and forms part of a culture change going on in CELT which is striving to create a learning community that consists of engaged students, staff and alumni. The positive extension of initiatives to engage graduates underpins CELT's commitment to embed this culture change.

The importance of evaluating student engagement

Since 2009 the University increasingly has sought to engage students through a number of university-wide initiatives. Before that time there were pockets of good practice and innovation around student engagement going on in isolation around the University but without a framework to bring these ideas together the potential for them to impact on the wider University was marginal. The initiatives have provided a framework for staff and student partnerships to operate within and have acted as a catalyst for a dramatic increase in the number of university-wide projects that engage students. These initiatives have been considerably praised, most notably the Student Academic Partnership scheme, in partnership with the Students' Union, winning a Times Higher Education Award in 2010 for Outstanding Support for Students.

The University saw that the ways in which students engaged in such initiatives was consistent with what Kay *et al.* (2010) call the 'change-agent' and Streeting & Wise (2009) call the 'co-producer'. Students engaged in an institution's processes have the potential to make meaningful change and can gain satisfaction from a sense of purpose as described by Harper (2006) and Trowler (2010).

Whilst the initiatives have provided a framework to allow more students to engage in the development of innovative ideas there is a concern that the potential for university-wide change is not being realised as innovation is happening in isolation. There is a tendency within the University for staff to operate within information silos; this is not conducive to the sharing and transferring of ideas and best practice. This leads to a situation where very good ideas being developed by staff and student partnerships remain within a very limited area rather than spreading to impact upon a larger number of students, as has been noted by Raiha *et al.* (2011:72).

As much of the work remains isolated the initiatives risk not developing as effectively as they could by building on the experiences and findings of all students and staff engaged in them. It is felt by students and staff that students develop personal skills such as communication, confidence, organisation etc. and that for the University these initiatives are worthwhile.

As Coates (2005, 2010) and Kuh (2009) have stated, when institutions monitor and evaluate student engagement initiatives thoroughly they can build a comprehensive picture of what work is being done and what areas need further development. This evidence can be used to effectively and strategically plan how the University can improve the initiatives by investing resources in the correct areas.

Why graduate interns have been used to conduct this work

These roles could easily have been taken on by appointing members of staff. The reasons why CELT decided to test the idea of employing CGIs will be explored in this section.

Through the Student Academic Partners scheme (SAPs) and other student engagement initiatives the University has seen the benefits that employing students can provide. It was felt that CELT, which coordinates many of the initiatives, should be seen to demonstrate that they were prepared to employ students and graduates as an example for others to follow.

As well as a demonstration of commitment to employing graduates it was seen as a chance to broaden the range of skills and support offered to student engagement initiatives. It was hoped that, as CGIs, we would relate to the students better than a member of more established staff as we had all been involved in a variety of student partnerships at the University previously and so had an in-depth experiential understanding of the student experience of such initiatives.

This experience also meant that we had a specialised skills base that was relevant to the work we were doing. Naturally, the three of us had a different set of skills; working styles and characteristics. This meant as a team we had a range of diverse and comprehensive ways to engage different groups of students within BCU. Summers *et al.* (in this volume) also discuss the benefits of employing graduates who have previous specialised experience for the field of work, a close association with the student experience and the benefit of offering a different way for students to engage with staff at the University which is less hierarchical.

On a pragmatic level, the opportunity to employ three of us came from the fact that a full-time member of staff left the University, thus creating a vacancy. Employing three CGIs with a broad range of skills was then seen as a more positive way to try to fill the gap that had been vacated. The fact that we preferred to work part time meant the funding made available by the departing staff member could be split in this way making us a very good value for money resource.

The role in which we have been employed could potentially have been filled by a range of people. We feel that graduates employed as interns are well placed to view the University from both a student and staff perspective. This allows us to transcend any potentially divisive us and them attitude and view things from an impartial stance which makes graduate interns ideally suited to conduct work around student engagement.

At the University, students have gained the chance to engage with curriculum developers and become part of the learning community through initiatives such as SAPs. Previously, the innovative ideas students had were remaining isolated as the bureaucratic nature of the University made it fairly inaccessible for individual students to provide radical university-wide changes. As CGIs we have an understanding of what students are trying to achieve but through our work we have also developed an understanding of the operating protocols of the University. Seeing both the student and staff perspective allows us to collate the evidence of the students and format it into something that can be presented to senior management, dramatically improving the potential for ideas to have a university-wide impact. Rowe *et al.* (in this volume) also discuss how the bureaucratic nature of the University can alienate students with the consequence that their influence is not so keenly felt.

Whilst we are able to decipher University protocols we do not feel constrained by them in the same way that staff might. Bartholomew *et al.* (2009) identify that barriers to innovation within university environments comes from an adherence to a culture of compliance and a fear of encroaching upon perceived regulations which are just as likely to be imagined. We are less immersed in the protocols of the University than more established staff which allows us to have a more 'can do' outlook. If not ignoring them altogether we try to find ways around the obstacles that University protocols create. We have been willing to take risks, experiment and adopt a heuristic approach to development of new initiatives which can promote action that fulltime members of staff can find difficult. Whilst our enthusiasm has had to be tempered by staff at times as there is a reason certain protocol exists, we feel learning organisations should always be looking at ways to improve working methods and challenge protocol to benefit students. With that outlook the University can learn even when ideas fail and graduate interns are in a prime position to encourage that learning and development.

Finally, just as we can produce student work for senior management we can also take official documents written by the University that are often indecipherable from a student perspective and translate them for a student audience. This has benefits for the University and students but ultimately, if the University wants to achieve the aim of genuine collaboration and co-creation, students should be involved in the writing of official documents so that translation will not be needed. In the meantime graduate interns offer another avenue for students to engage with the University, one that is more flexible than traditional structures that, as (Coates, 2010) points out, is more suited to students whose interactions with universities don't necessarily align with organisational structures.

In summary, the work we completed could have been undertaken by a number of students or a member of staff. As CGIs, we offered a different way of doing things, not necessarily a better way, but a different way that was appropriate for student engagement work.

What impact the CGIs had on the office environment and their colleagues

Whilst we may have been well placed to conduct the work we were involved in, we were not originally recruited purely as an extra pair of hands. CELT saw it as a chance to test a mutually beneficial, innovative new type of employee in a new role. It was anticipated that we would do more than just complete the jobs they were given. It was hoped that we would impact upon the office dynamic and challenge existing working methods. As graduates we have a different outlook that is well suited to challenging working methods which can have benefits for the people they work around and the wider University.

Something which all staff involved with us have identified is that they appreciate the insights that we have offered them into the student perspective. We believe that students, particularly those employed as SAP can also do this but students can often be reticent when talking to staff, particularly if it is to criticise something the staff member has done as it is not specific to their role. The graduate intern role has had greater scope to adopt a student and staff viewpoint and as a result we have had no such inhibitions. This allows staff to gain insight into how students will receive proposals for change. Several staff members have claimed it has encouraged them to reflect on what they are doing, which can enable valuable changes to intended learning and teaching practice, during its development, rather than waiting for student feedback at the end of the development process. We can give an opinion throughout the develop-ment process effectively providing a 'litmus test' for what is being done. A senior manager said:

> "I think graduate interns will help managers have a better sense of students in the University. It is very easy at senior manager level to be removed from students. I rarely have contact with students so it makes you realise what you are here for which is about students. It is

interesting to get another perspective so I think that is a real advantage."
(Senior Manager)

Not only are we able to give our own opinion but we have access to extensive networks of students from our course and maintaining connections with students from different student engagement initiatives (the SAP scheme) we were involved in. We have utilised these networks to test ideas, promote new initiatives and offer support throughout shared time in the office and it is access to these networks and the student voice which really benefits the work of CELT.

Colleagues in CELT report that the office dynamic has seen a positive change since the CGIs joined. Whilst CELT may not have suffered from institutionalised behaviour that leads to a formal, fairly inflexible environment there is still the possibility that staff can become cynical and entrenched in their ways if not encouraged to try new methods. We find that CELT, as a progressive and innovative department within the University, is receptive to the concept of employing students and we would like this enthusiasm to be shared within other departments and institutions. We are highly motivated and have an enthusiasm to do a good job that can be refreshing and inspiring to existing staff. We have little interest in University protocol so instead of perpetuating modes of behaviour we challenge them and try and find new methods of working. These methods might not be better but are often more fun, engaging and appropriate to a student audience.

Personal motivations and benefits

As well as earning a wage there are several ways in which graduate interns can benefit professionally from their employment, as well as gaining other less prosaic benefits. One such benefit is the sense of giving something back and contributing to the University. Markwell (2007:15) points out that: *"…how engaged students are and feel themselves to be during their student years will have a great bearing on how connected and supportive towards the institution they are likely to be in later years."* As CGIs we had all previously been involved in various student engagement activities and have appreciated the chance to help improve those initiatives that provided us with personal development opportunities. Much of that which the various student engagement initiatives at the University are trying to achieve is the building of a strong learning community where students, alumni and staff all feel valued for that which they can offer to the University and proud to be a part of the University. By employing graduate interns, this ideal of 'learning community' is being strengthened and builds upon the foundations of their engagement as undergraduates. This notion of giving something back is something we all identify as one of the main reasons we applied for the position and something we have appreciated as a benefit. It has also been noted by various staff members who have worked alongside the CGIs as something that is mutually beneficially for the university and CGIs:

> "I think your university has a very powerful influence on you and so you have an emotional link with that place. I think what the graduate internship programme is trying to build on that emotional link which gives you a moral sense of purpose. Obviously it's lovely to work for a university, but it's more than just working for a university, it's having that sense of contributing to improve the university and putting something back. That's what I've seen with the graduates I've been involved with participating in the internship process." (Staff Member)

This quote is suggestive of a transformative strategy for change involving employment of graduate interns across the University. Graduate interns have been described as having a real enthusiasm to make change which not only benefits them but their working environment.

The range of work undertaken has challenged the CGIs to push themselves far beyond their comfort zone but in doing so has proved to be extremely beneficial in offering personal development opportunities. For all the CGIs this was the first experience of working in an office environment and dealing with the requirements that that poses would have offered plenty of learning opportunities alone. Working in the office, however, has only been a part of what the graduates have done. Amongst other things the graduates have been:

+ Teaching;

+ Organising student focus groups;

+ Coordinating and working alongside students around the university;

+ Acting as line manager to other students employed within the CELT office;

+ Interviewing and having discussions with staff from across the university including senior management;

+ Presenting to senior management development panels;

+ Developing new initiatives;

+ Creating literature for internal and external use;

+ Writing and presenting academic papers at conferences.

Both the graduates and staff partners recognise this as being an impressive range of things to be involved in, especially for someone in their first role in an office environment. One staff member commented that:

> "This is about developing the graduates' skills so they are better placed to move on to whatever career they want to create... things like researching, leading, initiating a range of things; most people would be waiting five or six years into their career before they had a chance to do that." (Staff Member)

The chance to operate at these levels on such a range of activities means we have developed a range of skills that will help us in any career we should choose to go into. Having a chance to push ourselves and test our abilities whilst developing or improving personal skills was something which attracted us to apply for the role and something which we can demonstrate to future employers. One CGI noted:

> "I wanted to develop organisational skills, communication skills...I have always had those qualities but this has sort of pushed me to the next level by challenging me in that way. I see this as a stepping stone to my future career. Different people that I have spoken to, whether they are executives or in HR, think it is a good experience and range of skills to have." (CELT Graduate Intern)

As well as the range of jobs providing personal development opportunities it has also given graduates access to networking opportunities that could prove valuable as a first step on the career ladder. In one graduate's case her current job came about through a meeting she had with a manager during a conference she was attending for the University.

As a consequence of working for the university in a more formal role than previously experienced through the SAP scheme our personal identity has developed. A person's identity is affected by a myriad of factors including their social, educational and family circles. By adding employment as another factor to our experience of university our identity has developed in a new direction providing us with extra professional skills and personal confidence. Chapman and Ishaq (in this volume) discuss how the different factors influence a person's identity and the direction that they develop in.

A final benefit for graduates has been the insight into staff perspectives, how the University operates and the thoughts of other students from different areas of the University. A knowledge of how large organisations work and the internal politics that go along with that could be very useful in future careers. The chance to share ideas with students from different areas can broaden the range of knowledge a graduate has access to and seeing things from a staff perspective can help the graduates be strategic about their postgraduate studies. A CGI claimed:

> "I have gained employment and skills but it has also put me in a position where I have access to other students opinions so it can influence my own...I've also had a chance to sit on the staff side and see things from the tutor's point of view which was a really good experience...when I go on to do my MA exams I will probably be a lot better prepared." (CELT Graduate Intern)

Challenges

Having received the opportunities and benefits that come with participation in the graduate internship programme we were conscious that without care this chapter could project the impression the experience was only positive and there are no negative ramifications of employing graduates. We have no hidden agenda for this chapter and had the intention to devote as much attention to the potential downsides of employing graduates as the benefits. It is in our interests to look at the experience of employing graduates through a critical lens as by doing so problems can be identified and rectified to allow future graduate interns to have greater success and positive impact upon the University. However, everyone involved in the programme directly, and even those who have only been impacted in a very marginal way, were very positive about the experience and readily identified benefits whilst struggling to find any negative consequences. However, there are a couple of areas that have been suggested as inherent challenges when employing graduates that will be explored here.

As graduates are by their very nature in a state of transition and personal development it is highly probable that they will always have one eye on moving on from the University. This can cause a slight dip in performance of the work they were involved with for a couple of weeks whilst a replacement is found.

Whilst this is a challenge it should really be seen as a positive outcome; the graduate would have potentially been successful in a job application by demonstrating the experience and skills they had developed on the internship programme. Of course, this can add a sense of satisfaction for CELT as they see they have helped the graduate on the first step of their career. When a new graduate has been appointed they in turn will bring another set of fresh perspectives, new ideas and a unique range of skills which can help develop the work in a new direction. So whilst it might provide a slight challenge for a short while, the transitory nature of graduates can actually add net value.

In a time of cost-cuts and rationalisation of staff in our University (and the Higher Education sector more generally), there was a concern that employing graduates as interns could be seen as taking jobs from permanent members of staff. Of course we acknowledge that whilst graduate interns are a good value for money resource- a number of them can be employed on a part-time basis (which in our experience tends to be what graduates prefer), for the same cost as employing a full-time member of staff. However in our context the employment of graduates has not taken any jobs from permanent staff and there is little real threat of graduate interns ever being used to directly replace staff as what they offer the University is something different.

Graduate interns broaden the range of services offered to students and the scope of work that can be undertaken by offering something different.

Rather than replacing or taking away from existing work Graduate interns enhance the work that staff at the University does by offering a greater number of ways for students to engage with or gain access to the services provided. In our context, the departure of a member of staff created an opportunity to review the services the University wanted to supply and a direct replacement would not have fulfilled the new aims. By employing graduates and students to design and provide the services students will ultimately use, BCU has set up the framework to allow a climate where a collaborative, cooperative culture is able to emerge. Against the current backdrop of the changing context of Higher Education and the financial challenges that are a consequence of that, it is notable that BCU has found the funds to employ graduate interns again next year which suggests the University values the alternative services that employing graduates can provide.

Expansion

The number of graduate intern roles at the University is currently very limited but they are already beginning to become more prevalent. While our experiences are pertinent to us there are other lessons to be learnt from Montesinos *et al.* (in this volume). Those who have been involved in the programme have seen the benefits for the graduates, those who work with them and the wider University and, as such, would like to see more employed in a broader range of roles. It is anticipated that there will be challenges that have yet to be faced and these will no doubt emerge as a consequence of expanding the graduate internship programme.

For graduate interns to be successful they need to be appointed with a specific purpose in mind. It is important that through its desire to employ more graduate interns the University does not just appoint them without a specific function or role in mind. Whilst one of the notable benefits of employing graduates has been their flexibility it would be in nobody's interest, including the interns themselves, to be appointed on the basis they can be put to work on anything as and when it comes up.

It will also be important for the University to make sure graduates are clear about what their role is within the organisation and expectations of them in terms of behaviour. The graduates who have so far been employed have all been highly motivated and, in many cases, have been known to their staff colleagues previously through project work such as SAPs. As the number of roles increase the numbers of graduates applying to the jobs who have no experience of working within the University could also rise. It needs to make clear to these candidates that employment *is* employment, regardless of the fact that it is within the University. A student may be able to turn up to lectures as and when they like but an employee must turn up to work when they are expected to, and to do so in a professional manner which some graduates may need help with.

It is possible, as the programme expands, that graduates are appointed for much more specific and defined roles. On occasion we, as the first graduate interns, have been required to work on things that put us beyond our comfort zone and required us to use skills we had not yet developed. As the programme expands, it is important that staff members, in particular line managers, do not see graduate interns as a 'Jack- or Jill-of-all Trades' to whom any task can be given. As with all of the challenges identified this can be seen as an opportunity for the graduates to try their hands at a diverse range of work and develop many new skills.

As the programme expands to other areas of the University graduates may encounter environments less conducive to working methods which rely on an equal partnership between staff, students and graduates. The graduate interns were employed within CELT which, as has been mentioned previously, is a fairly innovative and informal department of the University. Within this environment the graduates have found it easy to conduct their work on an equal basis as a full-time member of staff. In other departments where this attitude does not yet exist, graduates may not enjoy the same success without difficulty. Whilst one of the benefits of employing graduates is to prompt a culture change with a department it is important that any department considering employing graduates prepares the right environment for success by adopting a philosophy of equal partnership.

Conclusion

There is very little within the literature, which we have come across, around student engagement initiatives that attempts to discuss any negative or ineffective methods of student engagement, the wider impact such initiatives have, or how any success can be built upon. This could be a consequence of much of the literature appearing to be based on assumptions and anecdotal reports without much empirical data. This confers limited ability to help universities further develop student engagement activities and takes for granted the worth of existing initiatives without celebrating them. As Coates (2005) points out the more research and data collection on student engagement is collected the better able universities are to make informed, evidence based decisions and strategically plan how to provide impetus for new student engagement activities or to aid development and improvement of existing initiatives.

Our chapter offers a narrative account of the experiences of those involved, principally that of appointing graduate interns to conduct the work alongside staff and students. Graduates' willingness and enthusiasm to perform on a diversity of work, including action at high levels within the University, makes them adaptable to a wide range of initiatives and work streams. This can have a positive effect on their fellow students' learning and experience and the wider University community while additionally enhancing their own personal and professional development.

By offering a rich narrative account we hope that other universities may see the benefits of employing their own graduates. We believe there should be greater demand to employ graduates as they offer a different resource to an institution. By utilising their insight to view student engagement initiatives and University protocol from both sides of the coin, graduate interns are ideally situated to become change agents in the student engagement realm.

About the authors

Mercedes Chambers is a graduate intern at CELT and has just completed her Graduate Diploma in Psychology from BCU. She can be contacted at **mercedes.chambers@bcu.ac.uk** or **mschambers1@hotmail.co.uk**

Luke Nagle is a graduate intern at CELT and has just started his Masters in Architecture at BCU. He can be contacted at **luke.nagle@bcu.ac.uk** or **l.nagle@hotmail.co.uk**

Chapter 5

Social Media and Employability – Creating New Resources with Students

Mark Ashfield, David Harte and Vanessa Jackson

Introduction

This chapter outlines the approach taken in developing new learning resources to support Media Studies students who wish to make better use of social media as a professional networking tool. Academic staff and students at Birmingham City University's School of Media collaborated on a project which culminated in the creation of a website offering guidance on social media use (socialmediatutorials.co.uk). Through qualitative and quantitative research we discovered how Media students were using social media in a professional context to develop a network of contacts useful in their future career. The project has been carried out over two academic years; the first year concentrated on the research phase whilst the second has focussed on the creation of a set of openly accessible learning resources. A postgraduate student studying Social Media was recruited to collaborate with lecturers on the research phase and a larger group of both New Media and Television undergraduate students were identified to help build the resources. The chapter draws on the experiences of all involved and finds that students were motivated to participate in the projects by a desire to enhance their own professional profile, to engage with lecturers outside of the context of assessment and by the nature of the subject matter itself – a desire to better understand their own and their peers' use of social media. This chapter draws together reflections from the academic staff and students involved. Written testimonies were sought from the students (four in total) and are quoted here.

Context

Perhaps more than other professions, there seems to be a competitive advantage to be gained in the media industry from being able to maintain a developed network of contacts. Whilst once such networks were sustained through face-to-face contact or phone calls, it's now the case that social media technologies play a major role in facilitating those connections. Both academic staff and students within the subject area of Media Studies understand that being 'connected' and being seen to be 'connected' are vital ingredients in attempting to sustain a career in this sector. Beyond the development of critical thinking skills (reading and understanding academic texts) and practical craft skills (mastering the use of media production equipment), it has been a feature of Media Studies programmes that they also develop curricula that address a wider set of professional skills such as networking and communication. But the widespread uptake of social media by media industry professionals has seen much of this curricula be disrupted and made to seem outdated, given its emphasis on such things as writing CVs and covering letters, see Gough, Morris and Hessions (in this volume). In general terms we are guided in our understanding of social media by Boyd & Ellison (2007:211) who state that 'social networking sites' are those that: *"…allow individuals to (1) construct a public or semi-public profile within a bounded system, (2) articulate a list of other users with whom they share a connection, and (3) view and traverse their list of connections and those made by others within the system."* In our research we set out to investigate what we seemed to observe casually in our engagement with students on such services; that is, students were using social media in relation to their employability. Although students were clearly following and sometimes conversing with media professionals with whom they had no offline relationship, it seemed they were not always using it effectively or in a strategic manner. Nevertheless, their use of the platforms made us consider the extent to which Birmingham School of Media's existing approach to employability in the curriculum took this activity into account. As a school that prides itself on producing 'industry-ready' graduates we were conscious of a gap opening up where students might see our existing approach as anachronistic.

Our solution then was to engage students in the research and development of new learning resources in this area: the development of a product. The process of creating this product ensured that both students and staff saw a specialist role for themselves and were highly motivated to complete work to a high level. The tangible outcomes that relate to the product were those predicted: new research, published in an academic journal; and a learning resource in the form of a website. However, below we outline other *process* outcomes that shed light on the underlying issues of student engagement. Specifically, they relate to a deeper understanding of extrinsic and intrinsic motivation amongst students; and the shift towards a more industry-like model of professionalism between teaching staff and students.

Researching social media use

Our initial research (detailed in Harte & Jackson, 2011) took the form of a questionnaire completed by 320 students, both postgraduate and undergraduate, followed by focus groups of between four and six students from different years of study and different levels of social media use. This was a Student Academic Partners (SAP) project. It produced useful data about the social media platforms the students were using, how they were using them, and what they were using them for. The most significant finding was that over a quarter of students were finding work experience or paid work through social media – the Twitter platform being a key tool in this – rather than traditional methods such as emailing, phoning, or writing to prospective employers. Students were building networks of industry professionals by: 'following' them; trying to engage them in conversation; 'reblogging' or 'retweeting' their status updates; and in general interacting with them to achieve the goal of creating a distinct professional online persona for themselves.

The research showed evidence that students used the 'Digital Native' (Prensky, 2001) discourse to their advantage, with employers seeking them out partly due to their age and the apparent ease with which they utilised a range of online services; in particular services such as Twitter, Facebook and a variety of blogging platforms. Of all the assumptions made about social media use the notion that young people are at ease with social media and that its use by them is 'natural', is perhaps the most persistent. Prensky, along with Tapscott (1998), seemed to forward the idea that those born in an Internet era think and learn differently, capitalising on the opportunities that new technology offers much more quickly than the previous generation. This is a popular but disputed view and Prensky himself takes on his critics ten years after he first coined the term 'Digital Native', making clear that his point was that young people have a *"comfort with digital technology"*, seeing it as a *"fun 'partner' that they can master, without too much effort, if they are shown or choose"* (Prensky, 2011:17). This might help explain the reluctance we found on the part of students for a prescriptive intervention in how they should be using social media. They did not want to be told what to do by lecturers, and did not want to be given one 'correct' way of using social media in relation to employability. Overall it was clear that many students showed a high level of sophistication in using social media.

Educators have long been aware that their students may well be ahead of them in their use of technology and in general, emphasis has shifted from providing them with specific skills and knowledge to *"critical engagement with media's changing forms and content and its impact on lifestyles, social norms and values"* (Hobbs & Jensen, 2009:5). However, the question of 'professionalism' and 'professional practice' is often dealt with in the curriculum as a set of skills to be taught in order to prepare students for the 'outside world', a world they presumably only engage with once they complete their studies. Ashton (2010, 2011), in looking specifically at Media Studies courses, has critiqued notions of 'industry-readiness' as being too narrow and instead argues for an approach that interrogates the ways in which *"professionalism emerges as a form of identity work bound to micro contexts and situated practices and understandings"* (Ashton, 2011:555). Although Ashton largely discusses the value of face-to-face rather than digital contact with local networks of practitioners, it is clear that students engage with the 'outside world' throughout their studies and social media is increasingly the mechanism by which they do it.

From the research findings in the first phase of the project it seemed that developing online resources would be a suitable response but that such resources should be built from the basis of student experience rather than academic assumptions. As a second SAP project, a group of six undergraduates with complementary skills was put together to produce instructive video content and develop and build a suitable website. The students were at the heart of designing and building both the website and the content hosted on it. The staff involved maintained a light touch, suggesting the structure of the site and possible topics to be covered, but leaving the development and content production in the hands of the students. The site includes video and written content, grouped under three sections: 'How To', 'Etiquette', and 'Case Studies'. The videos are under a Creative Commons licence, enabling users to download or embed the videos in their own projects. In some ways one could regard this as an attempt to create Open Educational Resources (McAndrew, 2010) although the intention was more to reflect the culture of the social networks within which students operate: *"In the economy of ideas that the web is creating, you are what you share"* (Leadbeater, 2008:6).

Intrinsic and extrinsic motivation

The first phase of the project was a relatively traditional academic research exercise, whilst the second can be likened to a real world media production project with a tangible product to be delivered to time and budget, and of course, to an audience. Each participant had a defined role to which they adhered. Although the similarity to industry practice was never actively discussed, the subtext was there in the background, making this a relatively authentic replication of industry production processes. The academic staff took on the role of executive producers, generally not actually contributing to the platform and content creation but setting the quality threshold, advising on design, content and structure, coordinating and chairing meetings, ensuring progress against the timeline, and bringing the different participants together.

The students were actively engaged in the process from the outset, motivated by a number of external and internal factors. The extrinsic motivators were strong, including the fact that they were paid for their hours worked, that they had been invited by the lecturers to participate, that the project was part of a recognised University scheme, and it was planned that their work would result in tangible products. The extrinsic reward of having a tangible output was mentioned by the students as an important driver: the first project delivered professional academic research; the second had the website as an artefact. The outputs meant the students' creative efforts were there for others to see in terms of product but there was also recognition of the value of the process:

"This project made me feel much more confident within my camera work and also made me much more aware of the importance of social media as a professional tool. It impacted the way I use social media." (Under-graduate 2nd Year Television student 1).

The motivational value of being paid for their work raises some seemingly contradictory responses in the students. One student mentions the money as being important, *"it definitely encourages you to work hard on a project and put it high in your list of priorities"* (Undergraduate 2nd Year Television student 2), making it more like a preparation for professional freelance work. Conversely, another student stated that the payment was not an issue, because of being habituated to working in a voluntary capacity on work placements.

Much student work is extrinsically motivated by compulsory assessment. Being involved in this project was voluntary and not assessed, although the work could count towards undergraduate work placements which are a compulsory aspect of the undergraduate Media course. There was the potential that the students would lose motivation during the project, because of its extra-curricular nature. This seems not to have been the case. The team dynamic seems to be one of the factors affecting the success of the project. Although this developed organically, it aligned to the stages of team development as described by Tuckman (in Karman & Weber, 1991:S12): 'forming', 'storming', 'norming', 'performing'. Certainly, the 'norming' stage of the project very much aligned in that it was characterised by *"trust, harmony, and the acceptance of identities [...] cohesion, participative decision making, and egalitarian leadership"* (ibid).

Paradoxically the students report taking the project more seriously than their University assessments; they became increasingly motivated, especially when they appreciated that no one within the group was, *"slacking, unlike some of the experiences of group work in University assessments*" (Undergraduate 2ⁿᵈ Year Television student 1). They enjoyed working as a group on the production: *"we were a real team as we enjoyed working on the project and wanted to be part of it"* (Undergraduate 2ⁿᵈ Year Television student 1).

The students also mention the positives of being able to work closely with lecturers outside of an assessed assignment, thereby building a learning community. Overall it seems that the project had a profound effect on them, changing their perception of what the student role was. This observation fits with Mezirow's theories of the transformational role of learning, and particularly the goal of adult learning: that the student's immediate objective may be seen in terms of mastery of particular skills and project related objectives, but that the ultimate goal is to become a socially responsible, autonomous thinker (1997:8). In this project it is clear that those tangible objectives have been met but it remains to be seen the extent to which this translates into the more intangible notions of 'autonomy' and 'social responsibility'.

Motivation from the students' point of view increased at two critical points: firstly, once the pilot video and website designs had been viewed, changes made and a style agreed on, and secondly, once the website went live, and there was fairly rapid and positive feedback from people outside the project. It can be argued that both these critical points were extrinsic motivators, but the combination of motivators is rather more complex. The signing off of the initial designs and content for the learning resources gave the students licence to take ownership of the content and design creation, sparking their intrinsic motivation. They felt secure in the lecturers' confidence in their abilities and knew what was expected of them. The fact that the students had creative freedom, and were working to established parameters, changed their motivation:

> *"I took ownership through working with the other Television students to articulate our perspective and experiences of social media into the project, where we would all organise and direct each video and contributor. This gave us a lot of creative control, as I was able to have an input in what types of videos we should make, how we would make them, what topics we wanted to cover and who the best contributors would be."* (Undergraduate 2ⁿᵈ Year Television student 1).

Developing this sense of co-ownership of the project was crucial for its success, and chimes with notions of involvement, belonging and community discussed by Bryson & Hardy (2010).

The postgraduate student involved in the initial research project cites professional interest in the subject matter as an intrinsic motivator, and this is almost certainly true of the students in the second SAP project as well.

> "I sought to consider, explore and understand a number of themes: general usage of social media platforms in the lives of 'digital natives' and whether this was quite as prolific as is often suggested; whether digital tools provide the opportunity for more strategic usage i.e. a legitimate and proven method of enhancing employability opportunities; and the extent to which these more strategic practices are evident among students. This proved an extremely valuable opportunity for academic development beyond the requirements or opportunities afforded by a degree course." (Postgraduate Social Media student)

This intrinsic motivation appears to have provided a strong impetus. Gibbs (1992) stresses that intrinsic motivation is more likely to promote deep learning, with students learning best in order to carry out tasks that matter to them. Learning by doing, when activity is planned and reflected upon, and when it involves interacting with others, is likely to be most successful. The students involved in both the projects had all these factors in their favour, and through their first hand testimony acknowledge that they learnt a lot through the project.

Media professionalism and creativity

Blended individuals are those who draw on both professional and academic experience, and are able to *"develop new forms of professional space, knowledge, relationships and legitimacies associated with broadly based institutional projects"* (Whitchurch, 2009:417). The lecturers involved in the project fit this profile, having backgrounds in media production as well as academia, and therefore perhaps found it relatively easy to adopt the role of media industry executives rather than teachers. It came naturally to them, in a way that lecturers without a practice background might struggle. Similarly the students, who have experienced industry placements and are used to producing media artefacts for assessed practical coursework, adopted their production roles with ease. The School of Media at Birmingham City University prides itself on a culture of intelligent media production, having the mantra of aiming to produce, 'thinking media workers'. The fact that both academic staff and students are imbued with this philosophy may account for the pragmatic adoption of a media industry production model.

Initially the lecturers were unsure if the students would have the expertise and motivation to be able to organise both the shaping of the content and the logistics. They were prepared to have to step in on initial shoots, to set the style and modus operandi, although this proved not to be necessary. The SAP scheme under which the project operated is essentially interested in *process*, because that's where the value of learning would be for academic staff and students. The desire to produce a tangible and quality *product* therefore came from within the team. 'Professional pride' from all involved ensured that a useful and high quality product was developed.

Fortnightly meetings were organised in order to plan the project and keep it on track. Both students and academic staff found these meetings useful in developing a collective understanding of how the learning resources might look and work: There was a shared vision, which facilitated collaborative working towards a common goal. One of the students comments on the meetings:

> "As a group we built the ideas from the research together, thus the meetings were where all creative ideas and direction were liaised and finalised. Also the group was kind of split into three sections, with the lecturers leading the project, the Web students making the website and blog content, and myself and the other TV students making the video content." Thus, meetings were great in updating everyone on each other's progress and problems we found which we could resolve in person." (Undergraduate 2nd Year Television student 1)

The value of the meetings cannot be underestimated, a view which is reinforced by Mezirow's (1997) research. The meetings were the venue for discourse, a space for social learning and meaning making, where judgements could be tested, and assumptions critically reflected upon, in the search for common ground. Mezirow (1997) finds that the ideal conditions for discourse are also those of effective adult learning.

Academic staff/student relationships

There was an unequal power relationship between the academic staff and students involved in the project. The lecturers instigated the project, and recruited the students, thereby immediately making the relationship uneven. The lecturers could have replaced students, if they had underperformed, in a way which was not reciprocal. However, there was a mutual respect, and in meetings everyone's opinions were listened to. The fact that the lecturers had a professional trust in the students was important to the relationship being a positive one.

For the second project, to build a learning resource, a production team with complementary skills needed to be put together. Recruitment of students with web skills and video skills was undertaken by recommendation and direct knowledge of the students in question. Within the media industry production teams are frequently assembled pragmatically from those known to the production company or recommended to it, providing they have the correct fit of skills and availability. Therefore, it can be mooted that industry practice prevailed. However, it could also be argued that a transparent system of fair selection, including applications and interviews, would have been preferable, particularly if involvement in this kind of extra-curricular project is seen to confer a benefit to those involved. A benefit that is two-fold in that it produces an external-facing *product* and involves a *process* that is rewarding in itself. With the increase in fees payable by students, there may be more pressure to get the most out of the Higher Education experience, and therefore to take part in these kind of non-assessed projects, see Chapman, P. *et al.* (in this volume) for details of further initiatives being developed by Birmingham City University. The proposed Higher Education Achievement Report (HEAR) is an attempt to formally acknowledge such non-assessed projects alongside students' degree awards (Universities UK, 2012).

The students reported finding the relationship with the lecturers productive, enabling them to develop ideas and have some creative control, whilst being guided and assisted. The fact that the lecturers trusted the students to work independently and to experiment with ideas made the experience feel different from University work. This collaborative working and *"notions of students as 'partners in a learning community' seem to be stronger in certain subject areas*" (Little *et al.*, 2009:4). Media and Communication, one could argue, is probably one of these subject areas, and therefore the project was to some extent building on an existing culture, see also Vaughan & Williams (in this volume) for a discussion of the learning culture within an arts discipline.

Mezirow (1997) is clear that to maximise the transformational impact of learning, the educator should create an environment which fosters self-direction and autonomous thinking, where students learn from each other and create problem-solving groups, and ideally where the lecturer ceases to be an authority figure and becomes a co-learner. Inadvertently, or perhaps instinctively, the lecturers seem to have created an effective learning environment which benefitted both the students' development, and the project outcomes.

Workload

Being involved in the project impacted on the workload of both academic staff and students, especially as it was an extra-curricular activity. Some of the students voiced the opinion that it would have been beneficial to be able to concentrate on the project to the exclusion of assessed work, although this would not have been practical, unless the project was confined to vacation periods. Students found the time management challenging, and frequently underestimated how long it would take to organise, film and edit each video. Juggling project activities with assessment deadlines taught the students transferrable personal management skills.

Designing curriculum resources

Curriculum resources are usually designed by lecturers, without consultation, let alone collaboration, with students. This culture potentially leads to lost opportunities, and is worth re-thinking. "*The engagement of students in learning design [...] can lead to students perceiving improvements in curricular relevance*" (Trowler, 2010:25). This statement seems to be borne out by the opinion of students involved in the creation of the learning resources. They felt that because they were more 'in touch' with other students, they were better able to understand how to target resources well in order to support other students.

It is to be hoped that because the site has been created for students, by students, and shares student experiences, it will not be perceived as didactic or dictatorial, in the way that the student focus groups from the initial research feared. The learning resources have not yet been formally utilised as part of the curriculum. This is planned for the next academic year, and analysis of the relative success of student-produced resources might be a fruitful avenue for future research.

Outcomes – predicted and unexpected

The social media and employability project has resulted in a number of outcomes, some predicted and tangible, like the website itself, whilst others have been largely unexpected, such as a subtle shift in the relationship between academic staff and students, and even improved student attendance. The relative success of the website surprised some of the students:

> "It was great making it, but showing people the finished outcome was so much better…..The website was really well received! Especially by all the other students and colleagues, who I think, would have loved to have got involved, when we had started!" (Undergraduate 2nd Year Television student 1)

The website has had some very positive feedback; it is openly available and can be used as a promotional and marketing tool by the School of Media and the wider University. Whilst there has been no financial benefit to the institution because of the project, there is a reputational benefit. Perhaps more subtly, simply having the website used by a network of people not only stakes an intellectual claim to the territory around the subject area, but raises awareness of the work of lecturers and students alike. Conversely there could have been a reputational risk if the quality of the site did not meet a threshold standard. If that had been the case the lecturers involved would have taken the decision not to publish the site.

Academic paper and presentations

The initial research was included in a presentation at an international Media education conference by the lecturers involved. This was written up as a paper, published in a peer reviewed Media journal in the United Kingdom (Harte & Jackson, 2011). The publishing of academic articles enhances the reputation of both the institution and the individuals involved. After the project website went live the academic staff and students involved were asked to present at a number of conferences, both internal and external to the University. For the students this was their first opportunity to present, and one which would not have occurred without the project. They were conscious that they received a lot of credit for their contribution to the project after their presentations.

Employability of students

Being involved in the project has had recognisable benefits to the students in terms of their own employability. This chimes with the views of Carini *et al*, that being actively engaged adds to the development of skills and attitude that are essential to a productive life beyond Higher Education, (2006, citing Shulman, 2002). The website itself offers the students a real world case study to add to their portfolio of work. Taking part in the creation of learning resources is an example of them working as 'freelancers' in a near professional capacity, which can be included in CVs. The students note that their practical film making and web design skills have improved, as well as their editorial knowhow in terms of content creation:

> "I have learnt quite a few technical skills that can be taken forward and I have developed a number of personal skills that will help me within the work environment." (Undergraduate 2nd Year New Media student 1)

One of the students summed up the impact of the experience personally:

> "I feel this project has prepared me for working to a brief in the professional world, as although we practice and undertake these types of assignments within University time, this project felt very professional and serious." (Undergraduate 2nd Year Television student 1).

We did not explore why the students perceived the output as more professional than some of their coursework, but conclusions could be drawn about the impact of close academic staff supervision, and the positive reaction to the website from external employers and others outside the students' immediate circle of contacts, such as other lecturers. As a result of the project one of the students was successful in applying for a very competitive broadcaster's work experience scheme. In the interview much of the conversation was directed around the scope of the project and the company was clearly impressed by the student's involvement. Two of the students have also been approached by other departments within the University to produce promotional videos for them, as a result of their work being showcased on the website.

The students also noted how participating in the project had enhanced their awareness of social media as a professional tool and improved their strategic use of it. This offers a further example of the students benefitting from the *process* and potentially improving their employability as a consequence. Importantly the students reported that the project had increased their confidence in approaching companies for work experience because they were proud of their creative input within the project and happy to showcase it.

The students certainly seem to have benefitted from participating in the project and to have developed a competitive advantage over some of their peers. This result reflects Kuh who argued that 'high impact' activities have very strong direct effects on engagement (2009:689). However, it introduces some ethical issues over the fair selection of students taking part in such schemes going forwards and whether such projects can be scaled up in terms of participating numbers. Kuh observes that where 'boutique like' projects are seen to work, that they ought to be made widely available (2007:B13). The SAP scheme whilst open to all is limited in participation terms by logistical issues such as: funding; the devising of suitable projects; and the impact on lecturers' workloads.

Shift in Attitudes between Academics and Students

Taking part in the project has resulted in a subtle shift in the relationship between the academic staff and students involved, see also Montesinos *et al.* (in this volume). One reason for this change is probably due to the familiarity of getting to know each other better as individuals; another is the collaborative nature of the project. For the postgraduate student involved in the initial research project, the process produced a more radical change of relationship:

> "Having a project-centred approach creates informal networks of students and academics alike, in a way that the institutions themselves cannot so easily facilitate. This was an entirely unexpected benefit of the process which had the effect of transcending the traditional roles of student and academic, contributing to a sense of blurring the lines that repositions the learning experience more as a guided discovery rather than a simple imparting of generally accepted knowledge." (Postgraduate Social Media student).

This position highlights the collaborative nature of the journey and presents an equality between lecturers and students not normally seen in the classroom. It also suggests a changed perception of the unequal power relationship in the project, as noted earlier. The identities of both students and lecturers and their relationship have subtly metamorphosed. Kuh (2007) sees opportunities for students to work with lecturers as having numerous benefits, not least because they have an additional source of encouragement and support when times are challenging.

In the second project the position of academic staff was different from their usual role in lecturing: they were not there to teach the students, but to shape, oversee and contribute creatively to the development of both the design and content of the website. This role is more akin to an industry relationship of executive producer and production team, rather than the traditional teacher-pupil stance. The students began to see the lecturers more as industry professionals, as one of them explains:

> "The project has reinforced for me the view that the lecturers have the ability to guide students and not just teach us." (Undergraduate 2nd Year Television student 1).

One of the elements that particularly pleased the academic staff was the independence demonstrated by the students. Once the style of the video pieces was established and signed off, the students took it upon themselves to research additional contributors and topics, to then record and edit the short videos, without the need to consult with academic staff. The fact that the students took ownership of the project in this way, and felt that they had licence within boundaries to create their own content, led to a greater number of videos being recorded, covering a greater number of subjects than originally envisaged. If the academic staff involvement had been more prescriptive, there is a danger that the students would have felt the need to have each idea signed off, slowing the creative process and potentially reducing the task satisfaction experienced by the students.

Student engagement

Student engagement is predicated on the importance of how the individual participates in educationally worthwhile activities. Whilst students have a responsibility for constructing their own knowledge, positive engagement also relies on institutions and academic staff generating conditions that stimulate involvement (AUSSE, 2009:3). Collaborations such as the social media and employability project seem to offer rich opportunities for students. Kuh (2007:B13) emphasises the benefit to students of being able to apply what they have learnt in class to real-world problems, finding that it deepens their learning and sharpens their critical thinking. Harper & Quaye argue that: *"Engagement is more than involvement or participation – it requires feelings and sense making as well as activity"* (in Trowler, 2010:5). The students involved in the project evidenced this form of engagement; they came to care about the project and understood its potential once the parameters were set. Kuh (in Bryson & Hardy, 2010:1) developed a framework for student engagement, based on five benchmarks:

- Level of academic challenge;

- Enriching educational experiences;

- Active and collaborative learning;

- Supportive campus environment;

- Student-faculty interaction.

Our project seems to meet these benchmarks: it was relatively taxing creatively for the students; it led to them learning new skills and knowledge; it was active and necessitated working with other students; the University was supportive of the project financially and in terms of arranging workshops and progress checks; finally, the initiative was a collaboration between academic staff and students. This combination of factors has probably influenced the success of the project. The recent 'What Works?' report (Thomas 2012) reinforces Kuh's philosophy in relation to activities that support student engagement, arguing that they should: *"...nurture a culture of belonging through supportive peer relations, meaningful interaction between staff and students, developing students' knowledge, confidence and identity as successful HE learners and an HE experience that is relevant to interests and future goals."* (Thomas, 2012:20)

Conclusion - reflection and externalising

All the students involved in the project described it as a very positive experience. One student said it had a tremendous impact on him, encouraging him to come into University more often and even to attend all his lectures. This was not an outcome that we were anticipating but demonstrates the wider learning benefits of schemes such as this in fostering the learning community. Increased attendance is likely to impact positively on progression and retention, and on the level of achievement. In fact this observation fits with conclusions made by Kuh & Hu (2001:21) that student-staff interaction encourages students to put more effort into other worthwhile educational activities. Several students found the skills they had developed transferred automatically into their University work. They had learnt a great deal through the project. This backs up much of the research into the positive effect on learning and development when students have meaningful contact with academic staff beyond the classroom setting and when academics engage with students as individuals (Astin in AUSSE, 2009:20; Kuh & Hu, 2001). Additionally the project seems to have resulted in the students becoming more ambitious about future plans,

> *"I think students could start approaching universities and lecturers with their own creative ideas and start building them into projects."* (Undergraduate 2nd Year Television student 1)

and

"I'd ultimately like the university to put faith in its students to create an advert for television for the university." (Undergraduate 2nd Year Television student 2).

They seem to have become more empowered through the experience and be excited by the prospect of more student-led projects, rather than academic staff-initiated ones.

In terms of how the project has impacted on the teaching of the academic staff in question, firstly, the website has proved the potential for the success of multi-media production teams. Secondly, the project has provided a model for collaborative working where the balance of power and control may be different from the classroom, thus engendering a positive culture of production. This can trickle down to the management of assessed group coursework, and demonstrates the benefit of academic staff taking on an overseeing role at the outset of a media production before taking a lighter touch approach after the parameters of the project are cemented.

The postgraduate student involved in the research phase made an unexpected observation about the subject matter of the project, and how it relates to the School of Media's activities:

"If students can use social technologies to bolster their relationships with employers, perhaps the partnership gave a glimpse at how academic institutions can deploy similar tactics to engage businesses. This not only builds strong links between them but also provides further opportunities for wider student engagement." (Postgraduate Social Media student)

This notion, whilst beyond the scope of this study, could provide productive ideas for future work in this subject area.

Questions remain about how projects such as this, where the *process* results in increased student engagement, can be made available to more students. It shouldn't be forgotten that in this instance, the *product* has had a wider benefit to other students and indeed a wider public. Kuh observes that when significant numbers of academic staff at an institution agree on the efficacy of an activity then resources and time tend to be directed towards it, meaning that it becomes available to a greater number of students and that participation is encouraged by the campus culture (2009:690). It is to be hoped that the SAP scheme is now established enough, and has been seen to have achieved sufficient impact, to be enlarged in terms of the number of projects funded and in the level of ambition of the projects.

About the authors

Mark Ashfield is a part-time postgraduate student at Birmingham City University studying for a MA in Social Media. He can be contacted at **mark@justaddlime.co.uk**

David Harte is Award Leader for the MA in Social Media at Birmingham City University. He can be contacted at **dave.harte@bcu.ac.uk**

Vanessa Jackson is Degree Leader in Television for the BA (Hons) in Media and Communication at Birmingham City University. She can be contacted at **vanessa.jackson@bcu.ac.uk**

Chapter 6

All Aboard: Using the Student Advisory Board to Engage Students with University Decision Making Processes

Sophie Rowe, Emily Cooper and Lynn Fulford

Introduction

This chapter presents a refreshing way to engage students in taking ownership of the decision making processes which ultimately affect their student experience. Using personal reflections from students and staff, it offers an insight into the successes and challenges faced by the formation of a Student Advisory Board (SAB) within a large faculty encompassing Education, Law and Social Science programmes. This chapter challenges orthodox processes, such as traditional Boards of Studies and the hierarchical power relationships they uphold. Instead it proposes that there is a case to be made for a shift in the ways of thinking about engaging students as active participants in their learning communities.

Provisions for students' involvement in university decision making originates from the democratisation of universities in the industrialised cities of West Europe in the 1960s and early 1970s (Luescher-Mamashela, 2011). During this time, formal student involvement in university governance became a feature of institution wide strategy, most often accomplished by extending existing committees' membership. Indeed, it is understood that following the 1994 Education Act there is a wider framework for representing the students' voice through Students' Unions, highlighted by Chapman, P. *et al.* in this volume. However, this chapter will focus specifically on the empowerment of students through faculty-based processes. This may be viewed as a subtle marginalisation of the Students' Union in student representation.

Student engagement as a sense of belonging

This chapter looks at student engagement in regard to students engaging with and taking ownership of university decision making processes. Student engagement is particularly elusive and difficult to define (Trowler, 2010). Kuh (2003:25) identifies it as: *"The time and energy students devote to educationally sound activities inside and outside of the classroom, and the policies and practices that institutions use to induce students to take part in these activities."* Whilst this definition is perhaps a useful starting point, it neglects what might be called the 'emotional' aspect of engagement that manifests itself in a kind of energy and feeling of connectedness to the institution. Evidence from a study across seven higher education institutions conducted by the Higher Education Academy found that between 37% – 42% of students think about withdrawing from higher education, with the primary reason being due the feeling of isolation (Thomas, 2012). An increased sense of belonging is therefore vital in addressing retention levels. The student interest in having personalised SAB merchandise, such as hoodies, represents an important symbol of engagement and identity.

Engagement, as understood in this chapter, means that students who wish to improve the institutional experience have the ability to suggest and discuss ideas with staff who are working towards the same goal. A key characteristic of the individuals involved in the SAB is that they are intrinsically motivated to make a real change to the student experience; this notion of self-efficacy is also discussed by Hutchings *et al.* in this volume. The collaborative partnership adopted by SAB fosters a model learning community because both parties have a genuine interest in the enhancement of academic and student life.

It is of note that students who engage with the SAB become more engaged and then often seek other opportunities to work within the institution. For example, those who participate in the SAB have also become university mentors, ambassadors and volunteers. It is this kind of wider involvement that gives student a feeling of pride in their institution and

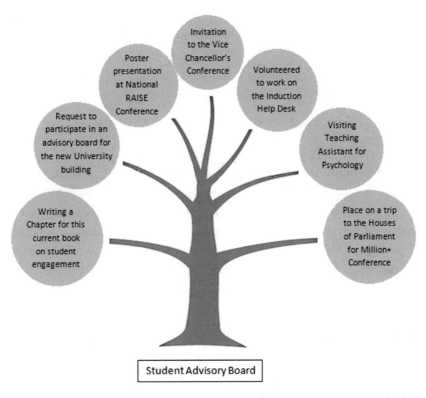

Invitation to the Vice Chancellor's Conference

Poster presentation at National RAISE Conference

Volunteered to work on the Induction Help Desk

Request to participate in an advisory board for the new University building

Visiting Teaching Assistant for Psychology

Writing a Chapter for this current book on student engagement

Place on a trip to the Houses of Parliament for Million+ Conference

Student Advisory Board

Figure 1: A tree diagram to demonstrate the network of opportunities a SAB member has subsequently been involved in

motivates them to achieve. Due to the different variables impacting on student engagement it is difficult to determine the relationship between involvement in SAB and further opportunities. However, through examining a student's participation in other university activities since becoming involved with SAB, the relationship was clearly causational in this instance (see Figure 1).

Through the experience of speaking to SAB members, students who are engaged in their studies and further activities understand that there is more to university life than 'grade chasing'. Experience to date tells us that students recognise that the university experience is multi-dimensional, providing a huge range of curricular and extra-curricular activities that will enable them to develop as professional individuals with excellent employability skills, and as members of their communities. However, simultaneously, they usually achieve highly in their studies because of their full participation, engagement and interest (Gibbs, 2010). This notion is reinforced by the claim from Lizzio & Wilson (2009:70) that *"extra-curricular activities foster academic and personal development"*. The most successful students, academically and professionally, are those who do more than simply comply with their programme's requirements; compliance is not the same as engagement.

Indeed, student engagement plays a central part in discussions regarding the purposes of higher education, particularly at a time when the wider political discourse uses market place metaphors – where students are 'customers' and universities 'providers' (Trowler, 2010). Such metaphors do not capture the transformative learning of higher education and its contribution to *"an individual's personal resources in ways that allow them to feel capable, to pursue meaningful activities, to have aesthetic experiences, to feel a degree of autonomy"* (Seaford et al., 2011:48). These emotions and experiences are at the heart of student engagement.

The Student Advisory Board: a new approach

The SAB is a faculty instigated project which assimilates the ideas of staff and students through a forum which promotes active participation. The SAB brings together a variety of student representatives and senior staff within the faculty, all with an active passion for enhancing learning and teaching. Student members invited to the Board are those who already represent their faculty as either university ambassadors or as student representatives who have been nominated by their peers. There are around fifteen SAB student members, including mature, part-time and postgraduate students. However, to move SAB forward it will adopt a supplementary forum open to all students who wish to share ideas regarding cross-faculty learning and teaching development.

Members meet twice a term – in the evening to accommodate students on placement – to discuss topics and to initiate creative solutions which positively impact upon the student experience. In between SAB meetings members meet as smaller project groups to develop action points agreed. Regular contact makes students feel as though the interpersonal relationships they build have stability, this helps foster a sense of belonging and identity (Baumeister & Leary, 1995).

Past resources designed by SAB Members aimed at enhancing the induction process include: student-friendly programme handbook, visual campus map, and a talking head video of lecturers. SAB members have also influenced faculty policy by initiating the Dean's Awards system of celebrating student achievement and participation, thereby demonstrating a move towards students as active participants in university decision making processes. Indeed, the honesty which arises out of students' feedback is invaluable and instructive of change. By engaging both staff and students in a forum which is separate from formal academic processes, such as Boards of Studies, students are able to set the agenda and direction of the meetings. This has the potential to empower students and promote a more proactive and meaningful approach to feedback.

In comparison, the structures of traditional boards originally designed for staff members are outdated and restrictive:

> "*The Board of Studies meetings are a dreaded date on the academic calendar.*" (Student SAB member).

Today it is common practice in the United Kingdom for universities to hold Board of Studies meetings for each programme. It should be pointed out that Boards of Studies still remain part of university protocol following the formation of SAB as a way to process minor modifications at a programme level. Contrastingly, the SAB is specifically focused on topics rooted in enhancing the student experience across faculty. Agendas for both Boards remain separate and minutes from both feed into faculty level learning and teaching and student experience committees.

Board of Studies members usually comprise programme directors, academic staff and at least two elected student representatives from each year group. However, they are noticeably poorly attended by students. Typically matters discussed include: programme director's report, staff feedback, student representatives' report, learning resources issues and equal opportunities.

> "*There is a feeling of going through the motions, ticking off points on the agenda as the meeting proceeds.*" (SAB Member)

Alternatively, students are empowered by the SAB process. They set the agenda, date and time of meetings, and take real steps towards resolving arising student concerns. SAB encompasses problem based learning which helps develop employability skills, as mentioned in Hutchings *et al.* (in this volume). By using a learner-centred forum, as opposed to a restrictive meeting, the SAB is able to discuss problems more deeply and foster sense of community between staff and students (Gerosa *et al.*, 2005).

> *"I felt more comfortable in voicing my opinions in the SAB as they are specifically focused on the views and ideas of students."* (Student SAB member)

This comment reflects the findings from a similar pilot participatory workshop style approach to committee meetings at the University of Lincoln, which found *"students and staff felt more able to speak out confidently, articulating their ideas and thoughts at times when they felt unable to talk"* (Bishop *et al.*, 2012:12).

Boards of Studies do not offer opportunities to develop collaborative projects or to conduct research. They are generally held as a quality assurance measure, to report back on matters rather than to innovate or to enhance the learning experience. Concerns are noted but are eventually lost amongst the vast number of pages of minutes. This leads to students feeling that the comments they raise are not taken seriously.

> *"The sad truth is that usually the thoughts and recommendations are brushed over and therefore, the issues that matter to those undertaking study at a particular university remain unnoticed. This fuels frustrations further, leaving those students involved in the Board of Studies meetings feeling disheartened."* (Student SAB member)

It is recognised that this may not be the case for all Boards of Studies; however this quote demonstrates how a lack of meaningful student engagement in quality processes consequently fails to *"enhance the collective student learning experience"* (Little & Williams, 2010 cited in Bishop *et al.*, 2012:2). When an issue is raised and no clear action is taken to rectify concerns students become demotivated. This in turn leads to students feeling they have limited ownership of decision-making processes and subsequently the inability to contribute to any kind of change.

On the other hand, SAB members are made to feel valued for their contribution. Students are paid for their attendance at meetings, time spent on creative projects and for the collection and consolidation of wider student feedback. The faculty acknowledges the increased financial pressure on students and offers an attractive hourly wage (£10 per hour) in comparison to service sector roles. Paying students creates accessibility for those individuals from a poor socio-economic background, and avoids discrimination against those who need to work alongside their studies to cover living expenses. According to a study conducted by Moreau & Leathwood (2006:34) which looked at the experience of working class students in higher education: *"a frequently mentioned strategy for coping with and managing the conflicting demands of paid employment and study was to limit social activities... such a strategy, however impacts on the extent to which students felt part of university life."*

The SAB overcomes this issue by offering a role which incorporates simultaneously a source of income and social activity. Payment symbolises that, just as staff are paid, so too are student partners: the payment sends a clear message that the university values the work that is done and, of course, it enhances a student's curriculum vitae because they are undertaking paid employment. Further discussion surroundings the benefits and shortcomings of paying students can be found in Montesinos *et al.* in this volume.

Student Advisory Board	Board of Studies
Students represented across faculty	Students represented across a programme
Attended by staff from senior management	Attended by academic staff
Agenda flexible, led by students	Agenda restrictive, governed by university protocol
Quality enhancement tool	Quality assurance tool
Exist to enhance the student experience across faculty	Exist to process minor modifications at a programme level
Regular committee meetings, held in the evening for students on placement	Committee meets once a term, date and time is determined by staff
Student members are paid for their contribution	Student members attend on a voluntary basis

Table 1: A table comparing characteristics of the Student Advisory Board and Board of Studies

Motivations for being involved in SAB

The following section provides testimonials from the Associate Dean for Student Experience and a student SAB member regarding their motivations behind becoming involved in SAB. The following extract represents the view of Associate Dean for Student Experience, and SAB member:

> "My idea to start a Board where students have an active voice began from my membership of a cross university group convened to discuss student representation. I had just been appointed Associate Dean with responsibility for student experience and it seemed to me that the traditional way of listening to students' voices through Boards of Studies was highly unsatisfactory. They are pseudo collaborative, existing in theory to hear the voices of all stakeholders but are, in reality, over-formalised, dominated by protocols and by senior staff. I believed that we needed something less formal, more student-led and more dynamic that would enable students to meet across programmes, to share ideas and experiences honestly and, above all, to allow changes to take place as a result of student initiatives and ideas."

The following extract represents the view of a psychology student, and SAB member.

> "As a student representative for my cohort of psychology students, I enjoy being actively involved in my university experience and offering advice and suggestions as to how to make academic life more fulfilling for all students at the university. When the opportunity arose for a position within the Student Advisory Board, I jumped at the chance. I wanted to be part of an initiative run by students for students. I have many a time represented my cohort in Board of Studies in which I have 'waited my turn' to feed back. In my experience staff have welcomed student participation on traditional boards, however I understand that this is not the case for all students. This perhaps demonstrates that the success of Boards of Studies is dependent on the enlightened academics which empower the student voice. However, in some respects I still recognise that the structure of the meetings is archaic in approach. Student representatives are simply there to comply with university protocol. Thus my main motivation for joining and partaking in the SAB was to help other students find their voice and become confident with their own ideas."

Positive consequences of SAB

SAB has positively impacted on student engagement through the redistribution of power, which in turn has helped to build a learning community and to enhance students' employability. The following section considers these positive outcomes through the exploration of student quotes.

Redistributing power

Students' participation in decisions surrounding their learning environment is often obstructed by power relationships (Schratz & Blossing, 2005). Similarly, Lizzio and Wilson (2009:71) claim: *"While conscious efforts are routinely made to protect students' rights in university policy and procedure, the often hierarchical structures of educational institutions can, perhaps inadvertently, privilege "staff discourse" and marginalise student views."*

Change at a faculty level can only be achieved by fully engaging those that make up the majority of the learning community. This section will therefore explore how the creation of SAB engages students through the redistribution of power from staff to students.

According to the UK Quality Code for Higher Education outlined by the Quality Assurance Agency for Higher Education (2012) student engagement needs to do and be more than just student representation. Having a voice is not the same as having power to enforce change. Quality enhancement processes only have a positive impact under certain circumstances (Gibbs, 2010). For example, collecting student feedback on induction has little or no impact on improving induction unless it is accompanied by other processes which implement change driven by feedback.

SAB gives students the opportunity to talk about their university experience and to bring about change through creative projects. The implementation of SAB demonstrates to the wider student body that the university is concerned about real student issues and is taking steps to address concerns promptly.

> *"Students were encouraged to bring our thoughts to the table without feeling like they were an unwanted necessity. This made me feel*

empowered both as an individual and as a representative of the student body." (Student SAB member)

Subsequently there is a natural respect for those that give up some of their power and who instead become learners themselves (Schratz & Blossing, 2005). For instance, the Faculty's Associate Dean handed over some power to enable students to steer the SAB discussion towards real issues that impact on the student experience and to suggest effective ways to change. Concerns are raised by Schratz and Blossing (2005:391) as to whether traditional staff roles can be maintained if students are given more influence; although it could be argued that this is not a bad thing when trying to challenge existing power relationships and building a learning community.

Protocol states that Boards of Studies should have student representatives present to give a wholesome and rounded view of university life. However, Boards are largely attended by academic members of staff, leading them to be hierarchical rather than collegiate and collaborative. This is problematic for two reasons, firstly the asymmetrical imbalance of students and staff means that the students are outnumbered in representation, and secondly because academics are systematically empowered to influence the outcome they desire. As a consequence Boards of Studies can be overwhelming for students especially if the student representative does not have a pre-existing rapport with the academic staff. Not only this, but students are further isolated by the unnecessary use of acronyms, abbreviations and managerial rhetoric, which sometimes even causes members of academic staff to stare in bemusement at each other.

"Board of Studies meetings can be a little intimidating as they are full of faculty members and are very formal in their execution." (Student SAB member)

"I found that I would become quite nervous when it came to giving the student representative report and sometimes this would cause me to tune out of the meeting altogether." (Student SAB member)

These quotes demonstrate a lack of student engagement. However, perhaps the best evidence of hierarchical structure can be seen by the order of the agenda. The student representatives' report is often situated in an ill-timed place, after the programme director's report and academics' feedback, near the end of the meeting. After waiting patiently for their scheduled five minutes students are often ushered to speed up to ensure that the meeting finishes on time. Even when students do feed back about problems, academic members of staff seem to dictate the direction of the meeting. This highlights that Boards of Studies have a quality, rather than enhancement focus.

> *"Staff are held 'accountable' for anything students are perhaps not engaging with. The prevailing attitude seems it be 'it's all your fault, fix it'."* (Student SAB member)

From this quote it is possible to see an emerging 'us' and 'them' mentality. Not surprisingly, staff often seem to be on the defensive within these Boards. This finding reflects data collected by Lizzio and Wilson (2009) from interviews conducted with twenty student representatives. Research investigated the issues typically initiated with staff and common themes were found: concern for the quality of student experience, the fairness of university procedures, or staff behaviours. Consequently, Boards which focus on accountability may have a detrimental effect on efforts made to foster a collaborative learning community.

Staff experience of SAB

Below is an account provided by the Associate Dean for Student Experience.

The development of the SAB is a fundamental part of the faculty's student engagement strategy, enabling staff not only to elicit students' views but to use them to impact on policy. From its beginnings in November 2010 the SAB has impressed staff greatly for a number of reasons:

- ✦ The high levels of energy, organisation and proactivity demonstrated by the students;

- Students' willingness to use innovative ways of engaging with their peers;

- Their ability to project manage, make presentations and communicate with staff and peers;

- The team approach students adopt as Board Members.

Central to the success of the SAB is its collegiate nature. Students are encouraged to set the agenda, to chair meetings and to decide how best to manage any projects that emerge from the meetings. Since the SAB's inception, students have been able to impact positively on a number of strategies, including faculty communications, assessment and student induction. SAB recommendations have led to programme materials being updated to a more student-friendly format.

Universities can sometimes, for understandable reasons, have processes and procedures that can seem slow and difficult to change. It is extremely refreshing and energising to work with students on the SAB, not just because they bring new ideas to the faculty, but because they bring a very powerful energy, a readiness to embrace change, to question existing practices and to make a positive impact on the experiences of students.

Building a learning community

As a result of redistributing power SAB has helped to build a learning community. Through participative processes staff and students are able to learn from experiences. A by-product of the meetings is co-learning: ideas continuously emerge from different perspectives, eliciting further discussion and reflection. This helps towards building a learning community because it encourages student engagement and ownership.

The SAB develops a way in which students can take real ownership of their learning experience, extending their capacity to implement change whilst working in partnership with staff. Students particularly appreciate advocacy from the Associate Dean:

> "The prevailing attitude seemed to be 'Could this be better?, let's work together and see what we can achieve!'" (Student SAB member)

"Being part of the SAB is an opportunity to work collaboratively with other students to implement changes and improvements to different aspects of a university. Staff play an important role too, as often their expertise and opinions are needed for a successful project." (Student SAB member)

The element of uniting students with staff means there is a sense of learning from both parties. In the same way Chambers & Nagle, in this volume, also recognise that students offer a key advantage compared to university staff as they are new to the institution and unencumbered by the burden of tradition. Students offer a view not contorted by rules and regulations; this gives them the ability to come up with innovative and unconventional solutions to student experience issues (Schratz & Blossing, 2005). Not only this, but also they are an invaluable resource of first hand student experience. Staff members are able to harness the passion, desire and interest that students have in improving their experience in order to make a real change. Academic staff have knowledge surrounding the mechanics of how to get things done, university processes and their restrictions. They also have experience and an archive of knowledge of what works and what doesn't. Without the cooperation of staff and students the SAB would become redundant.

Student experience of SAB

Students' articulation of their experiences highlighted a prevailing theme: a sense of belonging and identity, expressed as pride in the institution.

"I enjoyed being on the SAB and felt that it built bridges between students on various programmes, enabling a well-rounded view of student experiences at university." (Student SAB member)

"I feel that I have gained confidence in my own opinions and expressing these to others." (Student SAB member)

'The SAB was extremely enlightening, providing passionate students with the tools and opportunities to make changes for the better based on student needs and expectations." (Student SAB member)

Findings in this chapter are in line with wider sectorial evidence from the Higher Education Academy that a sense of belonging is most effectively nurtured through *"mainstream activities with an overt academic purpose that all students participate in"* (Thomas, 2012:12). Due to the changing role of students involved with the SAB there is a greater acknowledgement of the student voice. It is evident that students feel they are valued and respected participants in their learning community.

Employability

In an ever increasingly competitive jobs market employability skills amount to nothing more than clichés if they are not backed up with evidence. Through involvement with the SAB, students are able to build on their transferrable skills set through opportunities to project-manage, lead discussions, chair meetings and contribute to faculty strategy. As a result of active participation in the SAB, members become equipped with competencies and evidence which positively impact on employability.

> *"The skills gained such as project management and communicating with a variety of audiences have been useful within my current employment. I frequently participate in business meetings with a variety of colleagues from senior management to customers and I often manage tasks to ensure I see them through to completion."* (Student SAB member)

Two of the SAB members have since gone on to gain full time employment within the university, one as a Welfare Officer for the Students' Union and another as a Student Liaison Officer. The following extract represents the view of faculty's Student Liaison Officer, and SAB member:

> *"The SAB has equipped me with valuable skills such as the ability to work effectively as a team, delegate and to cope under pressure. Through the SAB I led a creative and innovative project aimed at developing online resources for students prior to course entry. My responsibilities included arranging fortnightly group meetings and taking comprehensive minutes with detailed action plans. These tasks prepared me for my current role which requires strong organisation skills. I have no doubt that my employer was impressed by my involvement in the creative aspects of SAB, which demonstrate my ability to think innovatively."*

Unexpected outcomes

Staff were pleasantly surprised by the students' ability to articulate issues in a professional manner.

> "All the students were really professional from giving their ideas for agenda items to attending the meetings and putting theirs and their peers' ideas forward in a collective and coherent manner." (Staff SAB member)

> "The students were excellent at engaging in professional discussions with senior members of staff and gave us all some food for thought for developing the student experience." (Staff SAB member)

Through SAB meetings it became apparent that senior staff were unaware of some cross-faculty student concerns. This is perhaps not surprising, given that there are usually long intervals between Boards of Studies which are only held three times per year. This infrequency of meetings results in easily resolvable issues building over time, consequently negatively impacting upon the student experience. Not only this, but due to their academic nature Boards of Studies are programme focused and, as a result, cross-faculty student issues can become hidden. SAB holds meetings on a more frequent basis and is attended by a range of students across the faculty; consequently cross-faculty issues have become more visible and are able to be resolved during the meeting or immediately afterwards. This is also helped by the process of raising concerns with senior members of staff.

Institutional barriers to student engagement

Although this chapter is focused on student engagement, it is important to acknowledge that similar initiatives are unlikely to succeed without the backing of a committed staff member, preferable in a senior role, with the conviction to challenge existing power relationships (Trowler, 2010). In other words, without the support from the current Associate Dean in SAB, it is debatable whether the structures which enable the success of the SAB would remain. Sadly, some staff will remain resistant to distributing such power. It is therefore vital to celebrate the success of staff who are proactively involved in engaging students in university decision making processes.

Plans for future

At present the SAB attracts mainly student programme and faculty representatives who are already often reasonably confident, highly motivated and engaged. The next stage, in line with the University's Centre for Enhancement of Learning and Teaching ethos, is to try to inspire a broader range of students to participate. The SAB plans to do this by expanding to include a supplementary unpaid forum element, in order to widen student access to debate. The current gap in participation in SAB from the Students' Union will be closed by extending invitations to the SAB to Vice Presidents of Education and Welfare and Campus Engagement. This will enable the SAB to impact on more students and staff and encourage higher and wider levels of engagement. Currently, the SAB meets twice a term, reporting to the faculty's Student Experience Committee which in turn reports at university level. During the 2012/13 academic year SAB members plan to meet every month and students will be required, rather than simply encouraged as they are at present, to take on key roles such as chairing, taking minutes, setting agendas, representing the SAB at Student Experience Committee and taking leadership roles in developing projects.

The students who have participated in the SAB so far are energetic, imaginative and innovative, unafraid to try out new ideas and technologies. These characteristics make them change-makers and exciting collaborators so the SAB need to find ways of allowing their voices to be heard more forcefully at every level, not just through the somewhat mechanistic way in which they report to the Student Experience Committee. In addition to representation at faculty committees, SAB will participate in: staff selection processes; the development and approval of programmes and their assessment; the university's progression, retention and achievement strategies. In brief, the key challenge is to rethink the faculty's structures, systems and processes so that Student Advisory Board participation is central – but to do so without sabotaging its energy and creativity by simply recreating a new set of protocols and formalities!

Conclusion

This chapter concludes by advocating that faculties have a lot to gain from adopting a Student Advisory Board approach. It is recognised that not all Boards of Studies are ineffective, although their structure remains restrictive to the student voice. This chapter has outlined a new approach which promotes the active participation of students in university decision making processes, through a forum which provides faculties with innovative and unconventional solutions to student experience issues. Whilst at the same time empowering students, opening up a network of further opportunities which enhance employability, and promoting a sense of belonging to the institution. Quite simply, the SAB benefits both staff and students by making board meetings more accessible for everyone. Indeed, a one size fits all model may not be replicable across different universities (Van der Velden, 2012). However, each university has a quality process in place which facilitates cross-faculty discussion which could be further enhanced by the approach adopted in this chapter.

In order to replicate this chapter's outcomes it may be appropriate to consider the following recommendations:

- Recruit a senior staff member, ideally one involved in a student experience role to help implement changes across the faculty;

- Initially approach student representatives and then expand to include other students who have been recognised for their involvement with extra-curricular activities;

- Hold meetings on a regular basis (ideally at least once a month), at a time which is appropriate for the students, taking into consideration students on placement;

- Redistribute power by encouraging students to chair meetings and to set the agenda;

- Promote the work of students and staff involved to encourage future participation.

Remember, student engagement is key to effective quality enhancement processes. Students provide essential commentary on the actions staff need to apply to make university change and improvement happen (Gibbs, 2010).

About the authors

Sophie Rowe is Student Liaison Officer in the Faculty of Education Law and Social Sciences, and Postgraduate Criminology student, both at Birmingham City University. She can be contacted at **Sophie.Rowe@ mail.bcu.ac.uk**

Emily Cooper is a Psychology student in the Faculty of Education, Law and Social Sciences at Birmingham City University. She can be contacted at **Emily.Cooper2@mail.bcu.ac.uk**

Lynn Fulford is Associate Dean for Student Experience in the Faculty of Education, Law and Social Sciences at Birmingham City University. She can be contacted at **Lynn.Fulford@bcu.ac.uk**

With special thanks for contributions from Ruth Sim Mutch, Jenny Bradshaw, Chesney Coleman and Jayne O'Keeffe.

Chapter 7

Student Employment and the Impact on Student Motivations and Attitudes towards University

Ixchelt Acevedo Montesinos, Derek Cassidy and Luke Millard

Introduction

Birmingham City University operates a variety of student employment opportunities, varying from Student Academic Partners and Mentors through to student researchers and administrators. It has now introduced a strategic initiative to employ over one thousand students across all aspects of the University's provision. This chapter will consider the impact of these student employment opportunities on students and staff using both quantitative data around student motivations and individual case studies. It will propose that student attitudes towards the University change as a result of the employment and it will consider the impact on staff on this new engagement. The conclusion will suggest that the benefits of student employment are multi-layered and far outweigh the financial cost.

Background for partnership schemes in Birmingham City University

Since 2009 Birmingham City University, in partnership with Birmingham City Students' Union (BCSU), has offered a variety of student employment opportunities within learning and teaching development projects.

This partnership approach led initially to students being employed on a Student Academic Partners (SAP) scheme as the University sought to enliven the process of curriculum change, engaging with the students to drive this through partnerships with staff. The nature of the partnership with BCSU is further explored by Chapman, P. *et al.* in this volume.

Feedback from many students who participated in this new initiative started to reveal some unintended and interesting outcomes. Not only were the students and staff talking of the enjoyment of working together to change the learning experience for themselves and peers, but they also started to signal an attitudinal shift in their perceptions of working for and with the University. This was encapsulated by one student who suggested that she now worked with the University rather than just studied at it. This perspective around a change in student perception and more of a sense of belonging reflected the University's desire to create a greater sense of learning community and recognised the philosophical shift in the University's approach to students as partners.

As the SAP scheme grew, the evidence provided by these unintended outcomes also developed. Not only were the attitudes of students changing towards the University; there was a greater sense of belonging and pride in their University, but also the project team started to hear of how the SAP experience had been deployed by students when seeking to gain jobs after graduation. The employability skills, developed in SAP projects, around leadership, project management, research and presentation were being seen by employers as making these students distinctive in the job market.

In 2010 key staff at the University attended a seminar presentation from Northwest Missouri State University, which focused upon the benefits of a strategic approach to student employment. Their evidence aligned with that being displayed by SAP students and the possibility of a more widespread and strategic approach to student employment, which went beyond just learning and teaching, began to become a possibility.

In 2011, the University submitted a bid to become part of the Higher Education Academy and Leadership Foundation for Higher Education, Change Academy initiative. The bid focused upon creating a strategic student employment initiative, across the University, which would, by 2015, employ over a one thousand students across all parts of the organisation. The project team included a Pro-Vice Chancellor, Director of

Learning Experience and the Director of Human Resources (HR) as well as students, BCSU and faculty-based staff. The year-long strategic development has seen SAP employment being supplemented and expanded into a whole host of student jobs which have been created across the University from librarians and academic mentors through to student researchers and administrators.

Birmingham City University is not unique in offering a student employment scheme for its students. Such opportunities have been available in the USA for many years and a small number of universities in the UK have also sought to develop job shops and similar temporary recruitment solutions. Where Birmingham City University is unique is the way in which the scheme has been adopted by:

+ The University's senior managers and embedded within the HR team, the gatekeepers to employment at the University;

+ Academic staff who see the potential of the scheme to augment standard learning, teaching and employability agendas through real employment opportunities.

This has resulted in all temporary and casual employment opportunities at the University now being scrutinised to determine if the role would be suitable for our students and could lead to a significant shift in the relationship between staff and students within the University community.

This chapter will consider the impact of these student employment opportunities on the students and staff. It will propose that student attitudes towards the University changed as a result of their employment and it will consider the impact on staff of this new form of engagement. It will also consider the implications for the University of such an engagement and the financial considerations such a scheme generates.

The results of student employment will be considered using a transformative learning model espoused by Mezirow (2000:8). This model suggests the following *"Transformation theory's focus is on how we learn to negotiate and act on our own purposes, values, feelings and meanings"*. Employment enables students to gain greater control over their lives *"as socially responsible, clear thinking decision makers"*. The locus of control and the power balance in these relationships is explored by Hutchings *et al.* in this volume. Clearly, this has benefits for the students as the skills they develop will make them more employable and enhance their citizenship credentials, but it will also benefit the university in which they develop these skills.

It is also interesting to note that this view is endorsed by the Quality Assurance Agency's UK Quality Code for Higher Education (2012:4) which states, as it seeks to define student engagement, that:*"Higher Education is not a passive process – it is transformational for the individual as well as having transactional elements. Higher education providers promote active involvement by students in all aspects of their learning and provide opportunities for students to influence their individual and collective learning journey"*

Through this chapter we will seek to explore the learning that can be gained through student employment.

Methodology

The authors utilised quantitative data from an online survey which was sent to 150 student employees utilising the 'survey monkey' tool. The survey explored the motivations behind students seeking employment, whilst also discovering the impact this has had on their relationship with the University. Of those contacted 82 students completed the survey giving a 55% response rate.

In addition, thirty case study interviews have taken place with student employees and those staff who work in partnership with them to ascertain more qualitative opinions on the value of student employment to students, staff and the organisation. These interviews operated on a semi-structured basis and were informed by the questions set on the survey monkey tool.

Findings

The interviews with students and staff revealed key themes around:

* New conversations between staff and students;

* Students as partners – enhancing the sense of belonging;

* Student motivations for engagement;

* Staff motivations for engagement.

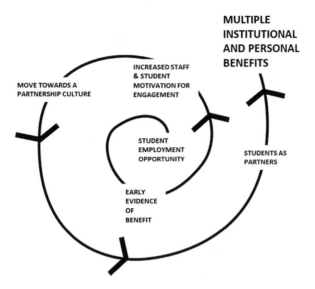

MULTIPLE
INSTITUTIONAL
AND PERSONAL
BENEFITS

INCREASED STAFF
& STUDENT
MOTIVATION FOR
ENGAGEMENT

MOVE TOWARDS A
PARTNERSHIP CULTURE

STUDENT
EMPLOYMENT
OPPORTUNITY

STUDENTS AS
PARTNERS

EARLY
EVIDENCE
OF
BENEFIT

Figure 1: Engagement escalation spiral

These key themes illuminated the journey that students and staff made as they as they moved from the mere principle of engagement as an employee to the impact on learning for students and staff and institutional cultures. The model we have developed hints at the evolving conversations and impacts that originate from this initial employment and lead to the layers of student and institutional benefits that develop. We have termed this our engagement escalation spiral.

New conversations between staff and students

Academic staff and managers identified that through working with students as colleagues employed by the University they had engaged with them in new ways. This is further developed within Chambers & Nagle, in this volume. The project lead for the introduction of student employment stated that:

> *"The vision is to see students employed in every aspect of the University's operations so that academics and students can't help but bump into each other. The mantra we use is that we want to make the informal*

conversations of staff and students normal, discussions in the café, in the library, in the finance office. I see student concerns, which could become major problems being intercepted through informal conversations created through these engagements."

An academic staff member highlighted that:

"It's about having the opportunity for us to hear the students' perspectives and for them to enter into a meaningful conversation rather than us just assuming that we know best. So I think it's all about creating those opportunities for a decent discussion and working alongside students is another way of doing it."

It is cited as an indicator within the QAA quality code (2012:6) that: *"Higher Education providers create and maintain an environment within which students and staff engage in discussions that aim to bring about demonstrable enhancement of the educational experience."* Student employment provides an excellent vehicle for such discussions that would enhance the student experience, but also improve the operation of the university.

Students as partners – enhancing the sense of belonging

A student employee expressed the view that her whole attitude to the University had been transformed through this experience.

"I now have a lot more respect for the University as an institution and lecturers as people rather than just instruments. That makes it sound very cold and machine like but I think many students just see the University as a building and feel that the lecturers are here to teach me and that is all they do. Looking at it from a staff perspective now it's so much more than that and so much more complicated."

This view was reflected by a Faculty Associate Dean who explained that when students are working alongside staff they *"..understand we are working as partners in a cohesive way rather than as some kind of hierarchy, so I think it has got so many benefits."* In addition, the enthusiasm of youth can also be engaged as *"the students really want to celebrate us so you get this sense of working together. It is great, it's just fantastic."*

The change in perception of role and identity through these new conversations is not restricted to staff. One student explained:

> *"I think when you come and work in an environment where they are talking more openly and freely with you, you get lot more of a sense of what they do so I have more respect for the course and how much time and effort goes into it. You see them in not just a lecturing role you see them more as real people."*

Mezirow & Taylor (2009) suggest that this awareness of a changing identity is a result of critical reflection by the students and provides development of another crucial skill for students as they engage in the perspective transformation identified by the same author.

Other students also talked of developing relationships with staff and establishing new respect for staff. In addition, for some students it impacts on their mode of engagement with the University:

> *"I enjoy my time at University now and spend more time inside the campus instead of just coming in to the library to do my assignment and leaving. I feel I am giving something back to the University community at BCU".*

Cranton (2006:5) talks of the ability of academic staff to foster transformative learning, *"that is the way in which adults reason for themselves and transform problematic frames of reference"*, in the classroom being dependent to a large extent on creating meaningful, genuine relationships with students. These are important to staff in developing trust, but appear even more important to students as that development adds value and respect to this interaction.

The survey of student employees (Figure 2) revealed that students perceived a move from an isolated student to a genuine partnership between students and staff. The graph shows that two-thirds of students strongly believed that they participated in a real partnership with staff.

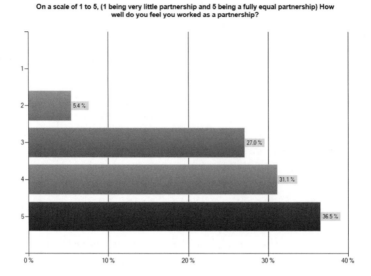

On a scale of 1 to 5, (1 being very little partnership and 5 being a fully equal partnership) How well do you feel you worked as a partnership?

Figure 2: Student perceptions of partnership with staff

The feeling of enhanced belonging was echoed by another student employee:

> "I feel more like I belong at the University. Since joining the scheme I have also found it easier to talk to people within the University; this has benefitted me in many ways as it has allowed me to network with professors and lectures but also make new friends."

Krause & Coates (2008:493-505) assert that students who worked in a learning community had a greater sense of belonging. This is reflected in the student's view that:

> "Yes, my attitude towards BCU has changed. As a student you take things at face value and don't fully appreciate nor understand the hard work staff members invest into the University to make students' experience and learning enjoyable. But working at BCU has enabled me to have greater respect towards the University. I feel proud to be a student and employee because it is a welcoming institution that is student focused."

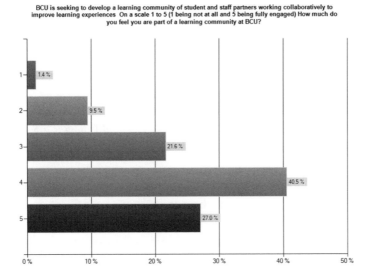

Figure 3: *Students perception of belonging to a learning community*

Another student said that:

> "It gives you pride in the University you are studying in as well because you are a part of it more so than just the sense of being student."

The student survey reflected this feeling of enhanced belonging and demonstrated that the majority of student employees felt that through student employment their learning experience had improved as they had become more part of the University learning community.

Student motivations for engagement

The reasoning behind the University's decision to initiate a student employment initiative, across the entire University was summed up by one senior manager who said he wanted students to say *"I work at this University I am proud of working at this University, I feel part of this University"*.

Student interviews did offer some resonance with this goal, but they also offered much wider reasons for engaging with the University in this way. The level of pay was an issue, as was the sense of being valued and respected.

> "When I worked in shop I came in did my shift and went home so the level of what you are doing is so much more at BCU. You get paid more at the University so automatically it shows that they respect you more and you also have more responsibility in decision making and an impact as well. I really liked that I felt valued for my time and I think it is a good thing that they are doing it."

Some students felt that being an employee of the University gave them an edge over other students on their course:

> "I think it allowed me to put that bit more into what I was doing. Yes I was doing my course but so was everyone else but it gave me the edge knowing that as well as doing my course I was doing something else that was of benefit to me and to the University."

A question could be asked of those promoting student employment as to whether as a result of this selection of students they are differentiating and offering advantage to those who are employed. The authors would argue against this by stating that all students can apply for these posts and that students pass through a standard selection process to become employed. If students are, through more effective networking, able to gain advantage as a result then that is their choice and demonstrates a further development of their skills as is further explored by Summers *et al.* in this volume. Entrepreneurial students will see opportunities and look to further their own ambitions and employment may provide them with one of these routes. Others talked of benefits beyond university:

> "Whilst having a degree is obviously important in the first place for getting the interview whilst you are in the interview it's the things that you've done extra to your degree which employers are interested in."

Some identified the self-growth they developed through these new opportunities:

> "It is a fantastic experience not only for yourself personally and your own

growth but on a professional level showing that you can study and work in the same place at the same time. To have that duality is an amazing thing to have on your CV and does so much for your self-esteem."

Another student identified that:

"The main benefit of my student employment is the process of self-eval-uation. I have been able to identify my strengths but also acknowledge my limitations and want to work on these to improve and grow as an individual which is a good feeling."

This personal growth is echoed in Chambers & Nagle, in this volume, and enables student employees to become critically reflective. This skill will be tested and developed in student employees as they grow into these new employment roles.

It is interesting to note the monetary benefit of employment did not dominate the discussions with students. However, it clearly impacts as the status of being a University employee influences the self-perception of students and the perception of those they work alongside. Would a volunteer worker be afforded the same level of respect as a paid employee and would the same demands be placed upon them? Students will use their pay in a variety of ways and most will see it as one of the primary motivating factors that enable engagement:

"I have been able to go through my Master's programme without incur-ring any fees and without having to get extra loans. Also, because I am working and studying at the University it is easier to be working within the University because you are here within the same environment so when I finish at 5 p.m. I can stay on and do a couple more hours of studying in the same environment."

The QAA Code of Practice (2012:11) requires that *"Higher Educa-tion providers recognise the value of the engagement of their students and ensure that students feel rewarded for their involvement"*. Monetary reward is clearly one vehicle for this, but it would appear the reward of devel-oping additional skills and having new experiences that place students in a more favourable position for gaining employment after graduation is also valued.

The student survey was slightly at odds with this view as students highlighted a wide range of ways in which participation as a student employee impacted upon them. Perhaps the most notable of these is the enthusiasm for learning and teaching, working with other students and motivation to become part of the wider University experience. These were all seen as having as much or equal impact as the development of specific skills.

Questions / Value	A great deal	To a certain extent	Some	Not a lot
Interest in wider learning and teaching issues?	46.6%	26.0%	21.9%	2.7%
Motivation to get involved in the University experience?	41.1%	35.6%	16.4%	4.1%
Confidence?	34.2%	39.7%	19.2%	4.1%
Communication Skills?	35.6%	37.0%	19.2%	4.1%
Project Management skills?	24.7%	50.7%	16.4%	4.1%
Enthusiasm for my own learning/teaching?	42.5%	39.7%	13.7%	0%
Enthusiasm in working with other staff/students?	53.4%	34.2%	9.6%	0%
Research skills?	37%	34.2%	13.7%	9.6%

Table 1: How has Student Academic Partners work impacted on the students' wider university experience?

These findings resonate well with the views of the Director of Human Resources who at the outset of the student programme talked of the students getting more than just a qualification through their University experience:

> "We are trying to help students feel more that this is their University. It is very easy for students to feel that University is just about the course they are on, when actually the University can offer a lot more than just that."

Staff motivations for engagement

The authors would assert that student employment has demonstrable benefits for students. However, they would also argue that there are many benefits for University staff and faculty:

"I think that the student employment agenda that we are pursuing here is just about the most exciting thing in which I have been involved in my time in this organisation, which is nearly 25 years now."

The transformational opportunity for the University and the student experience was central to this senior manager's perspective. The motivation for his engagement also related to the ability to impact change in the University and the status it gave the University in the higher education sector. However, this also hints at the greater job satisfaction that working with students can offer faculty. Within service departments, managers said that

"What we found in this department is that when we employ students it gives us a totally different perspective. We have some staff that have been around the University for a long time and may have forgotten what it feels like to be a student."

Another manager believed that student employment:

"will help managers have a better sense of students in the University. It is very easy at senior manager level to be removed from students. I rarely have contact with students so it makes you remember what you are here for, which is about students."

A programme director highlighted the freshness that these interactions with students brought. *"In terms of new technologies students bring a whole raft of different skills that young people are using. Some of them are quite new to me and they teach me"*. The ability of students to share their knowledge and provide faculty with new skills and perspectives is a powerful motive for staff engagement as faculty seek to keep pace with the social and technological contexts which new students bring to a university each and every year. Other staff saw the opportunity for impactful culture change within the student/staff relationship:

"We are at the start of something that is really exciting in the University. We are beginning to see students starting to act as the flag bearers for student engagement and there is increasing good will and understanding. The Student Academic Partnership Scheme has helped to do that too. I think we are gathering a critical mass that can see the value."

Conclusion

It is the belief of the authors that multi-layered nature of the benefits of student employment makes it an attractive proposition for all stakeholders whether it is at a personal and academic level for students, at a programme level for academic staff or as a cost effective method of providing vibrant new ideas and staff for the university.

For students there are clear benefits from the financial reward to the generation of new friendships and enhanced self-esteem. Hardy & Bryson (2010) offered the view that engagement increased student abilities and general thinking resulting in improved achievement and retention. This has been extended by them to suggest engagement is a combination of intellectual application, diligence and participation in the learning community, supported by a sense of purpose. This definition provides real resonance with the work of Birmingham City University's SAP scheme and is evidenced through Table 1 as students proclaimed a suite of skills that were developed through their roles.

In addition, there is the financial challenge for universities who are committed to student engagement of ensuring that funds will be made available year on year to maintain the momentum of student engagement and employment. Momentum for student engagement at the university has been developed over a lengthy period of time. If that financial tap is turned off it could result in a rapid return to the baseline.

The authors would argue that student engagement activities pay for themselves in improved student retention and achievement, not only for those students and staff who participate, but also in the impact of projects on the wider student community and the atmosphere that is developed within the university learning community. With students in the UK paying up £9,000 each academic year for their tuition the retention of 6 students, through these activities, who may otherwise have left would pay for the running of a university-wide engagement scheme such as the SAP scheme at Birmingham City University.

Thomas (2012:12) states that between 33% and 39% of students at UK universities think about leaving their course during their first year of study. At present 8% of students in UK higher education leave their course in their first year. Through student engagement and employment we would seek to show students that their university experience is more than just their course and offer them the opportunity to engage with a variety of supportive staff and students from other areas of the university who may provide the support their crave to enable them to remain and succeed at university.

Thomas (2012:11) believes that the feeling of belonging can contribute significantly to improving student retention and success. Her study finds that institutional approaches that promote belonging have key characteristics of: "*...supportive peer relations; meaningful interactions between staff and students, developing knowledge, confidence and identity as successful (Higher Education) HE learners, an HE experience that is relevant to interests and future goals.*"

Moxley *et al.* (2001:93) talk of the important work of universities "*... in helping students reach their potential and to find their niche as citizens who contribute socially, culturally, economically and interpersonally to the quality of life of a community and a society*". This requires universities to address the social realities today's students face which will include how they can afford to pay for and live alongside study. The creation of student employment opportunities within a student engagement framework may be a significant step in this process.

The second key challenge is the need to make student engagement for everyone, not a select few. The University pays students for its engagement activities because it does not want to disadvantage students who need to work to fund their studies. Many universities rely on volunteers to create student engagement activities and whilst this is laudable it disenfranchises those students who need to work to pay the bills. Through payment we ensure most students can access engagement activities. However, the challenge is to move from a very successful model that engages 10% of the University's student population to one that draws in 50% or 75%.

In addition, universities have a moral obligation to students to help them to achieve. They should be able to assure themselves of the quality of the students they produce. As one senior manager said:

> "*By employing our own students the university shows a sign of faith in their abilities, a sign that we recognise the strengths of what our students have to offer.*"

Students see the bigger picture of preparing themselves for their future, but also of giving something back. The most powerful advocates for this work are students themselves and as identified by Austin & Hatt (2005) the messenger often becomes the message.

Student engagement through employment empowers students to shape the skills they develop at university and helps universities to move towards offering more individualised learning routes. Students are starting to recognise this broader context and understand the wider implications of student engagement whilst also demonstrating one of the strongest motivations for student participation.

> *"I look forward to the next day at work because I feel like a valued member of the team. I now appreciate students are not passive customers of their learning experience but are able to personally enhance their learning and social development."*

About the authors

Ixchelt Acevedo Montesinos is a final year BA (Hons) Business Psychology & Marketing student and a student employee within Birmingham Institute of Art & Design at Birmingham City University. She can be contacted at **Ixcheltacevedo@googlemail.com**

Professor Derek Cassidy is Associate Dean (Academic) within the Birmingham Institute of Art & Design at Birmingham City University. He can be contacted at **Derek.Cassidy@bcu.ac.uk**

Luke Millard is Head of Learning Partnerships within the Centre for Enhancement of Learning and Teaching at Birmingham City University. He can be contacted at **Luke.Millard@bcu.ac.uk**

Chapter 8

Differential Student Engagement: Lessons Learned

Caroline Hutchings, Nicola Bartholomew and Oonagh Reilly

Introduction

This chapter presents a mutual learning journey based upon the experiences and reflections of three project partners (and co-authors) involved in a Student Academic Partners (SAP) project in the Faculty of Health at Birmingham City University (BCU). We, as co-authors, represent both student and staff perspectives and we share our exploration of the motivations that underpin student engagement in this context and the power relations between partners that may have influenced levels of engagement.

The SAP project in question emerged from a staff/graduate discussion on the challenges healthcare graduates may experience in maintaining key skills whilst seeking their first professional post. The creation of a Virtual Employability Centre (VEC) to support graduates was identified as a vehicle for collaboration within the SAP scheme; a resource *for* students and graduates generated *by* students and graduates with academic support. Four students were recruited to the project, one group comprised two students from the discipline of Speech and Language Therapy and the other group comprised two students from Diagnostic Radiography. The four student partners were supported by two academic staff partners: one from each discipline. Additionally, a graduate was employed to oversee the project.

The focus of this chapter is not about the generation of the VEC itself but about the *process* of staff–student engagement, which enabled this project to succeed. As the project unfolded, it became apparent that the levels of engagement were inconsistent across student partners, which prompted the academic staff partners to consider why this might be; were all student partners equally motivated to engage from the outset?

The chapter draws from two theoretical models to discuss the varied levels of engagement: Social Cognitive Motivational theory (Linnenbrink & Pintrich, 2002) and Forms of Power (French & Raven, 1959). The first part of the chapter reviews the selection and recruitment of student partners and discusses social cognitive motivational theory in relation to the motivations that prompted staff and students to participate in the first place. Initial motivations are further explored to highlight potential markers for the varied levels of engagement we experienced and the factors that may have imposed an inhibitory effect on engagement.

The chapter then explores the balance of power within the student–academic relationship as our experiences suggest that this had a significant effect on levels of engagement. Traditional power relationships (Toker *et al.*, 2002) are considered as students may harbour latent expectations for a paternalistic student-tutor relationship, which may promote a more passive approach to partnership working from a student's perspective. To test these theories, we gathered narratives from two student partners, one from each discipline who had demonstrated converse levels of engagement with the SAP project. The narratives reveal opposing views on the degree of ownership student partners felt they held over the project, which may be associated with their perceptions of power and their initial motivations for engagement. Reflections from academic staff partners are also considered.

As we begin to disembark from our journey through this SAP project, we can reflect on the methods of project management that were adopted and how these may have exerted an inhibitory effect on student engagement. We therefore offer our recommendations for partnership working, based on our lived experience, to be considered by others as a framework for success.

Recruitment and motivations

In 2011, undergraduate students from the two healthcare programmes were invited to participate in the SAP project to create the VEC. SAP schemes run across the University and explicitly aim to create opportunities for staff and students to work in partnership to build a learning community on and off campus (Birmingham City Students' Union, 2012).

Concepts for SAP projects will, ideally, emerge from students though project concepts may also be constructed by academic staff, perhaps as mechanisms to better meet strategic requirements within a faculty. Student partners in this context may be invited to participate in a project as a development opportunity. Our SAP project was a vehicle for collaboration between staff and students to meet the specific needs of a graduate population. The resources envisaged for the VEC relate to continuing professional development, career management and profession-specific skills maintenance.

Factors influencing student engagement and motivation

Differing levels of student engagement used in the sense of Kuh's description of time and effort (Kuh, 2009) were observed throughout the duration of the project. One student reported that they felt they *"sat back a bit when [they] should have been trying to work with the partners that had put themselves out to try and work with me"*, contrasting with another who stated that they felt *"the ownership is all [theirs]; currently [they're] the only undergraduate working on it"*. This dichotomy is further evidenced by one group of students delivering the entire VEC content and one ceasing contact with the project prior to delivering any content.

This dichotomy prompted further exploration and the lived experiences of two of our student partners, one from each group, have been used as case-studies within this chapter to help us identify the successes and challenges of SAP project management. We should caution that our recommendations and conclusions refer only to our experience on this project. However, viewed in the context of theories of motivation and power, principles of successful engagement and strategies to avoid disengagement could be extracted and applied to future SAP projects and indeed to learning and teaching practice in general.

Our student partner from the group that delivered (Student A) proved to be highly motivated and has been exceptionally active in bringing the project to fruition. In contrast, our student partner from the group that did not produce content (Student B) demonstrated significantly lower levels of engagement. So what were the factors that may have influenced such different engagement levels? We have examined information provided by the lived experiences of these two students in the light of Social Cognitive theories of motivation to help steer us in this.

Intrinsic and extrinsic motivation

Intrinsic motivation has been clearly linked with achievement in motivation theory. Students who are intrinsically motivated will foster a deep-seated interest in a given activity and their engagement with this activity will generate its own reward (Miltiadou & Savenye, 2003). Krapp *et al.* (1992) suggest that interest is an interactive relation between an individual and aspects of their environment. These students need no further incentives to engage as their deeper interest provides the intrinsic motivation.

We would expect a student-owned project concept to have emerged following students' interaction with the (learning) environment and the student's inherent personal or situational interest in a given area may have prompted them to develop it further within the SAP scheme. Both students in our project were in fact participating in a project that had been created *prior* to recruiting the student academic partners although both appeared to recognise the value of the project: *"people needed this and they wanted it and there was a market and appetite for it"* (Student A).

Extrinsic motivation is the motivation to engage in an activity simply as a means to an end (Miltiadou & Savenye, 2003). Students who are *invited* to participate in a SAP project rather than those who construct a project proposal themselves may wish to contribute for monetary reward and for evidence of extra-curricular experience. This was evident in some of the comments from both student partners A and B who recognised the value to their CV and ability to show to employers a tangible product that they had helped create.

When it came to reasons for applying, alongside the chance to gain new skills, Student B focused on extrinsic motivators including wages and CV augmentation. Student A focused on more intrinsic factors such as the chance to use existing skills, enhancing student academic relationships and learning more about the University resources and support available. Whilst we should endorse students who make a pro-active decision to bolster their employability status based on extrinsic factors, it is suggested that students who are extrinsically motivated are more likely to suffer from anxiety and burnout (Levesque *et al.*, 2011) and in this context are more likely to drop-out of the scheme altogether. We would argue that due to the adaptive cognitive dimensions we discuss later, this is also a risk for intrinsically motivated students. Perhaps part of the role of the academic partner could be to ensure that students develop the skills needed to balance and manage workloads effectively.

Linking motivation to achievement

If we consider social cognitive models of motivation in an educational context, it is suggested that there are other facets to student motivation in addition to intrinsic motivation including: self-efficacy; adaptive attributions; and achievement goals (Linnenbrink & Pintrich, 2002). Self-efficacy is self-belief in one's own capabilities relating to a given task. If an individual believes that they have the skills to be successful in a particular task then naturally they will be more interested and motivated to engage with that task. This principle is certainly upheld by the first student's experience: *"The SAP project was in an area I already had experience in…I knew I could do it."* Individuals who demonstrate such self-efficacy will work harder, will be more likely to achieve and will demonstrate the ability to self-regulate their learning.

It is also suggested that self-regulated learners generate motivational beliefs that may be used to keep them task-focused when a conflict of interests threatens to divert their attention (Bembenutty, 2011). Our student partners certainly identified challenges with fitting project work around academic workloads and work placements with Student B talking about challenges such as *"going on placement, constantly having deadlines to fill and my dissertation, things like that as well as worrying about getting a job"* being a barrier to success for them. Student A identified similar difficulties but went on to demonstrate that they had prioritised the tasks for project delivery *"I've had to be really flexible and I've found that I've been missing out socially …but it's worth it for the project and for the experience."*

Achievement goal theory proposes two goal orientations, namely mastery and performance goals (Elliot & Church, 1997). Whilst performance goals focus on short-term, surface level achievements in comparison to the achievement of peers, mastery goals reflect a deeper approach to learning for the purpose of knowledge and skills acquisition. Mastery goal orientation may be associated with self-efficacy, self-regulation and achievement.

The theories briefly outlined above may be subsumed into an integrated model of student motivation linking motivation with achievement (Table 1). This model presents four key groups, (Martin, 2006) with 1 and 2 anticipated through mastery goal orientation and intrinsic motivation:

	Dimension	Characterised by
1	Adaptive cognitive dimensions	Self-efficacy, valuing and mastery orientation
2	Adaptive behavioural dimensions	Persistence, planning and task management
3	Impeding cognitive dimensions	Anxiety, failure avoidance and uncertain control
4	Maladaptive behavioural dimensions	Self-handicapping and disengagement

Table 1: Model of Student Motivation, adapted from Martin, 2006

Adaptive dimensions promote student engagement and achievement whilst impeding and maladaptive dimensions inhibit engagement. We have already referred to difference in the achievement of the two groups in shaping the VEC.

So how might motivational theory influence SAP project management? On reflection, selecting student partners who demonstrate adaptive cognitive and behavioural dimensions and are intrinsically motivated is perhaps a crucial component of recruitment if we are to ensure that project outcomes are met and that students have a positive learning experience during the process. The same principles may be applied to the academic staff partners who must also value the project concept and prioritise their time accordingly to create a fertile environment for an equal partnership to flourish.

Our recruitment and reflection on methodology

In retrospect, we admit to adopting a recruitment process that over emphasised extrinsic motivators and performance goals in its strategy for securing student buy-in. Our recruitment process was purposefully goal-orientated as a means to foster student interest during their busy academic schedule. The opportunity for paid employment was emphasised at advert in addition to the opportunity to augment curriculum vitae through extra-curricular activity. Four out of sixteen potential candidates were selected as student partners based on personal tutor recommendations rather than any formalised selection process, for the purposes of expediency.

This method disregarded the need for intrinsic motivation and the adaptive behaviours associated with engagement and achievement, and these were not assessed as part of our recruitment process. We contend that some of our student partners demonstrated impeding / maladaptive dimensions of motivation and disengaged from the process. Nevertheless, we were fortunate to employ a student partner who clearly demonstrated adaptive dimensions of motivation and perhaps this is largely due to her previous experience of project management.

In order to discover our student partners' experiences of the partnership, we adopted a qualitative method to promote open-ended responses to semi-structured questions. Although self-report tools such as the Motivated Strategies for Learning Questionnaire (Pintrich & DeGroot, 1990) may be used to assess student motivation, engagement and learning strategies, and are clearly scalable for large groups, such tools can only collate short responses from participants. We wanted our students to be free to describe and expand upon their experiences within the project.

It must be noted that a narrative inquiry methodology (Riley & Hawe, 2004) was not adopted in the true sense. Rather than free story-telling, the open-ended, structured interview questions were intended to guide their narratives as we felt it was necessary to gather feedback about specific issues relating to perceived levels of motivation, engagement, ownership and working in partnership. Nevertheless, it was essential for student partners to provide open and candid responses to these questions to enable us to capture a true depiction of their lived experience. As academic staff partners we felt there was an element of risk associated with introducing 'researcher' bias whilst gathering this student data. This issue was addressed through the implementation of a Voxur* unit. This portable computer unit supports video capture and enabled an impartial colleague to pre-record our interview questions. Student partners were left to review these questions, reflect on them and record their own responses when ready.

The recorded response from each student partner was then transcribed into a word document. A thematic analysis of responses was subsequently undertaken by another impartial colleague from within the Faculty. The main themes identified were: opportunities for self-development; working outside the student role; opportunities to influence/ownership; staff support/partnership; working with others/partnership; uncertainty. The themed responses largely revealed causes for differing engagement levels and matters relating to project support structure and partnership working. We look at these later in light of the development of the student–academic relationship.

While there were shared responses between both student partners in relation to the perceived value of the project, there was clearly a dichotomy in terms of perceived levels of project engagement and ownership. Student A demonstrated high levels of engagement but also revealed robust intrinsic motivations in part due to their previous experience of project management. In contrast, Student B who was more extrinsically motivated (valuing pay and CV evidence) revealed a degree of frustration relating to inter-partner communication and limited direction from academic staff partners. So, were academic staff partners' expectations of partnership-working significantly different to student partners and how does the student–academic relationship influence these perceptions?

Student and academic relationships

Both academic staff and student partners revealed some pre-conceived expectations of partnership working within their narrative accounts. *"As an academic, with a clear idea of project outcomes, I anticipated a need to be didactic in my approach to the project"*. Student A initially *"felt constrained by my expectations of the academic relationship"*. Furthermore, academic staff partners admitted to seeing the project as an efficient way to bring an idea to fruition as they had limited time allocated to engage with the work. Although a didactic approach had been anticipated, both academic staff partners ultimately expected that the project in general would be handed over to the student partners to complete. We contend that this initial conception of the project was not conducive to partnership working but rather to student delivery with limited academic guidance.

Student partners had also anticipated a way of working more allied to a traditional, didactic teaching relationship in which the academic directs the student, which leads us to an exploration of power within the academic-student relationship.

Power within relationships

Toker *et al.* (2002:636) refer to the 'old paternalistic teacher-student relationship', which cannot be deemed a partnership since the balance of power was held by the 'teacher'. The use of power (where one person has authority over another (Kantek & Gezer, 2008)) in academic-student relationships cannot be ignored. Discussing power in supervisory relationships, Markham and Chiu (2011) suggest that any such relationship, reflecting long established pedagogical norms, is hampered by the default positions of expert and learner with the associated inhibitory self-talk of the academic needing to be right and the student needing to wait to be told what is right.

French and Raven (1959) describe a taxonomy of power which we have adapted to discuss our student–academic relationship:

> **Reward Power:** The student perceives that the academic can provide them with desired outcomes (e.g. improved grades or references)
>
> **Coercive power:** The student believes the academic has the ability to punish them (e.g. lower grades, inhibit future employment)
>
> **Legitimate power:** The student feels they are obligated to do as the academic says due to their position (pre-conceived ideas of paternalistic student-teacher relationship and the university hierarchy)
>
> **Referent power:** The student wants to be associated with the academic (i.e. elevated status amongst peers, perceived success, access to opportunities, and access to the university community)

> **Expert power:** The student perceives that the academic holds specialist knowledge (i.e. project management and academic writing skills, to provide the student with additional learning opportunities)

The narratives revealed that both student and academic staff partners anticipated the project operating within a traditional student–academic relationship i.e. the academic providing some direction to the student. This would have meant the academic drawing on their 'expert' power, with the student recognising this as expert and as legitimate power. Motivation under this framework would then be linked to reward or coercive power and performance goals. Student A recognised the expert power, which they felt was an advantage to their work *"I'm lucky really, I've got two academic partners so I've got a subject-expert academic partner, and then I've got a partner who is the technology expert".*

Although this acknowledgement of 'expert power' suggests that a more paternalistic relationship would ensue, Student A's narrative revealed that they experienced a considerable degree of autonomy in the project: *"I feel accountable for it and supported but I feel my ideas can drive it."* For Student B however, this degree of ownership was absent and perhaps reflected levels of disengagement: *"I would say that because I perhaps didn't contribute as much as other partners did I would say that I personally didn't have much ownership of it".*

Both sides reported more parity than expected. We would suggest that the influence of the SAP scheme rationale, aimed at supporting students and academics in moving towards a more student-directed (student 'pull') method of learning, played a part. This method required academic staff and students to become partners in "learning encounters" and thus our collaborative project became an opportunity to create a new discourse within the traditional student–academic relationship.

Student and academic roles

We have already revealed that the initial stages of the project did not anticipate this new discourse arising from joint learning encounters. Furthermore each participant has an established role as an academic or a student outside of the project where the two must interact simultaneously in a more traditional academic-student relationship; occupying 'parallel universes' as it were. Student A felt that the tutor-tutee encounters had become more positive with the academic staff partner understanding more about them and thus able to consider aspects of their life more fully when offering tutorial advice outside of the project. Within the tutorial situation, the tutor offered advice in line with that of their role of academic staff partner; explaining the system and options and expressing support for whatever decision was made by the tutee; no expert power was claimed at all. It is impossible to know whether this approach is inherent to the tutor, or as a result of the student–academic partner relationship translating easily to other settings. Certainly multiple opportunities for interaction were provided as part of the project (a result of the dissemination of information about the VEC), and it may be *these* opportunities which enhanced the student–academic relationship.

Equity

Whilst we are striving for an equitable relationship within the project, true equity cannot always be achieved for the following reasons:

+ Legacies of traditional power relationships between academic staff and students;

+ The on-going requirement for a teaching relationship to be maintained outside of this relationship (e.g. marking work, providing expert knowledge, deciding upon pedagogy);

+ Environmental/infrastructure restrictions (people and systems e.g. lack of access to university processes such as room bookings).

We believe there were several factors that enabled us to create a more equal 'parallel universe'. With limited time allocated to the academic staff partner, the student narratives referred to a period of uncertainty at the start of the project when they were unsure what was expected of them and how to progress. There was an initial lack of structured encounters between students and academics "*I think that at the beginning… I did feel like I was kind of designing this in the dark*". Conversely though, this autonomy gave students an opportunity for ownership as they were allowed to scope the work themselves. Students additionally felt that this gap was a "*reminder to be proactive and to take the opportunities that are given to you*". Although students felt it took time to understand what was required of them, it allowed them to work up the ideas themselves: [*academic staff partners*] "*...have let me get on with it. I kind of feel that it is my project*". Flint & Roden, in this volume, raise parallels to this issue albeit from a social media context, in that over-moderation can discourage student ownership and participation.

With a delay in recruiting a graduate who was planned to supervise the project, Student A who had more flexibility around their timetable, grasped an opportunity to develop ideas and plan independently. This resulted in the academic staff partner being used as a "sense check" with the student; proposing ideas and solutions, and created an early degree of expertise with a deep level of involvement for the student. This had the effect of turning the partnership into more of a collegial relationship and gave some expert power to the student. It also meant that the student gained some reward power, being involved in providing part of the project outcome.

Barriers to partnership

Some forms of power may be perceived by the student but not the academic and may well be a barrier to true partnership. The use of expert power may inhibit the student in taking initiative within the project. For the academic, it may be difficult to find an appropriate balance between allowing the students to develop their ideas and autonomy within the project *and* ensuring delivery and supporting the student in what may be a new role to them. A solution may be to employ a mixture of student partners with a range of different skills and experiences; allowing for peer support. This would alleviate this role for the academic staff partner and potentially increase the power of the student voice.

McAllister & Lincoln (2004) identify barriers to a successful student-tutor relationship within a clinical context. We have adapted this based on our analysis of the partner narratives. We recommend consideration of the following barriers prior to embarking upon student–academic working partnerships:

+ Failure of academic to balance their focus between the task itself and maintaining the team dynamic;

+ Failure to respond to an individual's ways of learning and working;

+ Academic wishing to supervise rather than partner and student abdicating responsibility for self-management;

+ Not seeing the relationship as an opportunity for mutual growth and development;

+ Putting in too little time and effort;

+ Lack of shared goal between partners.

Shared goal

We propose that the academic-student interaction, if it is to be equal, is helped by a shared goal: in this case the development of the VEC, which provides a vehicle for a more collaborative way of working. The student narratives clearly indicated that the project goal was important to them and they recognised its value to their fellow students: "I think it would be really hard to be that focused on it if it wasn't for the fact that new people needed this and they wanted it and there was a market and appetite for it". Not only did students indicate they found this motivational, but the goal and indeed the opportunity to work alongside academics (referent power) was recognised as valuable by their fellow students who wanted to know more and offered to get involved. This allows a different model of inter-action to be showcased to students as well and creates the 'student pull' method of learning that the SAP scheme aims to inspire.

The academic environment

Our student–academic relationship exists within the current university environment. Within this context Student A felt they had difficulty assuming a staff role alongside academic staff. They were unable to easily transfer the positive student/academic partner relationship to other academics, restricted by their own expectations of academics' views of them. The academic partner also noted areas of constraint introduced by working with a student partner: constraints such as being careful what was discussed in shared offices. Health profession students are bound by the Health and Care Professions Council's standards and the code of ethics and professional behaviour applies, since no formal contract existed for the SAP scheme. Faculties or courses where this is not applicable may wish to consider a formal contract with a confidentiality clause for the project.

In some ways the constraints of the university system created greater parity of roles. Student partners could not access staff systems which were something we could not control, so administrative tasks such as booking rooms or printing had to be completed by the academic. This may have provided a fixed level of parity during the tasks and physically prevented the student from being an administrative resource. This could be retained to visibly show academic staff "rolling up their sleeves", subconsciously setting an expectation that the project team will work together on whatever tasks are required. The structure of the encounters also contributed towards an equitable staff-student relationship. Face to face meetings away from the tutor's office allowed us to forge a new relationship in more neutral spaces. Giving students access to areas they did not normally enter (even the staff kitchen) made them feel included as staff, giving them a sense of belonging.

Application of skills to a clinical environment

Health-based courses require an element of practical training, where work-based placements allow students to apply theory whilst primarily developing professional skills (McAllister, 1997). The skills acquired during this project may be transferred to the clinical context.

Employability and transferable skills

We have discussed previously the need for a recruitment process when selecting students. This was also seen as an opportunity to start developing the student's employability skills: responding to a person specification; being able to articulate on an application form and at interview their motivation for applying; demonstrating their suitability for the role. We are also proposing that it would allow exploration of candidates' motivating factors, team working and development needs.

In addition to ensuring that student partners are engaged and intrinsically motivated, they require the maturity and confidence to engage in this mode of partnership working that is also mirrored in the professional health context. Furthermore, students are expected to develop employability skills such as timekeeping, communication skills and work management. As student partners may not demonstrate these skills from the outset, we might expect a period of support, similar to that provided on placement, depending on their level of training.

Ostergren (2011) refers to the continuum of supervision where the supervisee gradually gains more skills and becomes increasingly responsible for their own reflective practice and decision-making, eventually achieving independence of practice. This continuum model could be used when working with students to create a partnership; initially providing students and academics with formal opportunities for observing and reflecting on practice being created.

Toker *et al.* (2002) discuss how student–academic interaction can induct student health professionals into the working practices of professional-client relationships. The social philosophy underlying many health courses promotes treating the client or patient as an individual, a human being with their own set of needs rather than a collection of symptoms. We would argue that the student–academic relationship has to be based on this individualistic principle. Additionally, if the relationship is to succeed, certain values in relating to others need to be present. These include the values of authenticity, trust, empathy, empowerment, mutuality and openness about humanness and fallibility (McAllister, 2001). Such values are mutually exclusive to some of the types of power discussed above.

Although our narratives revealed that limited thought had initially been given to fostering an environment explicitly supportive of partnership working, they also revealed that the student–academic interaction had developed to achieve a degree of parity within this relationship. Both sides were prepared to work to forge a new type of relationship, setting aside traditional expectations.

We should note that we are not advocating the removal of a professional distance between academic and student. Neither academic staff nor student partner wanted, or felt it appropriate to become friends since this was a professional relationship within a working environment (see Flint & Roden, this volume). However, being open and invoking a degree of appropriate disclosure was seen as germane to enable a working relationship to flourish. In line with the intrinsic motivational factors discussed previously, we feel it also helps if both parties are 'people-oriented'. This requires an ability to balance the logistical aspects of the job-in-hand with the needs of the people involved; by being alert to each other's working and learning styles and affective needs. It could simply be described as finding and bringing the best out in people and a solid framework for communication set within a supportive environment is essential here.

Additional factors for success

While we anticipate a need for student partners to project-manage, they must also be given time and support to develop appropriate project-management skills. A recruitment process could allow academic staff partners to balance the overall composition of a student team and enable peer support. Self-assessment of learning and development needs against a person specification could be completed by student partners following appointment, and would provide a baseline for evidence of development at the end of the project.

We have argued that the period of delay at the project start essentially promoted student empowerment, but narratives also refer to this as a period of uncertainty for students where a lack of engagement may become apparent. We would recommend therefore that more structured engagement opportunities are offered at the start of a project with regular meetings between students and academics which would allow reinforcement of inter-student relationships as well as student/academic relationships. Some student partners felt the pressure of their existing academic workload and early sessions could be used to provide a clear project plan and timescale, allowing students to manage their workload and meet their academic requirements. Regular contact would allow the whole project team to be aware early on of any changes in partner's circumstances meaning they were subsequently unable to participate. In the event of student disengagement, small, more directed tasks could be allocated by academic staff partners to offer a way back into the project and support students to re-engage. Work could also be reassigned should new students join.

Analysis of student narratives indicated that a lack of work produced may not be due to lack of motivation. Difficulties working with fellow students; feeling overwhelmed with other areas of their life; feeling left out of the project as other students progressed, could all be inferred as reasons for non-contribution. This supports the need to build strong, professional relationships between student partners and for regular monitoring of students by the academic staff partners. They felt strongly that they had a duty of care to the students to ensure that they could balance what was effectively an extra-curricular activity with their studies. Supporting students to progress in spite of these difficulties will be of benefit to the project and will also help to develop student resilience within a supportive environment.

Student partners also felt it incumbent upon them to be proactive in the project context. Although support was deemed readily available, it was not always sought. As project partners, students were assumed to take on responsibility for their own workload and professionalism in the sense of maintaining their commitment, building positive relationships and interacting with staff and students professionally. Again, student partners may require extra support to acquire these skills which was not felt by us to be a reason for non-selection. However, appropriate peer or academic support should be made available within the project framework or via other appropriate departments within the University.

Although we have already discussed some of the motivating factors that led students to apply for and engage with the project, there were some unexpected rewards for those participating. Student A revealed that they had become more cognisant of resources offered across the university community and also relished the chance to develop and demonstrate previous skills, which would not easily have been recognised within their new professional field.

Experiences associated with the project served to enhance further the student–academic relationship. As co-authors, the student and academics felt that this opportunity to write for publication in addition to the opportunity to present at a professional conference enabled both parties to reinforce the levels of equality within this collegial relationship, albeit within a different context. Such associated activities should be actively encouraged.

Preparing work for publication also provided an on-going reflective opportunity to critically appraise the experience of the project and clarify areas of success and those needing improvement. These have been distilled as recommendations at the close of this chapter, allowing us to identify elements we found to contribute to our success.

Recommendations

+ Encourage students to generate their own project concepts to foster ownership and intrinsic motivation;

+ Prompt students to consider their own academic and extracurricular commitments before they apply for the scheme to ensure that workloads may be managed effectively;

+ Consider writing a project job description and personal specification to identify required key skills and attributes;

+ Consider holding interviews to a) help with the selection process and b) to offer wider employability skills development (to include feedback on student performance at interview);

+ Encourage student candidates to submit a written statement explaining why they want to apply; their skills / attributes and how they might best fit into a team;

+ Provide early team-building opportunities to establish team roles and expectations; project plans, and milestones;

+ Academic Staff Partners may consider their own development needs in relation to interview experience, writing job descriptions and project management;

+ Establish regular and frequent team meetings in the early phase of the project but becoming less frequent in the later stages as student partners develop their autonomy;

+ Provide opportunities for pastoral support but in addition, emphasise the fact that student partners also have a duty of self-management;

+ Be mindful of issues relating to confidentiality when engaging in student/academic partner meetings;

+ Consider the on-going management of the project (where necessary) to include succession planning;

+ Encourage student partners to disseminate project work in a variety of forums.

Conclusions

Of course, we do not deny that a project within student–academic partnership schemes such as the one described in this book offer useful opportunities to bolster capacity in relation to work; and, just as 'performance goals' were (perhaps naively) used as extrinsic motivators for student recruitment, they may also be (mis)used to engage staff. We understand that this may be reflective of the perceived pressures to meet a wider strategic agenda and that this principle may work should all parties continue to perform well. However, should challenges arise then anxiety, burnout and disengagement may ensue. If staff and students are to embark on partnership journeys similar to the one described in this chapter, they should do so with their eyes open and consider deeply their reasons for involvement. We contend that such awareness will help to ensure that partners are sufficiently intrinsically motivated to stay on-target and to fully benefit from the partnership.

As we reflect on our argument, we need to reiterate that our conclusions do not emerge from a high-level strategy of student engagement but from one that is small and localised in scope as acknowledged by Chapman, P. *et al.* in this volume. Through our exploration of our student–academic partnership experience we have recognised the importance of establishing a robust yet flexible framework that allows local partnerships to flourish and achieve project outcomes. Our reflections have also led us to find that the inherent opportunities for mutual growth and development have far exceeded our initial expectations. Such opportunities should be seized as they arise and perhaps even be fostered within the curriculum so as to build a wider learning community with a shared vision for the future.

The VEC will continue to be developed and marketed; prompting further SAP opportunities with opportunities for cross-pollination between the staff and students of our faculties of Health and Business. Finally, as we consider where we go from here, we are aware of growing scope for this local project to inform a nascent institutional agenda to award credit for extra-curricular activity; credit that reflects the development of inherent transferable skills that cascade from student engagement in projects such as ours.

About the authors

Caroline Hutchings is a Speech and Language Therapy student in the Faculty of Health at Birmingham City University. She can be contacted at **Caroline.hutchings@mail.bcu.ac.uk**

Nicola Bartholomew is the Senior Learning & Teaching Fellow in the Faculty of Health at Birmingham City University. She can be contacted at **Nicola.bartholomew@bcu.ac.uk**

Oonagh Reilly is a Senior Lecturer in the Department of Speech & Language Therapy & Rehabilitation Studies at Birmingham City University. She can be contacted at **Oonagh.reilly@bcu.ac.uk**

Chapter 9

Problem-based Learning: Student and Tutor Perspectives

Kathleen Donnelly and Naomi Francis

Introduction

Problem-based Learning (PBL) as a classroom technique has been used extensively in teaching the sciences, particularly medicine, since the late 1960s (Smith *et al.*, 2005). More recently, partially due to the efforts of the faculty at the University of Delaware, its influence has spread to other academic disciplines (Ahfeldt *et al.*, 2005). The PBL technique ideally shifts the responsibility for learning from the tutor to the student and can lead to increased student engagement.

PBL has been used in our core Marketing, Advertising and Public Relations Practice module (MAPR Practice) since its inception as a double module for second year students on all our marketing, advertising and PR courses. After a programme restructuring, MAPR Practice was changed to a single 15-credit module delivered in the spring of the second year. The portfolio assessment was retained, and, in addition to a common one-hour weekly lecture slot, four groups of students, between 20 and 30 in a group, are scheduled for weekly two-hour seminars.

Each group is assigned a 'problem' in the form of a real-life client who presents to the class in Week Three. Classroom activity combines a variety of experiences: guest speakers, lectures, seminars, visits to and from the clients. All these are to aid the students in the completion of their individual portfolios.

The PBL approach allows students to work independently from tutors, choosing their own portfolio items, including events plans and marketing materials such as brochures, advertisements, press releases, web pages, etc., for their tutor-chosen clients. In the last week, students have the option of presenting their work to the client.

The structure and content give the students real-world experience in their chosen field, but also require a considerable amount of independent learning. Similar to the programmes in the School of Media, described by Gough *et al.* (in this volume), students enhance their employability by interaction with a real client, and end their second year with a portfolio of their own independent work.

For this project, the tutor determined that working with a student researcher would provide a different perspective and possibly uncover more honest feedback from students who had taken the module. The student was recruited by posting a notice on a forum which was sent to all those who had just completed MAPR Practice.

Based on both primary and secondary research, this chapter presents the findings and reactions of both a student from the most recent class, and the tutor who co-created the module, in alternating sections.

Introduction by the student

The MAPR Practice module was challenging but very motivating; not only because of the innovation and creativity needed to put together a portfolio, but also for the pleasure of gaining experience working with real-life clients. This gave me an important insight into the marketing world. Within the module I felt that I fully engaged with my client, which assisted me in choosing the ideal portfolio items to really improve my client's marketing.

The reason I chose to take part in this project to undertake research into PBL was the experience I would gain and the opportunity of writing a chapter for this publication, which would help me in my future career and education. Furthermore, I was surprised to hear about PBL as I was not aware of it, and did not realise the module was based on this theory. Therefore taking part in this research for me was not only to gain key skills but to also learn more about the PBL technique.

Introduction by the tutor

PBL appeals to me as a teacher because it places the onus on the student to take responsibility for his or her own learning, and therefore 'engage.' But why does this not always happen in practice?

Based on a weeklong seminar I attended at the University of Delaware in 2001, PBL inherently involves (1) a problem, (2) a tutor-facilitator, (3) individual and small group learning, and (4) an assessment of the process. According to Duch *et al.* (1997-1998:10), the tutor in PBL *"guides, probes for deeper understanding, and supports students' initiatives, but does not lecture in advance on essential problem-related concepts nor direct or provide easy solutions."* Having the client come to class to present information about their organisation to the students early on is an invaluable intro- duction to the real-world of client-agency relationships. By keeping the module schedule open-ended, related concepts are presented as and how the students request them. Extensive use of e-mail, meetings and Moodle, the University's Virtual Learning Environment (VLE), shifts the responsibility to the students to present their work-in-progress and receive feedback.

The module has had mixed success; last spring the average mark was 49%, with a median of 50%, based on 40% being a pass. Predictably there are those who disengage from the beginning, throw a portfolio together at the end, and then resit. Some are enthusiastic from the first class when their client is revealed, and either rise to the challenge or fade away.

What motivates those students who do engage, and what hinders those who don't? What factors impact their performance? Can this be measured by marks? As Hutchings *et al.* (in this volume) point out, students who are intrinsically motivated would want the experience of working with a client on activities they choose. But even students who are extrinsically motivated should engage based on their desire to bolster their CVs and gain practical marketing experience.

By having the student author conduct primary research with the others in her class, as well as alumni, I hoped to identify the factors affecting engagement and make recommendations for teaching PBL modules in the future, including this one.

PBL and engagement

Drawing on a variety of sources, Ahfeldt *et al.* (2005:9) when explaining about measuring and analysing engagement state that PBL "*...involves confronting students with a problem related to the class material as opposed to traditional didactic approaches to education. The problems...are loosely structured situations designed to create an environment that allows students an opportunity to explore and learn.*" In this module the real-life client organisation serves as the 'problem.'

In reviewing the research done into using PBL in the classroom, Ahfeldt *et al.* (2005:9) identified two key elements: "*...its shift from focusing on the teacher to a student-centered education with process-oriented methods of learning, (and its emphasis on)...understanding concepts, thinking critically and working collaboratively with others. Self-direction and reflection are key contributors to the process, which is of greater importance than the product.*" This shift and emphasis have been built into the module since its inception.

Ahfeldt *et al.* (2005) began with the hypothesis that more PBL would lead to more engagement. They measured this using a questionnaire adapted from the American National Survey of Student Engagement (NSSE), an ongoing programme ranking universities on their levels of student engagement. The survey addressed three key areas of engagement: collaborative learning, cognition, and personal skills.

Using their own university's ranking on the NSSE as a benchmark, Ahfledt *et al.* (2005) found that the greater degree to which modules incorporated PBL the higher they scored on engagement.

In addition, Allen *et al.* (2011:26), in their discussion of PBL and engagement, state that "*...by requiring students to talk to each other and collaborate on projects important to their academic success, PBL addresses student alienation and failure to form social networks, major reasons for students dropping out of college.*" They also cite research which shows "*students frequently (view) PBL as both a challenging and a motivating approach*" (Allen *et al.*, 2011:23).

Methodology

The definition of student engagement by Kuh (2009, in Trowler 2010:7), used by Warmington *et al.* (in this volume) states that: "*...the time and effort students devote to activities that are empirically linked to desired outcomes.*" To find out more about why students do or don't put in the 'time and effort' in this PBL module, primary research was carried out by the student and secondary research by the tutor.

To avoid bias for or against the tutor, the student researcher designed and conducted all primary research, including a survey distributed online, by e-mail and in a class, as well as follow-up interviews and e-mail exchanges. As Hutchings *et al.* (in this volume) point out "*The use of power...in academic–student relationships cannot be ignored.*" Having a student survey and interview other students removed this power difference which would be present if the teacher was the researcher.

To avoid any problems of confidentiality involved in the student researcher having access to class records, the tutor analysed secondary research, including marks, frequency of tutor meetings, e-mail exchanges and use of Moodle.

Primary research by the student

All surveys, questionnaires and interview questions were devised by the tutor and myself. I took suggestions from the tutor and then formatted the questions into the relevant research method. Many students were at first reluctant to answer questions, being concerned about what the information was needed for. When the research project was explained, many were happy to complete the surveys, not only giving honest feedback in the multiple-choice answers, but also in the open-ended questions that many often leave unanswered.

To format the survey I used the layout on Survey Monkey which allowed for an unlimited number of questions to be asked with various response types such as multiple-choice and comment boxes.

Questions one to five were answered with 'strongly agree, somewhat agree, somewhat disagree and strongly disagree.' These questions determined the students' impressions of the module's approach, tasks and requirements. The respondents were given the choice of four answers instead of five to eliminate the opportunity of choosing a middle neutral answer.

The next group of questions presented statements of students' perception of their client, for example:

Which one of the following statements best describes your feelings about your interaction with your client (Please choose only one):

> *I felt I needed lots more interaction with the client.*
> *I felt I needed some more interaction with the client.*
> *I felt there was enough interaction with the client.*
> *I felt there was too much interaction with the client.*

I then went on to ask for an overall insight into what the students felt towards the module, allowing them to choose all answers that applied.

The last 11 questions were open-ended, allowing for more extensive answers, asking for the students' views on the teaching they experienced, as well as how they felt they did within the module and ways of improving.

The survey was comprised of 24 questions with an additional 'Any comments?' box; a link was then created to post with guidelines on the Moodle forum to all fellow students who undertook the MAPR Practice module this past semester. In addition, the tutor posted the link to the final year students, and to any alumni she was in touch with who had taken the module. These respondents were instructed to return their surveys directly to me, not the tutor. In addition, once classes began again, surveys were distributed to students in two final year sessions who had taken MAPR Practice. All of these methods led to a total sample of 64 respondents.

Interviews were conducted as an alternative to holding a focus group. The interviews were made up of extended questions from those asked on the survey, with each interview being recorded for confirmation, only by audio to allow more confidentiality. Questions via e-mail were distributed to students who had agreed to answer extra questions but were unable to attend an interview. Questions included what helped and hindered students to engage in university study.

All these methods of research were undertaken by myself, without any assistance from the module tutor, to allow students to participate confidentially and give honest feedback.

Secondary research by the tutor

In an effort to determine the level of student engagement in the module, I turned to the secondary data which had been collected in the most recent semester. These included (1) the students' required 500-word reflective essays; (2) my records of students' in-class activity, meetings with me and e-mails; and (3) Moodle usage statistics. I felt it was more important for me to analyse this data rather than turn it over to the student researcher, who, for confidentiality reasons, couldn't have access to student marks, for example.

Findings from primary research by the student

After downloading the data from 20 surveys completed via Survey Monkey, and combining this with the 44 surveys completed by final year students in class, I was able to analyse the findings.

In all methods of research the students were asked to fill in information about their course and client. The students were also asked if they had held any employment while taking the module as this can be a factor in student engagement. The results showed that a significant number of students were in some type of employment, with 38 out of the 64 working outside of the University. The remaining were not in any employment or chose not to answer this question. As no definition about the number of hours involved was given, students self-reported themselves as working part-time or full-time.

In the MAPR Practice module the work was hands-on, requiring creativity and innovation. Question #1 was related to this approach, stating, 'I prefer the hands-on approach in this module to the usual textbook-based modules.' Out of the 64 students who responded, 36 of them chose that they 'strongly agreed' with this statement, with the rest of the answers falling into 'somewhat agree' (22) and 'somewhat disagree' (5).

We were given four mandatory items which we were required to include in our portfolios – questions to ask our clients, a secondary research report, an agency brief, and a reflective essay. We also chose seven optional items from a list including web pages, budgets, advertising, etc. With that in mind the next statement was, 'I liked the idea of deciding what tasks to work on for myself.' This was divided evenly between 'strongly agree' and 'somewhat agree,' with the other two answer choices receiving no votes.

Over the years the MAPR Practice students have worked with clients such as the Birmingham Royal Ballet, National Express and the Big Brum Theatre in Education Company. The clients came to lectures within the first weeks of the module, giving us insights into their organisation, its views and values, and the opportunity to question areas which we could work on for portfolio items. It was necessary that students engaged with clients at this face to face meeting to gain a full overview of who the client was, as the module expected us to work independently, gathering all information on our own. Therefore it was essential that I asked questions to gain an understanding of how students felt about the clients that they were given.

For the question, 'Which of the following statements best describes your opinion when you first heard who your client was?' I decided to look into any similarity in answers chosen between this statement and two others: 'Which of the following statements best describes your feelings about your interaction with your client?' and 'Which of the following statements best describes your opinion about your client at the end of the module?'

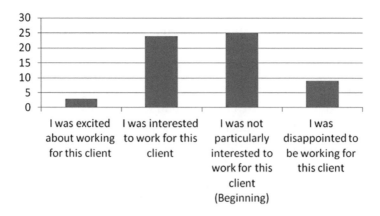

Figure 1: Which of the following statements best describes your opinion when you first heard who your client was?

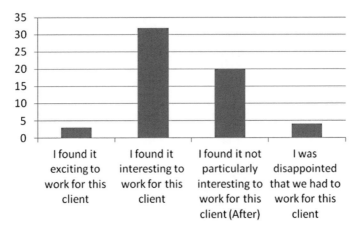

Figure 2: Which one of the following statements best describes your opinion about your client at the end of the module?

The Figures evidently present a difference of opinions about how students felt when first meeting their client compared to how they felt after the module. I decided to see if having enough interaction with the client could have been a reason for this. Below in Figure 3 the figures show that the largest percentage felt there was enough interaction. The highest percentage for client interest was 'not particularly interested,' but many felt that there was enough interaction. This was reflected in the figures for client interest at the end of the module when the majority found their client interesting to work with.

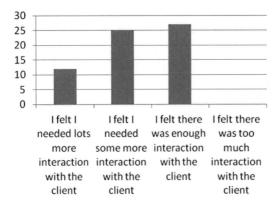

Figure 3: Which of the following statements best describes your feelings about your interaction with your client?

The question asking the students about their overall perception of the course gave them a variety of statements and they could choose all that applied (See Table 1). As the MAPR Practice module was different from any module many of the students had taken, there were different views on how they felt towards it. Many of our other modules are built on an assignment basis, with information and resources found throughout our learning. In MAPR Practice we the students were expected to identify areas that we wanted to learn about.

Thinking about your overall perception of this module, choose any of the following statements that describe your feelings about this module (Please choose as many as apply): N = 64		
Answer Options	**Response Percent**	**Response Count**
I felt this module was challenging.	41%	26
I felt this module gave me real-life experience.	41%	26
I felt that I should have challenged myself more in this module.	28%	18
I felt this module helped me with my career choices.	27%	17
I could have got more out of this module if I had spent more time on it.	22%	14
I felt lost at the beginning of this module, and so I didn't spend as much time as on it as I should have.	22%	14
I wasn't interested in my client and so I didn't spend as much time on this module as I should have.	17%	11
I feel that I got all that I could out of this module.	17%	11
I felt the tutors didn't do very much in this module, so I didn't spend as much time on it as I should.	8%	5
I felt this module required too much independent learning.	8%	5
I could have got more out of this module if the tutors had helped me more.	6%	4
I spent too much time on this module.	5%	3
I felt this module did not fit well with my course.	3%	2
I felt that the requirements of this module didn't challenge me enough.	3%	2
I didn't feel this module had much to do with the real world.	3%	2
I didn't have anyone to work with in my seminar group, so I didn't spend as much time on it as I should have.	2%	1

Table 1: Overall perception of module

Table 1 shows that finding the module challenging and gaining real-life experience scored the two highest percentages. The next group of similar percentages indicated how the students felt they had done in the module, with many feeling that they could have challenged themselves more and that they should have spent more time on it. However, others felt that they had no interest in the client so they didn't spend the amount of time they should have.

As the module was expected to help with our career prospects and future learning, it was significant that I asked what helped and hindered their learning. Many students felt that having the one-on-one tutorial with their tutors helped them the most. The online resources on Moodle and the presentations from their clients were also noted. What may have hindered their learning was that they did not understand what was needed or having unclear directions, as well as not being interested in their client. For example, commenting on what hindered their learning, they said, 'trying to find what portfolio items to choose,' 'my lack of interest with the client,' 'not turning up to lectures' and 'too much to do as the module had so much (work) to do.'

I then went on to ask what they or the tutors could have done to make the learning experience better. Several felt that the tutors had done all they could, whereas providing more information throughout the course would have been more supportive. However, when asked what they could have done better, they highlighted aspects such as time management, motivation, attending one on ones with the tutor, and putting in more effort.

Although MAPR Practice is a compulsory module, as a last question I asked if students would recommend the module to fellow students and why. Everyone said that they would highly recommend the module, due to its hands-on approach and real-life experience. Many then went on to give their views on what fellow students should do if they were to take the module, such as starting work earlier, and concentrating on all materials given by the tutors throughout.

As much of the research took place during the summer months, gaining interviews with fellow students presented some difficulty. This meant that one interview was conducted with a third-year student, Student A, on the PR and Human Resources Management Pathway. Unlike the survey questions these were open ended, allowing for more in-depth answers. This continued through e-mail questions with two students – one from the second year, Student B, and one from the final year, Student C. The questions were based around what three things each student liked best about the module, and what they may not have liked.

All three students were happy to participate and gave very honest feedback; Student A stated that she felt the module was very hands on which allowed for independence. As it was linked to the course they were taking they all felt that it was giving them the experience they needed. Working in groups within the module also developed their key teamwork skills. Students B and C also added that the real-life experience, guest speakers, and having the freedom to work on portfolio pieces of their own choice were the areas of the module they were most fond of. Not being able to choose their client was something all students felt would disengage a student. Their overall perception of the module was that it allowed for their independent learning as well as their creativity.

Questions were also asked such as, 'What makes you engage with the whole of university life?' They revealed that being engaged in the whole university experience can also have an effect on your attitude to university work. This is confirmed by the findings of Montesinos *et al.* (in this volume), who found that students employed by the university had more enthusiasm for their own learning and teaching.

To link with this I also asked if they took part in any other university activities. Student B was a member of the Business School Student Council and Student C a black student representative and a writer for the University magazine.

Findings from secondary research by the tutor

Reflective essays: Ahfeldt *et al.* (2005:9), point out that *"self-direction and reflection are key contributors"* to PBL, so I analysed the reflective essays students were required to include in their portfolios. They were told to address three questions; the first asked, 'What did you learn from the feedback from your tutor that you applied in this module?' 52% discussed feedback specifically on their own coursework, usually written comments by one of the tutors. 40% mentioned tutor meetings. 25% cited feedback given in class, which would be much less specific, implying that they hadn't received individual feedback, or didn't feel that it was helpful. Only

10% mentioned feedback via e-mail, although my records show that I had e-mail exchanges with more than half of the students and also with students from the other tutor's two groups.

The answers to the third question, 'What could you have done differently to get more out of this module?' reveal some of the students' thoughts about how they could have engaged more.

Mentioned most (41%) was better use of the tutor, either for more meetings or general feedback. About a third of the answers dealt with choosing different items for the portfolio (35%), doing more research (30%), including taking advantage of opportunities to visit the client, and 'more time' (29%). Other regrets mentioned, in declining order, were better organisation and/or planning on their part, choosing to do the optional presentation to the client, doing more work in general, learning to use the software covered in some sessions, and, surprisingly last, given the poor attendance record of the module, attending more. Overall, these regrets seem to reflect a distinct lack of motivation to become engaged.

Student records: The average mark across all four seminar sections was 49%, with a median of 50%, not counting those who did not submit (DNS). This average varied from a high of 60% in one of the other tutor's seminar groups, to a low of 42% in one of my seminar groups. It is not clear whether that group's scheduled meeting time of 9 am was a contributing factor to the low marks, but they did have an overall attendance level lower than the other group that met at 11 am.

Looking at the e-mail exchanges, which I saved, 14% of the students had only e-mail contact, with no recorded meetings with me or the other tutor; 25% had met with me, but had no e-mail exchanges, and 28% had no recorded or remembered contact with either tutor, indicating a disturbing 'lack of engagement'. 33% had both e-mail and personal contact through tutor meetings.

There were three portfolio items required to be submitted early in the semester (three questions to ask the client, a research report, and an agency brief). There were only four students who did not submit their questions for the client, but 7% of the class of 137 did not turn in a research report and/or an agency brief. This relatively high number who ignored early deadlines, designed to keep them on track from the beginning, is also a key indicator of early dis-engagement.

The data collected through Moodle usage showed that, on average, each student accessed the site for this module on 1.5 days per week, and clicked on about five pages and/or resources while there.

Also interesting was at what point during the semester the students actually enrolled on Moodle, given that strong encouragement was given in the first class session. 34% signed up the first week; but 46% waited until Week Two, as the deadline to submit the three questions to ask their clients loomed.

Analysis

Combining both the student's primary research and the tutor's secondary research unearthed some common themes.

Analysis by the student

The choice of client was a major factor in the non-engagement of some students. Figure 1 illustrates that a high number of students found their client not particularly interesting at the beginning. This came up again in the overview question (Table 1) as well as in the interview where the re-sitting student showed different reactions to the two clients she had. Having interest in and fully engaging with the client is a must from the beginning to gain a full understanding of the company's profile and to be motivated to submit a quality portfolio.

Over 50% of those students who took part in the research mentioned time management as a factor relevant to their engagement with MAPR Practice. With over half the students being in some type of employment, the factor of time management very much affects the prioritising of work. When students were asked what they could have done to make their learning experience better, the majority cited issues such as more one to ones with the tutor, greater interacting with the client and the need to become more motivated, all of which require time. I feel that time management is a concern that can only be addressed on the students' side.

Although all students were expected to hold regular meetings with their tutors throughout the module, many students failed to do so. Even though the PBL technique requires independent learning from students, these meetings were designed to benefit them in gaining guidance on their finished portfolios. The majority of students realised that failing to attend regular meetings did have an effect on their knowledge, final portfolio and mark. Although it was stated by tutors in the first class what was expected from a PBL module, having the theory fully explained to us may have given us a broader understanding of what tutors required in our portfolios as well as why the tutor meetings and client presentations were so crucial.

Analysis by the tutor

As shown in Figure 1 there was a split between those who were 'excited' or 'interested' when they first heard who their client was (42%), and those who were 'not particularly interested' or 'disappointed' (58%). But this shifted to 55% and 45% respectively by the end of the module. Only 17% said it affected how much time they put into the module. 39% wanted more interaction with their clients (although 42% felt there was 'enough').

Given that this is an issue for all students, engaged or not, it is interesting that 42% of our full-time students had part-time jobs, and 23% even reported that they were working full time. That's 65% of our students who are balancing work and school, in addition to family obligations. Most tutors would have estimated this as a much smaller percentage. Although time management is covered in their first year Personal Development module, more emphasis needs to be put on it. Hutchings *et al.* (in this volume) also found that lack of engagement was not only due to lack of motivation, citing 'feeling overwhelmed with other areas of their life,' as one of many other factors that can distract students from their coursework.

It is not clear whether students' final marks in the module are an adequate measure of their engagement. However, the 50% median for the class, and the 41% of respondents who said that the module was 'challenging' and gave 'real-life experience,' could indicate a real split between those who engage and those who don't. The fact that 34% enrolled on Moodle during the first week, but 46% waited until Week Two, may indicate that there is a small group, about one-third, who engage right away, with a larger cohort, about half, coming along a bit later.

In the survey 28% felt they should have challenged themselves more and almost as many said they should have spent more time on it (22%).

This was a theme in the reflective essays as well, with quite a few stating that they should have chosen more challenging portfolio items to work on.

Student and tutor analysis

Based on our findings, the following questions were posed to the student researcher:

Tutor: What do you think students' actual attitude to the module, and specifically to the PBL technique, is?

Student: I think that overall students had a positive attitude to the module. MAPR Practice expected something different from the students. Instead of the usual assessment and exam we were putting together a portfolio that not only showed creativity but also marketing techniques we had learnt so far. The module also gave us an insight into the world of work which many of us will be taking up in a few years. Having real-life experience is something that every student is looking for within their time in university, so the module did indeed help break down the barrier between university life and employment. As for the PBL technique, unfortunately students didn't have much understanding as to what this was and what it entailed. But with factors such as independent learning, many were happy to adapt to this as it also gave us insight into what employment may hold.

Tutor: How much do aspects such as which client they are assigned to affect students' engagement?

Student: From what I was able to identify, having a client you are interested in has a major effect on the engagement you have in the module. The client is someone you will be working on for over 12 weeks; not engaging from the beginning can be an obstruction to the work you produce. In my case I had a client who was willing to allow us to visit them within their environment and witness how the company operated. Opportunities such as these do allow you to submit portfolio items that you feel could really make a difference as you are able to connect with the client.

Tutor: Many students said they should have challenged themselves more. How can we motivate them to stretch themselves?

Student: I do feel that, during lectures in which there was extra time, students could have benefited from bringing in work that was in progress to get some opinions and thoughts from tutors and other students. As the module was based on independent learning, many students felt that they had left the work in the module until it was too late. Other modules that had heavy workloads kept them engaged and motivated to get the work done, leaving less time for MAPR Practice.

Tutor: From your personal experience in the module last semester, what do you think worked and what didn't?

Student: The face-to-face meetings with the client definitely worked, as this gave us that little insight into what you could create for your portfolio that could really have an effect on the company. The guest speakers within the seminars were very beneficial. These seminars gave quality information on different subjects that our other modules may not have covered. Each seminar focused on something different which motivated us to come and find out what was next. Unfortunately I don't think planning the one to one meetings ourselves worked, as many students did not complete this. In the end they realised what a benefit it could have been.

Tutor: Thinking back to how you felt during the module, have your thoughts about it changed since you've been doing this research?

Student: Since undertaking this research I indeed feel that the module has many benefits from the real-life experience to the independent learning to the creativity you can include within your portfolio. All these factors have made not only me but also my fellow students aware as to what to expect as we get ready to leave university life and place ourselves within the working environment. The module really opens up your understanding of the different aspects of marketing as well as developing the attributes employers look for, such as teamwork and motivation, along with independence.

Tutor: Overall, what do you feel you got out of the module and the experience of doing this research, good and bad?

Student: I felt the module made me think out of the box, instead of just finding relevant articles and information to present in an assessment like many modules. I was presenting a piece of work that only I could solely produce with the information I had collected from interacting with the client. Out of the research I was able to gain more confidence about my writing and the skills needed to produce quality work. I was also able to communicate with the majority of my class members that I may not have done otherwise.

The student's conclusions

Since taking part in this research I have been able to see how the PBL technique provides effective learning that can benefit us, not only in university work but also within employment. I also feel that such a technique could be used in other modules that would actually benefit the students more than a textbook, didactic approach. Independent learning encourages you to open up more to the module and genuinely take the learning with you, whereas, in other modules, surface learning is undertaken to complete assessments but lost straight after. I have enjoyed taking part in researching into the PBL method and hearing the response to it from my fellow students. As a student I am aware that it is fundamental that you engage with your module to achieve the grades and skills which university can bring. Taking into account the different factors that were brought up by students, such as time management, prioritising, having the interest and motivation, I believe that these are the definition of student engagement.

The tutor's conclusions

I would make three recommendations for this specific module. Firstly, that after they have seen presentations from more than one client, students could be allowed to choose which seminar to attend based on their preference for one client over another. Secondly, as 59% of the students surveyed either 'agreed' or 'somewhat agreed' that it would be better to have studied MAPR Practice as a double module in one semester, making this change could lead students to devote more time to it. Thirdly that Moodle could be used more for resources, and also to track student engagement during the semester, intervening when a student appears to be waning.

For the larger issue of PBL, there are other patterns that can be identified. The type of problem students are assigned to work on can have a big effect on students' engagement. Students like the challenge of independent learning, but they often have other commitments that we as tutors aren't aware of and need extra motivation to take full advantage of the opportunities offered. Problem-based Learning does not appear to be for everyone. Based on this sample, only about half of the students engaged, with approximately one-third feeling committed to the approach.

About the authors

Kathleen Dixon Donnelly is a senior lecturer in Public Relations at Birmingham City Business School. She can be contacted at **Kathleen. donnelly@bcu.ac.uk**

Naomi Francis is a final year student in Marketing and Human Resource Management at Birmingham City Business School. She can be contacted at **njfrancis@live.co.uk**

Chapter 10

Media Industries Beyond the Curriculum: Motivating Blended Professionalism for Enhanced Student Engagement and Employability

Kerry Gough, Jamie Morris and Amie Hession

Within the Birmingham School of Media at Birmingham City University (BCU), we employ a wide range of strategies to encourage student engagement in order to enhance the employability prospects of our media graduates. These include the development of student and staff partnerships to enhance close industry engagement practices through co-curricular activity, the co-development of course content and a fostering of personalised tuition through the Professional Media Practice arm of the BA (Hons) Media and Communication programme. This chapter examines how these strategies have been employed through the Student Academic Partners (SAP) programme, as discussed throughout this volume, to engage our students in order to enhance their employability, to strengthen the reputation of our School and to feed the media industry with the next generation of creative media thinkers. Our School ethos of *"blended professionalism"* is one in which we actively encourage our students to practice through fluid professional relationships across placement and outreach activity within the media industry environment (Whitchurch, 2009; Trowler, 2010).

The Media and Communication programme at BCU consistently performs well within national league tables; ranking 8th in *The Guardian* (2012) league for Media Studies, Communications and Librarianship and reporting excellent National Student Survey results of 93% for student satisfaction; with 89% of those students going onto work or further study and 65% of last year's cohort entering graduate level jobs (Unistats, 2012). Part of the ability to 'obtain employment reasonably quickly' comes from the adaptability required of our students through the complex nature of the degree programme, the embedded nature of our professional development provision, but also through the close working relationships and collaborative partnerships that we actively foster with our students (Gibbs, 2010).

The success of the School's employability figures at BCU can arguably be attributed to the complexity of a programme which crosses multiple media platforms, and as such by its very nature, forces our students into a mind-set of resourceful adaptability through the wide-ranging skills performance required to succeed not only on the programme, but within the industry upon graduation (Wisby, 2011). This is reinforced in three different ways: firstly, through the embedded academic provision for professional media development, which provides personalised tuition across the three years of the undergraduate programme; secondly, through close industry engagement practices which convert industry demand into the academic preparation of our students and thirdly through the added-value activities of engagement through student and staff partnership.

The BA (Hons) Media and Communication degree is by design a difficult programme of study; with nine distinct specialist pathways (as of 2012-13), which include Television, Radio, Journalism, Photography, Public Relations, Music Industries, New Media, Events and Exhibition Management and the all-encompassing Broad Course. This enables our students, in effect, to 'build their own degree' in the selection of modules from an array of media disciplines. Students of the course are expected to engage with the demands of 'adaptable expertise', across a range of different media which necessitate cross-collaborative working relations and interdisciplinary networking, all of which are designed to mirror the demands of the media and creative industries (Gibbs, 2012). As one student states:

"The course is tough, but it prepares you well for work placement and industry experience as we are constantly being pushed to work outside of our comfort zone and to pick up challenging assessments that force you to dive straight in."

While another student identifies an added benefit, whereby staff:

"set industry level standards for their assignments which helps us when we leave and go on to get placements to be at professional standards already."

Each of the Professional Media Practice modules across the three years are structured around assignments and assessments that encourage our students to reflect critically upon the industry. Building upon their experiences acquired whilst on the course, they encourage the production of critical self-evaluations and focus upon strategies for continuing professional development.

Work in all modules is orientated towards providing individualised, comparable experiences of the actualities of the media and cultural industries business; be that of recording a radio show, producing a music promo, starting a record label, creating a magazine, researching television audiences, or making a documentary.

As we enter the 2012/13 academic year, in a time of increased university tuition fees and institutional uncertainty, the added demands of a personalised curriculum and the necessary extension of the undergraduate offering through value-added activities has lingered, indeed a key theme of address at the 2011 QAA Annual Conference, featured around the position of students as consumers versus their role as cohort and community (QAA, 2011). The emergent debate overwhelmingly sought to define the student body in polar terms; either as an active cohort who were immediately involved in the development of their community, or that of a consumer group who were making value-for-money demands of their education and the institutions providing it (Blease-Dudley, 2011; Corfield, 2011; Jessop, 2011; Oliver, 2011; Stuart, 2011). At the Birmingham School of Media, we address both ends of that spectrum, taking into account not only demands for student satisfaction and the role of *"student-as-consumer"* as outlined by Dobozy (2011:11), but also through a desire to ensure that we provide an enriched student experience where we engage our students at the heart of the School as *"active and productive participants in their learning endeavours"* (*ibid*, 2011:25).

In this chapter we examine how we can match these demands through a process of student engagement and the provision of experiences that allow for competence development in the face of a changing media employment landscape. We are in the business of producing graduates within a testing climate; the shift towards independent media production evident across the last decade has led to a rise of the freelancer and the development of the 'portfolio career' necessitating an adaptability of skill set. Exacerbated by the global economic turndown, portfolio careers are fast becoming the industry standard; long gone are the secure career pathway jobs within the media industry – instead, the multi-skilled, multi-faceted temporary recruit has fast become the human resource of choice.

While the cost of a university education has not increased disproportionately in real terms, the increase in costs to the individual remains a very real and immediate one. As a result, the recent Graduate Employability (2012:1) conference documentation identifies how:

> *"In a time of economic difficulty, students require diverse skills to stand out to prospective employers and will look to institutions with strong employment records. As fees rise universities will work harder to attract students and employability will be a focus for many prospective students. Desires and demands from all sides must be more transparent to ensure today's student is supported to become tomorrow's valuable employee."*

When laid out in such pragmatic terms, the necessity to add value through employability enhancement, and to encourage student engagement through co-curricular planning and extended provision becomes self-evident (1994 Group, 2009).

In response to this, through the SAP scheme, our students have been employed in a paid capacity on a range of projects that are designed to enhance student engagement and co-creation in a way that supports increased employability potential and skills development. Students within the School of Media have been employed across numerous projects, however within this chapter, we will be focusing upon the work conducted around enhancing employability with the redevelopment of the Professional Media Practice programme, the development of a Creative Media Networks events programme and the ongoing Media Industry Outreach project in which the motivation for student engagement emanates from our shared desire for employability success.

Embedding media employability and blended professionalism through collaborative practice

Employability has become an increasingly important motivator in light of the 2012 increase in university tuition fees (Harrison, 2012). As Gibbs (2010:40) identifies, justification for higher education participation relates directly to the nature of employability. He argues: *"The extent to which graduating students are able to obtain employment reasonably quickly, in graduate jobs, in fields relevant to their degree subject, and with a salary that justifies their investment of time and money in higher education is a commonly used dimension of quality."* However, while employability has come to the fore as a key indicator of success for academic institutions, Gibbs (2010:42) cautions against a reliance upon *"narrowly focused vocational education"* or the inclusion of *"generic 'employability skills'".* Instead he proposes a more developmental emphasis upon *"higher order intellectual capabilities involved in adaptable expertise"* (*ibid*). It is through the student-staff partnerships at work within our School, that opportunities for applying and rehearsing these adaptable capabilities occur. Hutchings *et al.* (in this volume) also discuss the issue of employability skills nurturing in relation to resource development.

This increasingly necessary focus upon employability has motivated staff and students to work together in the creation of a learning community, which encourages continuous and on-going student engagement in the development of teaching materials, content and strategies for the enhancement of our students' continued professional development. Within the Professional Media Practice strand of learning, this occurs *within* the curriculum through a process of perpetual feedback and engagement. Student evaluation of the taught content, support materials and their experiences of employment and placement activity, are then used to feed back into the module redesign. These revisions, conducted alongside our student partners are then experienced and re-evaluated afresh by the wider student body. Through a process of engaged partnership, we have developed course materials to build upon the external placement experiences of our students to bring these back into the taught environment. Through engaging our students in the programme development, this has not only given them ownership in the construction of a personalised programme of tuition, as identified by Wisby (2011), but has also allowed for the expansion of their university degree provision in a way that marks each student out as unique.

Working alongside the Professional Media Practice programme, student academic partnership has enabled a redevelopment of taught provision to provide a challenging assessment that assists our students in the building of unique portfolios for their professional development and the willingness of students to get involved came as a delightful surprise. Two additional SAP projects, designed with student engagement and employability in mind, have run in parallel to the development of Professional Media Practice. The Creative Media Networks SAP project has sought to facilitate the generation of networking opportunities, while the Media Industry Outreach Project, acts as a co-curricular extension to taught provision, offering up employment enhancing experiences and work placement activity. The importance of these activities is reflected through student commentary:

> *"Professional Media Practice was essential to enable me to plunge myself into the industry confidently... Without the numerous placements I have undertaken on this course, I wouldn't be as aware or confident that this is the right career for me and would enter the work place post graduation with little knowledge of how media organisations operate."*

The interlinked nature of these (employability-focussed) projects contributes to the development of a culture of *"blended professionalism"* in which identity, according to Whitchurch (2009), is extracted from *both* the academic and professional environment. However, while Whitchurch (2009) and Trowler (2010) have examined the role of the blended professional from the perspective of the academic, and their transitory existence between education and professional employment, we maintain that these fluid professional relationships extend the role of the student

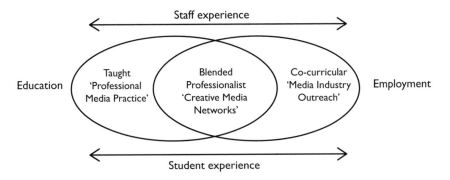

Figure 1: Combining taught programmes with co-curricular activity to create blended professionals

to one of usurping transitional space between their university education and the employment opportunities with which they engage. Just as the professional experiences of the *"blended professional"* educator 'bleed' into the educational environment through taught provision, so too the work placement and employment experiences of our undergraduate students feed back into the educational context through redesign of the taught employability provision ensuring that graduates are fit for purpose.

When examining graduate capability, Reid & Solomonides (2012:146-147) have identified how: *"such graduates would have the ability to integrate knowledge, skills, personal qualities and understanding in their personal and professional lives."* These modular redesigns act as a tool to enhance employability through the emergence of *"blended professional"* graduate media practitioners (Whitchurch, 2009:407). Also, teaching staff bring professional engagement activity into the School, whilst simultaneously testing the climate for media graduate skills requisites within the industry. This perpetual feedback loop is outlined in the diagram below (see Figure 1).

In this way, the taught Professional Media Practice programme aligns itself with the co-curricular provision of the Media Industry Outreach Project. Staff and students working together in the redesign of the learning programme, foster a learning community which enhances employability through a two-way blended professional experience which facilitates the development of the blended professional graduate. The immediate experiences of students, the desires of educators and the concerns of employers are addressed as part of a dynamic learning community in which all groups become invested (Taylor and Wilding, 2009). The students become a vital lynchpin in this process, acting according to Kay *et al.* (2010), as agents of causal change in reaction to the ever-shifting demands of industry. Here our students become actively engaged in a process of leadership for change, by which their engagement feeds back into the School through the perpetual feedback loop, which in turn fosters further co-creation activity (Wisby, 2011).

However, not only are staff and students actively engaged in the co-creation of taught content for Professional Media Practice and the development of industry outreach opportunities, but according to Copper (2012) this 'comes full circle' to encourage input from the media industries in the crafting of future generations of media industry workers.

The ability to combine skillsets has become an essential ingredient in the composite of the successful media graduate (Skillset, 2009). Increasingly, media-industry workers are making use of newly emergent social media and online portfolios in the pursuit of employment (Skillset, 2009), and as is further identified by Ashfield *et al.* (in this volume).

Together we have adapted the academic tuition for Professional Media Practice to become more responsive to the shifting nature of media industries employment and through this combination of embedded professional development and co-curricular planning, our joint aspiration is to produce engaged graduates who have the prerequisite blend of skills demanded by the industry.

Engaging students in professional media practice

Our students are expected to engage in a range of activities that will supplement their formalised education and reinforce their employability as media graduates. The close working relationships developed as a part of the SAP process has had a transformative impact upon both staff and students alike; students involved in the process have commented how *"The atmosphere is really great between staff and students"*, while another comments *"Instead of lecturers teaching you, they assist you and guide you, giving you full opinion and creative view over the project."*

Staff have also felt the benefits of these dynamic working relationships:

> *"Working with our students has been a joy. It is so refreshing to be able to test out ideas prior to delivery to the wider student cohort, particularly for projects that are designed with the student experience in mind. They soon tell you if you get it wrong and often come armed with much more engaging solutions."*

Motivated in our shared desire to enhance the employment prospects of our students through the personalised tuition of Professional Media Practice, to enhance work placement opportunities through the projects described in this chapter, we have developed close student / academic staff working relationships. As a direct result, over the last two years, we have seen a shift of mindset within the School in which the opinion of our students has increasingly influential in the decision-making processes; indeed, in relation to the redevelopment of Professional Media Practice, the student voice has become absolutely central.

The Professional Media Practice modules are embedded across each year of the degree programme. Work in these modules involves locating and preparing for work placement in the creative industries, coupled with a critical reflection upon personal and professional development. In bringing professional development into the first year of the undergraduate programme, we are better placed to prepare our students for the demands of work within industry in a way that enables them to rehearse the articulation of those skills acquired, and learn from those processes. Here we have established a developmental pathway that adheres to the following process:

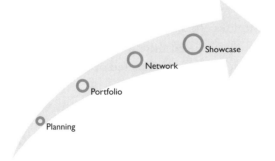

Figure 2: Development process for the Professional Media Practice pathway

Embedded throughout the undergraduate degree programme as a core strand which students must pass in order to progress into subsequent years of study, Professional Media Practice engages our students with a range of different approaches to gaining employability skills.

In the first year, students begin planning for their chosen career pathway and assess the feasibility of their own career aspirations. Reid and Solomonides (2012) have identified a need for students to account for their employment capabilities, so in conducting an audit of initial skill sets, our students evaluate what they need to do to achieve their career ambitions and time is subsequently spent developing the format for their CVs and the nature of their professional presentation to potential employers. Coupled with this, they run their own media production event requiring all students to engage in organisation, co-ordination and delivery activities utilising a full range of media competences; thus providing students with a hands-on experience of the demands of working with other media producers. As a part of this process senior students are engaged with the implementation of the event, assisting and advising their junior colleagues in its orchestration and delivery.

Many of the skills here are not taught, but rather are *experienced* through a process of *"active learning"* (Winchester-Seeto et al., 2012:426) whereby their experiences not only contribute to their awareness of industry practices, but also prepare them for the uncertainties of a role within the media industry. In this way, teaching can be defined in Mathiasen's terms as a *"social event"* (2008:111).

Encouraged to employ the VUCA principles of Vision, Understanding, Clarity and Agility, as outlined by Johansen (2007) our students employ these tools to aid their swift entry into the job market, as they learn to react and adapt rapidly to the ever evolving media landscape through the engagement opportunities offered up by taught practice. These principles are then rehearsed and reinforced through the completion of 70 hours of placement activity, which must be completed in order to progress into the second year of study.

While the first year is focused predominantly upon curriculum vitae planning and portfolio development, second year students build upon the frameworks laid out in year one to develop their own unique professional media practice portfolios and begin networking and sharing those portfolios with professionals working within the media industry (See

Figure 2). A drastic overhaul of the second year Professional Media Practice programme has been facilitated through the development of SAP projects that have allowed students to take charge of their own learning. For example, by embodying the person-centred democratic approach to learning, as highlighted by Fielding (2011) staff and students collaborated on the development of a form of assessment that focused upon individual personal assessment. In this way we performed in what Fielding (2011:11) terms a *"lived democracy"*, recognising a shared responsibility for the development of a creative and individualised community for the shared benefit of all.

While portfolios developed in year one are largely safe, internally-facing and produced for assessment and critical reflection activity; in the second year, through our SAP project, we adapted the assessment to accommodate student choice in their self-presentation and production of their own professional media development website. The ambition here was to create a space in which our students could actively reconstruct their professional selves through an active *"critique of their own knowledge"* as advocated by Reid & Petocz (2008:35). These sites are external to the university, housed on free-to-use websites, including Wordpress, Blogger and Tumblr, through which they showcase their unique talents and highlight their skills in branding themselves as independent, thinking media professionals in line with the School's philosophy of *"blended professionalism"* (Whitchurch, 2009:407).

Historically, we have used Mahara (the University's e-portfolio system) as a tool for the creation of these portfolios, however during consultation surrounding second year Professional Media Practice provision, one student commented that *"Mahara just isn't used by the industry and as creative media people, it's a bit of a joke that we are made to use it."* While successful elsewhere, it very quickly became apparent that the Professional Media Practice portfolios, in their original format, had little life beyond the assessment and became redundant post-assessment. Mahara, as open source e-portfolio and social networking software, while allowing a sustainable means of monitoring consistency of content and formatting in a first year context, offered little by way of the creativity necessitated for successful self-presentation in the *creative* industries.

Previously, students had performed the requisite critical thinking and collation of professional development activity for the assessment, only to rework this into other formats for their prospective job applications. Across our discussion with students relating to their experiences of the second year professional development, the repetitive nature of reworking their CV and Mahara portfolio elements became a recurrent issue. Prior to its redevelopment, the strength of feeling came as a complete surprise, as one student complained, *"There are only so many times that you can rework your CV within the classroom context"*, while another SAP working on a different project highlighted how *"Redoing your CV on Mahara as a part of your second year professional media development is a bit shit!"*. In response, these complaints became our primary motivator for improvement in the redesign and co-creation of the revised portfolio assessment and its renewed allowance for creativity.

Working together, we devised a programme that allowed students free choice from a range of free-to-use software and provided guidance through a series of support materials that we co-wrote. Building upon Rowley's (2011:54) acknowledgement of students as *"digital natives"* and a recognition of their inherently immersive use of media technologies, students selected the most appropriate format to echo the industrial practices of their chosen media sector. Initially this represented a huge concern surrounding assessment, and the ability to assess different portfolio formats equitably became a prominent point of discussion when we revealed the materials to the students' personal tutors (who would be marking them). One tutor remarked:

> *"I had initial concerns about how the new assignment would work, and I was reluctant to lose the traditional CV, as that is still necessary when applying for the majority of jobs in the television sector of the media industry. I also had qualms about how the students would illustrate knowledge of industry issues within their specialism."*

However, with some minor adaption of the learning outcomes and a finessing of the assessment criteria, we were able to overcome these concerns. We included an element which assessed the appropriate selection of format in relation to the media industry sector identified by the student as aspiring media industry professional, along with an account of materials which demonstrated their understanding of industry related issues. This facilitated a far more *"enabling"* and responsive approach to assessment as promoted by Fielding (2011:18), whereby the *"flexibility"* extended the usefulness and longevity of the portfolio for the students' professional development. The same staff tutor, who raised concerns, went on to comment upon their reaction to these portfolios at the point of assessment:

> *"When I marked some of the blogs/websites that the students had produced, it was easy to see how valuable a tool they could be when engaging with potential employers... ...I was so impressed by what the students had achieved through their blogs/websites that I was inspired to set up my own site along similar lines... ...I'm a convert!"*

With the new free-format Professional Media Practice portfolios, our students have in effect taken ownership over their own professional development. As Rowley (2011:45) has identified, this allows students to *"sort, classify, select and collate evidence to demonstrate their holistic degree learning achievement"*. These professional development activities are all co-ordinated in-house and have the added advantage, as advocated by Thomas (2012:6), that the careers advice and professional development coaching that our students receive comes directly from members of teaching staff within the 'academic sphere' who have experience of working within the industry.

As an added advantage, one student partner involved in its redesign also identifies how *"the impact of the portfolios being student-led has also impacted upon the quality of work on the module"*. In having a heavy personal investment in the presentation of these portfolios, the outcome of such work is one in which the students are motivated to engage. He goes onto identify how:

> *"As a student also participating in the module, I felt a real determination to ensure my work was of a high quality to make sure I represented myself to the best of my best ability."*

We would contend that this curriculum change has resulted in motivation for the creation of a self-branding portfolio that consists of all of the distinct work produced and accumulates experiences gained into a coherent portfolio of 'brand-me'. In line with Reid & Petocz's (2008) thinking, it would appear that a personalised interest and direct invest-ment stimulates a heightened motivation for student engagement.

In addition to the development of their Professional Media Practice Portfolios, second year students complete an additional 105 hours of work placement activity. At this stage, their Professional Media Portfolio becomes a useful tool in their self-promotion, as one student commented:

> "I think the creating of a portfolio is essential in the development of students as media professionals. The production of these help us to put theory and practical techniques into practice, enabling us to showcase the work we have been able to manufacture due the work experience we have gained."

We strongly encourage our second year students to make use of these portfolios when prospecting for work and placement activity. This is also the place where our most successful undergraduate students invest time evaluating their work placement activity *in-situ* in a manner that is fresh and engaging (Cottrell, 2012). Rowley (2011:57) identifies how this use of reflection aids in bringing the *"curriculum alive"*. The vivid imme-diacy of the experiences that are documented encapsulates enthusiasm and maintains detail in a way that does not become muddied over time, as memories of placement activity often can. This offers up a means of life-long, on-going, critical reflection, in which the direct impact of such activity results in the production of engaged thinking media professionals who are well rehearsed in self-evaluation and are aware of the professional impact of their own activities (Grosjean, 2012; Rowley, 2011; Samways & Seal, 2011). As one student identifies:

> "Because the module is extremely focused on gaining employment, there was a lot of emphasis on the fact that these portfolios could be a contrib-utor in getting employed when applying for a job. There is just a really prominent theme from the School to make sure we provide ourselves with the best possible future."

While the second year of the Professional Media Practice strand is focused upon portfolio population and networking, the focus of the final year shifts predominantly towards continued media industry networking and the showcasing of each student's individual talent. Rehearsing these skills across the three years of undergraduate study, our students enter their final year of the programme with a wealth of accumulated experience. With a commitment to producing creative media thinkers and blended professionals, the programme's ambitions include matching those experiences as closely as possible to the professional environment. Final year students organise their own networking event at the end of year show, which acts to showcase their final year products and projects. A further part of their exit strategy sees each student receive individual feedback on their performance during mock interviews and pitches.

Importantly, while direct taught educational engagement with the enhancement of key skills has resulted in the enhanced employability of our students, none of this would be possible without close collaboration with the media and creative and cultural industries. Alongside our co-development of the taught programme, with the advent of Professional Media Practice portfolios and the development of the Creative Media Networks events, additional co-curricular activity as embedded in the Media Industry Outreach project assists in the generation of *"blended professionalism"* through the bringing of employment into the educational environment (Whitchurch, 2009:407).

Graduate employability and media industry outreach: co-curricular engagement with the media and creative industries

While the media industry talent pool grows in relation to the contraction of media industry jobs, it is in our shared interests and motivation to ensure that our students gain as much industry experience as possible in preparation for entry into the job market. While Professional Media Practice prepares our students for employment within the media and creative industries, the Media Industry Outreach project serves to augment those employment opportunities by capitalising upon the wealth of contacts and media industry networks that the School has at its disposal. Acting as a means of initiating and bolstering work placement activity, with the use of our online placement advertising portal 'Job Book', the site acts as a promotional mechanism which enables effective communication between staff, students and potential employers around paid employment, work placements and collaborative production opportunities.

As a student initiated project, the Media Industry Outreach Project was developed to assist students in gaining placements. Encouraging supportive relationships with local media business, the project assists in developing regular placements and more long-term internships. While our students have a good record of securing placements with a wide range of media practitioners – including the BBC, *Country File, The Gadget Show Live, Kerrang! Radio, Loaded* Magazine, *More* Magazine, *The Guardian, Channel 4 Online, ITN, East Midlands Today, Endemol* and *NEC Birmingham* amongst others – locating and securing work placement represents an area of ongoing concern, particularly with our first year students.

Through maintaining these contacts and building a database of School-of-Media-friendly placement providers, we are able to pass on the benefits of placement activity to our students, whilst supporting a contracting industry sector through the provision of trained undergraduate assistance in a tight economic climate. Our students identify the value of this activity; as one student comments:

> "It really puts you out there in the professional world and lecturers really push you to gain as much work experience as you can, which is really vital in this industry."

Our industry partners have responded in similarly favourable terms, identifying how on the reverse of this, placements and internships have offered them an opportunity to test out our undergraduate students, putting local media business in a position to cream off the talent in advance of the competition. As one employer states:

> "Taking students on work placement offers us the chance to test out the potential that they have to offer. We benefit from their assistance during areas of peak workflow while they benefit from our critical feedback and credit for any work that we use."

In this way, the Media Industry Outreach Project has seen the brokering of a mutually beneficial networking of relationships in which local media businesses benefit from working with our students, whilst simultaneously supporting their professional development.

While the *Graduate Employability* (2012) conference raised concern over the exploitation of graduates, we found that increased competition has led to media businesses making more careful selections in the recruitment process. Although the unpaid internship has become a 'necessary evil', it is a vehicle through which media graduates have benefitted from a more sustained period of employment experience. A fuller discussion of student interns can be found in this volume (Chambers & Nagle).

Enhancing employability through collaborative partnership and mutual blended professionalism

Working in partnership on projects such as those discussed in this chapter has benefitted student engagement in two ways: firstly by directly engaging the students involved in the planning, set-up and implementation of the projects themselves and secondly through the added benefit of engaging future generations of media students through the co-curricular outreach activity generated as a result. The benefits of such value-added activities of engagement have far exceeded our expectations as a School in the generation of closer working partnerships and the fostering of an enhanced sense of community. Blended professionalism has emerged as a two-way process in which student experience has fed back into the taught programme through the perpetual feedback loop. Students working on the project have commented how: *"Working as part of a team within the University really makes me feel like I am an integral part of the University and makes me look forward to coming in."*

Through working in close partnership on these collaborative projects, and motivated in our shared desire to enhance employability for *all* of our students, we have benefited from the fostering of a collegiate atmosphere and supportive environment in which our working relations have added to the satisfaction of both our staff and student cohort alike.

In addition to our initial ambition for students to gain work placements and garnering a set of excellent industry experiences, students and staff have been able to think creatively about ways of improving their own experiences within the School and to capitalise upon the improvement of that experience for future generations of media students. Through collaborative working processes our students have taken ownership over their study, enhanced their environs and made recommendations for change as valued members of the respective project teams (Wisby, 2011:34-35).

Thomas (2012:8) has identified how these relationships between students, staff and peers *"promote and enable student engagement and success in HE"*; as such, these collaborative projects not only enhance the employment prospects of our students, but they also foster a mutually supportive collaborative community. By developing strong cohesion between staff and students, BCU becomes *our* shared home for creative collaboration. These emergent values, while initially unexpected, have had the additional benefit of fostering close working partnerships that have extended beyond the classroom and through which a shared pride and mutual respect has come to the fore. As one staff member comments:

> *"Five years ago I would not have dreamt I would be giving my mobile number out to my students, or taking after hours calls and being happy about it. But now I see those students as an extension of my work colleagues. We work together on common projects and learn from each other whilst having fun in the process."*

These practices have become so natural that student consultation and co-working has now become an embedded part of what we do within the Birmingham School of Media in which we are all, according to Taylor and Wilding (2009:3), engaged as *"collaborators"*.

Through a series of interlinked student and staff partnerships we have revamped the Professional Media Practice programme to incorporate unique portfolio development and the fostering of creative media networks. Together we have developed an extended programme for sourcing student placement activity through the Media Industry Outreach Project and facilitated a means of advertising and recruiting for those placements in a way that has allowed us to meet the demands of both the industry and the individual needs of our students in the construction of unique career pathways and portfolios. The great thing about this whole process is the affirmation that we produce high quality graduates who are capable of performing within a variety of employment roles and contexts. By offering meaningful employment to our students and giving them the opportunity to hone their craft skills, this can only aid in their preparation for paid employment outside of the university upon graduation.

The strategies we have employed have been designed to enable our students to hit the ground running and enter the creative media industries as well-informed, creative media thinkers and *"blended professionals"*, not just graduates of a media degree (Whitchurch, 2009:407).

As a direct result of our activity, our student partners have found themselves in employment elsewhere across the university on a number of different projects through Birmingham City University's in-house student employment agency, 'OpportUNIty Student Jobs'. Building upon their specialist knowledge to deliver media content and using their own experiences as a student to inform their performance, the practice of *"blended professionalism"* becomes an inherent part of the learning process, as one student identifies: *"Participating in these activities has contributed massively to my professional development".*

With direct support from our Centre for Enhancement of Learning and Teaching (CELT), the *"blended professionalism"* of our students is something that will continue to be embedded across our institution. Through such relationships the trust and faith in our students to perform on a professional level has become a given. This is highlighted in this volume by Montesinos *et al.* who comment that the students who work alongside us come with a tried and tested guarantee reinforced by the philosophy of the university's student employment agency, OpportUNIty Student Jobs, which starts from a position of valuing our students so much that we employ them ourselves.

About the authors

Dr Kerry Gough is Senior Lecturer in Film, Television and Media Theory at Birmingham City University. She can be contacted at **Kerry. Gough@bcu.ac.uk**

Amie Hession is a third year BA (Hons) Media and Communication student at Birmingham City University. She can be contacted at **Amie. Hession@mail.bcu.ac.uk**

Jamie Morris is a third year undergraduate studying the BA (Hons) English and Media at Birmingham City University. He can be contacted at **Jamie.Morris@mail.bcu.ac.uk**

Chapter 11

Student Engagement: Enabling Academic Success through Dynamic Partnerships

Wal Warmington, Trevor Hodge, Sheikh Sela and Anil Kainth

Introduction

This chapter emerged from a project based at Birmingham City University (BCU), between Autumn 2011 and the Spring of 2012, and involved Student Academic Partners (SAPs) working alongside staff within the Centre for Academic Success. The Centre provides tutorials, workshops, bespoke sessions and specialist English language support for international students. It operates from its own resource rooms, across BCU's City North and City Centre campuses and through print and e-based resources. As a result of a bid submitted for student engagement funding to develop a Student Academic Partnership initiative, the Students Targeting Active Academic Resources for Students (STAARS) project was born. The aim was to discover how students could be motivated to promote the academic resources available at Birmingham City University (BCU). The activities of the STAARS project involved the SAP's helping to deliver a relevant, stimulating and meaningful academic support service which aimed to enhance students' academic achievement. Together our story of positive student engagement reflects McCulloch's (2009) notion of students as co-producers within productive partnerships.

Our chapter begins with a brief exploration of the literature around student motivation, engagement and learning and it then moves on to describe examples of activities from the STAARS project. The conclusions draw attention to learning from the project, envisaged changes in practice and the significance of being co-producers of learning. Overall we argue that a dynamic partnership based on collaboration with students and the development of significant caring relationships can enable academic success. Here we understand success to mean:

+ Enhanced student motivation;

+ Increased ownership and involvement in their learning;

+ Greater recognition of the student voice.

Student engagement

So why is student engagement so important in our context? At the core of student engagement is the degree to which students feel motivated to actively participate in their learning experience. For the purpose of our chapter we adopted the following definition of student engagement by Kuh (2009, in Trowler, 2010:7): "...the time and effort students devote to activities that are empirically linked to desired outcomes ... and what institutions do to induce students to participate in these activities."

Gibbs (2010:43) highlights how all-encompassing 'student engagement' has become: "what best predicts education gain is measures of educational process: what institutions do with their resources to make the most of whatever students they have. The process variables that best predict gains are not to do with the facilities themselves, or to do with student satisfaction with these facilities, but concern a small range of fairly well-understood pedagogical practices that engender student engagement."

These definitions point towards the need to recognise what students do in and out of class that can lead to improved outcomes, as echoed by Kuh (2009; 2007), along with the activities universities can undertake, which aim to involve and empower students in shaping their learning experiences (Higher Education Funding Council for England, 2008). These concepts of student engagement are important to students in relation to how they approach their work and their desired academic aspirations. They are also imperative to the University with regard to, for example, the provision of curricula, learning environments and staff expertise.

Furthermore, significant issues linked to the importance of learning and learning outcomes have been highlighted by Otter (1992), who found that students experienced difficulty attempting to understand their learning outcomes in terms of assessment, what was expected of them as students and how such learning was communicated to employers. The project described in this chapter highlights how SAPs have been active in helping other students to understand their academic journeys. The development of such understanding can assist students in owning and articulating their learning outcomes more effectively (Allan, 1996).

Other authors have identified the need to respond to the student engagement agenda by adopting innovative approaches to teaching (Nygaard *et al.*, 2011); and giving critical attention to how curricula is planned, structured, delivered and experienced (Bartholomew & Bartholomew, 2011).

Despite the positive effects of inclusive approaches to pedagogic practice and learning (May & Bridger, 2010; Coates 2005), the challenges of increased student engagement are clearly not confined to the quality of teaching and learning. Other dynamics relating to, for example, extrinsic/intrinsic motivation and forms of assessment (Beard & Senior, 1980; Brown *et al.*, 1998) may need to be present if authentic student learning is to occur. Also institutional activity that motivates students toward greater participation can also impact significantly on students' perceptions of belonging (Hawk & Lyons, 2008). An example of this is described by Rowe *et al.* (in this volume). These forms of student engagement, as highlighted by Rice (2001) and Hawk & Lyons (2008), illustrate the need for positive relationships that motivate students to develop and sustain their own learning and involvement with university. Attempts to develop and maintain such relationships are explored in the next part of our chapter.

The Centre for Academic Success

From the perspective of the Centre for Academic Success at BCU, 'student engagement' is primarily concerned with motivating students to develop their approaches toward, and responsibility for, their own learning. In developing students learning, academic tutors working in this area are themselves supported through both the institutional and individual membership of professional bodies such as Adult Learning in Higher Education (ALDinHE) and the British Association of Lecturers in English for Academic Purposes (BALEAP).

Our SAP project also attempted to build on the specific findings of a previous SAP initiative entitled, 'Improving Student Access to Study Skills Support'. Research outcomes from this work commented on the need for improved Centre visibility and publicity. Further suggestions included sending emails at strategically important times across the academic year, for example, pre and post course assessments, along with exhibiting at the International Student and Freshers' Fairs and providing students with welcome packs and details of the Centre's activities.

Data collected by the Centre for Academic Success between Autumn 2010 and 2011, shown in Table 1 below, reflects an increase in tutorial and workshop take up. From this, Centre staff responded to:

1) A greater need for support across faculties to enable academic success; and

2) Increased numbers of motivated students wanting to participate in learning activity.

Number of Tutorials & Workshops	2010/11	2011/12	% Increase/Decrease
	7515	8401	+12%

Table 1 Source: Centre for Academic Success annual review

The above data was supplemented with feedback from students attending tutorials and workshops. Overall, contact was made with approximately 450 students and six staff members from different faculties. Despite the slight increase in use of Centre provision, the thematic analysis from recorded conversations and written comments highlighted inconsistent initial awareness of services. This was linked to students being unable to articulate their needs precisely or holding imprecise perceptions about how the Centre for Academic Success could impact on their approaches to study. Further themes underlined an appreciation of how particular academic skills had been acquired and used, resulting in improved grades and increases in students' confidence. These related to, for example, being more proactive and realistic about managing time and also, especially within domestic settings, 'voicing' their academic activities to others, in ways that secured boundaries and an appreciation of the need for quality space in which to study. Lastly, a distinct theme drew attention to how the learning development provision appeared static and immobile, thus narrowing students' interpretation and simplifying their understanding of the range of available provision in the Centre for Academic Success.

With these indicators from our feedback, it remained important to consult as widely as possible and ask students to specify what academic support services they would ideally require. The question then became: How do we communicate our services in order to motivate and engage students in meeting their academic needs? This question drew attention to reviewing how aspects of the Centre for Academic Success are communicated and the degree of flexibility that could result in learning development provisions being more widely known and more effectively utilised. Therefore, guided by these concerns and issues from the literature, the initiative was designed to give students a more prominent voice during their academic journey, which could result in greater student engagement and, in turn, increase progression and retention rates across multiple faculties.

The birth of STAARS – a mechanism for change?

This section outlines activities of the STAARS project covering data gathering, involvement in awareness raising workshops and further work with student representatives and academic staff.

Having identified two students to be SAPs, the STAARS project was carried out within three distinct phases, namely: the Investigative Phase, the Development Phase and the Implementation Phase. The 'Investigative Phase' of our project involved our SAPs, together with supportive academics from across various faculties and staff from the Centre for Academic Success, exploring a number of issues. These related to students and staff perceptions and observations about the diversity and delivery of our current services and their impact on student achievement.

We also wanted to identify how students themselves articulated their learning needs. We decided to conduct individual survey questionnaires, focus groups, and use an analysis of existing data (the Centre's findings from the previous year) to determine what was needed and how it could be developed.

During the latter part of 2011, 209 individual questionnaires were completed by a representative sample of students (male-female; home-international; undergraduate-post-graduate etc.) from across the University. Interviews with 4 focus groups, each consisting of 5 students, were also undertaken. This activity enabled our SAPs to develop their leadership and research experience and provided valuable data for the development phase of the project. Findings from these questionnaires pointed to the need for increased awareness about activities at the Centre for Academic Success, responsiveness as to how it relates to students, and communicating how it for many students has had a positive impact on their approach to learning, given the diverse ethnicities of students at BCU. As universities continue to focus more on progression, and in particular graduate level employability, student engagement has become even more vital (May & Bridger 2010). This is consolidated by the reality that certain students, particularly males of colour, appear to be disproportionately marginalised when it comes to graduate employment destinations (Birmingham City University, 2010b). Harper and Antonio (2008) draw attention to the need for student engagement to be all encompassing, regardless of race, ethnic background, religion, class, gender or socio-economic background. This sentiment is further echoed in Harper and Quaye's (2009) writing on inclusive student engagement and the need to engage positively with international students.

The 'Development Phase' was guided by feedback from the SAP research activity and highlighted a number of themes:

+ Many students would welcome the chance to share their experiences of learning with others;

+ Some paper based resources needed to be redesigned;

+ Some website materials were difficult to locate and were not as widely used due to students preferring direct relational contact;

- Many students appreciated the approachability of centre staff and their caring, relational approach;

- Those students who felt most affirmed had experienced being at the Centre or had it recommended by other students;

- Many related stories of change and success were linked to: improved grades, getting to grips with the course, managing time and life balances more successfully. These occurred after applying tutorial or workshop advice, for example, using planners and working with other students in pairs/groups; and

- The need for communication approaches, both formal and informal, that enable students to locate and use various resources supported by the Centre for Academic Success.

These themes related to a number of strategic objectives of the Centre involving developing and re-designing resources that support students' academic achievement. These included resources and activities, such as goal setting and motivational exercises and staff/student led awareness-raising developmental workshops. The themes also drew attention to issues of adaptability and usage of resources across different faculties, accessibility to all students, particularly students with disabilities, students ability to use technology, and how they could prepare effectively for tutorials and receiving feedback. This led to the SAPs, Centre staff and focus group members, evaluating current resources and linking these issues to the types of relationships that students would wish to have with staff. This extensive 'student to student' and 'student to staff' contact was at the heart of the STAARS process and would inform the 'Implementation Phase' of our SAP project, involving the SAPs adopting peer tutoring roles and co-facilitating workshops.

This work continued in the Spring of 2012 and involved our SAPs, working alongside Centre professional staff, delivering resources that enhanced student engagement and improved the students' holistic experience of teaching and learning. This involved undertaking a limited number of successful one to one tutorials and small group sessions (formal and informal). In these roles, the student partners collected further feedback and were attentive to earlier student comments about relationships and possible resource development using current popular social media such as Twitter, Facebook, etc. The use of social media appeared to be a factor, emerging from the STAARS project findings as it represents 'real-time' active networking. This approach will be discussed by Flint & Roden (in this volume).

The STAARS project highlights how relationships and communication approaches between students and their university can nurture involvement and belonging. This reflects an important challenge for universities of varying types and sizes that seek to listen and respond effectively to students' voices, as consumers of education. Such realities are particularly acute especially when students' experience of teaching and learning is assessed (via, for example, student satisfaction surveys) and evaluated on how successful they feel they have been in trying to engage with the learning processes. We would also contend that key aspects of these relationships are driven by the primary involvement of students, as they develop supportive and collaborative relationships. The use of relational experiences, specifically meeting students at locations around the university to promote the Centre's services, was critical in their perception of their agency in their academic journeys. This demonstrates students' need to hear testimony or to be shown (especially by their peers) the Centre's usefulness:

"It's [learning development] something you just need to keep hearing about."

"I like working with other students, especially when you have chance to explain what you've been doing and come to realise that you actually know more than you think."

"I wasn't aware that you helped us with our work in this way."

There is still a need to promote services at induction and beyond. This needs to be shaped by listening to students through formal relationships, dialogic and written course feedback, faculty and university questionnaires, student union involvement and informal caring relationships between students and staff and students to students. The SAPs involvement in promoting services and aspects of student engagement is described in the next section.

Awareness-raising workshop

After producing a poster about the work of the STAARS Project, staff members from the faculties involved were invited to attend an event to heighten their awareness of student engagement issues. This provided a key opportunity to share our research findings and listen to staff concerns around student engagement and learning development. It also provided another opportunity for staff/student partnerships in terms of joint planning and facilitating workshops.

The workshop began with an awareness of the challenges BCU faces. The facilitators then drew out key moments and memories of learning and studying from the staff participants that focused awareness on the dynamics of learning development and student ownership of their learning processes. Factors highlighted included:

+ The importance of finding out your own learning style and being able to articulate it to others;

+ The use of healthy competitiveness as a means of motivating students;

+ Being influenced positively by inspirational, 'wacky', passionate teachers who have a love for their subject…and help you develop similar approaches and enthusiasm for the same or other topics/subjects;

+ The need to develop an identity as a mature student based on making the transition from work to education and applying time management and organisation skills;

+ Taking a targeted approach and recognising the value of experience as a mature student;

+ Appreciating that 'learning is never a waste' and is a continuing process of 'thirst and desire' to find out more…to make discoveries;

+ Having positive role models and learning from others/peer learning in groups and 'gangs of friends';

+ Working hard for someone who believes in you.

Most apt in relational terms were the comments of one participant who spoke of how the activity helped, not only to learn from experience, but 'to put yourself in the students' shoes'. The discussion proved useful in identifying and recognising key moments of individual learning development. Further participant evaluation referred to the importance of ensuring enough time for such reflection, both within their curricular planning activities and through increased communication with subject lecturers around the process of learning whilst at university. Additional evaluative comments highlighted how such activities helped staff maintain accurate knowledge of the Centre for Academic Success and were useful in enabling staff to assist students in accessing helpful learning resources. We feel that this outcome is an example of good practice of staff and student collaboration which could be replicated with key members of academic and non-academic staff. It is also a way of promoting a dynamic partnership, whilst having a positive impact on students' educational development, as illustrated in the 'student representatives' and 'engaging academic staff' initiatives below.

Student representatives

A further outcome was linked to the establishment of student representatives within faculties to communicate the existence of the various types of learning resources and development material both at the Centre for Academic Success and on the centre's website. These student representatives communicated in both formal and informal contexts and, in the case of the main University campus, helped mitigate the localisation which occurs when students do not necessarily visit or identify with other buildings beyond their faculty. As a centralised BCU-wide provision, the Centre for Academic Success is in a central building, occupying a corridor suite of rooms and offices, near one of the cafeterias, and appears to have had a limited impact on the awareness and perceptions of students.

To help counter this, the student representatives have been effective in introducing small groups to the Centre by conducting focused 15 minute tours to and around the Centre from different parts of the main campus. These walks also enabled the student representatives to share their experiences of the Centre and to communicate how they have transformed their approaches to study in the process.

Engaging academic staff

A further meeting involved giving feedback to course team academics on how their teaching had encouraged participation and given confidence to a number of international students who felt empowered to participate in classroom discussion (Palmer, 2009). One lecturer's approach encouraged an authentic sharing of personal experiences across the student-teacher divide. This involved some clear references to past educational learning styles and expectations of their roles as students and the lecturers' roles as teachers. Such approaches allow students and lecturers to examine their pre-conceptions, stereotypes and myths. It also allowed them to bring comparisons and issues from their different contexts into classroom activity (Carroll, 2005; Mortiboys, 2010).

Despite our feelings about the need for forms of student engagement that recognise the significance of relationships, we do not suggest that such frank and caring relations are the only way to achieve academic success. There is a need for different relationships at different times and with different students (Gatfield, 2005). Clearly student engagement needs to benefit both home and international students. In this respect, initiatives like STAARS positions universities to satisfy their progression and retention agendas. Securing students' academic success and progression increases the likelihood of them achieving their ultimate goals, and for universities to achieve theirs.

Conclusions

Based on the project's outcomes and the Centre's aspirations, we envisage the following developments:

+ STAARS led staff awareness workshop opportunities across the university, to reflect on and factor in the student voice;

+ '24/7' library sessions – providing support at key times of academic stress to students;

* 'Lunchtime Labs' – active, informal tutorial sessions where students are located;

* Mentoring and co-ordinated peer assisted learning initiatives across schools and faculties;

* Disseminate findings beyond BCU;

* The strategic on-going review of the publicity, marketing, and resources of the Centre for Academic Success.

Such forms of student engagement can increase levels of student satisfaction and, as this chapter has demonstrated, lead to more desirable academic outcomes (Carini, Kuh and Klein, 2006). The STAARS project, and the part played by our SAPs, in particular, has taught the staff from the Centre for Academic Success much about the need to ensure our learning and academic resources remain dynamic and widely known. These resources need to be relevant and accessible and need to be offered in terms of a holistic relationship with individual students. This awareness must also transcend the students' reality and filter into the larger institutional domain and show itself in different activities related to peer learning. The narration of the on-going student educational journey, academic staff awareness and the use of the Centre for Academic Success as a resource have resulted in many students making important intrinsic links with their own motivation and approaches to study:

> "The staff at the Centre for Academic Success took me seriously, believed in me, were caring and clear in what I was good at and could go on to achieve."

Such students have also gained significant extrinsic outcomes through improved grades, active use of feedback and increased ownership of the learning development process through effective self-directed learning:

> "Before I came to see you I got 31% for my coursework for Analytical Methods and 32% for Science and Materials. In the exams, I got 94% for Science and unbelievably – for the one I was most scared of – 74% for Analytical Methods. So combined, I got merits in both. I also got merits in all my other subjects and a distinction in Technology. I'm really happy. Thank you for your help."

These changes convey the power of the lived experience (Reason and Bradbury, 2008) and an understanding of this power underpins the STAARS project and its future. The evidence of such dynamic relationships has helped the Centre become more reflective of the qualities that can contribute positively to students' learning experiences and the promotion of academic success.

Within the context of student engagement, these elements are essential pre-requisites in enabling successful student achievement:

- The importance of effective and affective communication;

- The valuing of dynamic and dialogic relationships; and

- The promotion of increased ownership by students of the learning experience and increased responsiveness of staff to student 'voices'.

Indeed, as a University and a resource for learning development, if we are to continue to motivate students to achieve, then we need to be consistent in hearing and heeding student voices. This requires on-going forms of collaboration and partnership that are effective, and affective, as we seek together to become co-producers (McCulloch, 2009) of useful knowledge.

About the authors

Wal Warmington works in the Centre for Academic Success as a Lecturer/ Academic Skills Tutor in the area of Learning Development at Birmingham City University. He can be contacted at **wal.warmington@bcu.ac.uk**

Trevor Hodge is Head of the Centre for Academic Success at Birmingham City University. He can be contacted at **trevor.hodge@bcu.ac.uk**

Sheikh Sela was a SAP in the above project and has recently completed an LLM in International Human Rights at Birmingham City University. She can be contacted at **sfsela@hotmail.co.uk**

Anil Kainth was a SAP in the above project and is currently studying for a MSc in Construction at Birmingham City University. He can be contacted at **anil.catherine@gmail.com**

Chapter 12

By Appointment to Birmingham City University Students: Promoting Student Engagement through Partnership Working

Amanda Andrews, Joanne Jeffries and Bernie St Aubyn

Introduction

By way of offering some context, it is useful for the reader to know that nurse education is going through a period of great change in the UK. The increasing demand for knowledgeable, professional practitioners has led to a review of nurse education programmes. Prior to September 2011, nursing education programmes in the UK were delivered at Diploma and Bachelor of Science level. Now however, nurse education provision is now available at Bachelor of Science level only. Such changes call for new approaches to the delivery of curricula – approaches that are consistent with new expectations for nursing practice.

Of course, nurses must be able to apply their knowledge with care and compassion, working in partnership with patients who are at the centre of their care – but during the writing of this chapter we came to the realisation that the practice of lecturers must mirror this practice; we must be able to apply our knowledge with care and compassion, working in partnership with students who are at the centre of their academic responsibility.

This chapter will look at the prevailing student engagement ethos within a community-nursing module (on a nursing programme) by deconstructing its delivery and will show how lecturers and students working in partnership have had a positive effect on the engagement and learning experience of all partners. The partnership approach improves student engagement, not only with the academic element but also with the professional elements of the module; furthermore it has features that are replicable for the teaching of other disciplines.

The success of the partnership approach is supported by the analysis of student commentary and a reflective student account working within the partnership. The student commentary was captured by evaluation forms completed by the students at the end of the module. These collected comments will be used throughout the chapter to support of claim of positive effects of the partnership approach on student engagement. Four themes emerged from the student feedback:

1. The positive approach and attitude of the lecturers;

2. The fun, enjoyable, interesting delivery of the lectures;

3. The structure and range of teaching methods employed helped learning;

4. Partnership working within groups was enjoyable and encouraged participation.

These themes resonate with those outlined in the framework for enhancing student engagement at the institutional level which include staff interactions and the variety of learning methods employed (Trowler & Trowler, 2010b). A variety of learning experiences delivered by enthusiastic lecturers is seen as an important aspect of student engagement (Thomas, 2012). This is also discussed in the chapter 'Social Media; an effective way to prompt student engagement and support student induction' by Flint and Roden (in this volume).

Student engagement

The ethos of the module from its onset is one of student engagement through partnership working. The essence of partnership working is sharing; this is marked by respect for one another; defined roles; rights to information; accountability; competence and valued individual input (Tunnard, 1991). For partnership working to be a reality there needs to be open and effective communication and co-operation between the partners. Establishing this from the lecturers' view point helps create a fun, safe and positive learning experience for everyone, with set parameters for the duration of the module. Partnership working is not only nurtured between the students and lecturers, but also between student and student (in group working) and between the lecturers themselves by the demonstrable close and successful working within the module team. The module in question is called *Adult Nursing in Primary Care* and is taught in the second year of the programme. The students learn about the roles and responsibilities of professionals working in the community setting with the overarching aim of the module for the students to develop the knowledge relating to caring for patients/clients in settings other than hospitals. Students also learn the need to work in partnership with other professionals and patients/clients to provide high quality care; once again resonating with the module ethos of partnership working.

Students and staff participate in the setting of ground rules to identify accepted levels of behaviour from all parties. The 'playing field' is levelled by the acknowledgment that learning is a two way process where all partners are co-producers of knowledge and learning. However, we do recognise that it is still the ultimate responsibility of the university, in the climate of educational consumerism, to design engaging learning experiences (Nygaard *et al.*, 2011). To dispel the 'them and us' culture it is noted that the lecturers are there by virtue of time and experience within nursing and they are not the principal source of knowledge but in fact learning partners. This ethos of partnership working sets the scene for an effective working relationship between students and staff that enhances student engagement, participation and learning outcomes (Kember *et al.*, 2001). The following selection of students' comments support this view:

> "From day one, the lecturers built a rapport and trust very quickly. An open approach was laid out by the lecturers, we were all there to learn from each other, and this became self-evident as the module progressed."

> "Thank you for treating us like humans and equals. It made for a good learning environment."

"I enjoyed the friendly environment, a very good way of teaching by the module co-ordinators."

Partnership working is considered to be the implementation of a joint programme where information, tasks and rewards are shared (The Audit Commission, 1998). Workers within a partnership have a shared ownership of common interests and goals and work towards a clearly defined purpose within an ethos of trust and commitment (Ball *et al.*, 2010). Other ingredients for a successful partnership include regular open and effective communication within a supportive environment, clearly defined parameters and effective leadership (*ibid*). The enthusiastic, humorous, fun and lively demeanour of the staff in creating an open and engaging forum for dialogue enhances the opportunity for honest communication, which is essential for partnership working. A main emerging theme from the student evaluations was that lectures were fun, enjoyable, interesting and well delivered. The overwhelming majority of comments stated how interesting and enjoyable the lectures were:

"I thoroughly enjoyed this module. It was the best module I have had on this course so far. I looked forward to each lecture... ...It's rare that I put such positive feedback for all questions asked but I did feel very interested in this module all the time."

"Really enjoyed the module. Always looked forward to coming to the sessions. Best module so far!"

Students commented on how the lecturers made the lectures fun and had a sense of humour:

"The module co-ordinators made this module fun and enjoyable which helped us to concentrate and learn better."

Some clearly defined parameters are established by creating negotiable ground rules for all partners to follow. Negotiation is a key feature of any interactive partnership (Dillenbourg, 1999) and devising these ground rules enhances ownership and encourages participation in the structure within which the module is delivered. Ground rules not only outline roles but also confer ownership. Some ground rules devised include rules about general behaviour, for example late arrival and early leaving, the responsible use of mobile phones and a reinforcement of the expected behaviours reflective of a trainee professional. The ground rules reduce some of the common barriers to partnership working by outlining partners' potential roles and establishing and stabilising a consistent learning environment. These ground rules also establish direction and a contract for successful partnership working.

The benefits of effective partnership working include students' active engagement in their own learning, an increased level of classroom interaction and the generation of a fun and positive learning environment. This is resonated in the students' account of participation; many of the students commented on the approachable and supportive nature of the lecturers. Some additional words used to describe the lecturers were 'friendly', 'enthusiastic', 'helpful' and 'engaging'. Students also commented that the lecturers encouraged learning: *"Lecturers were enthusiastic and wanted us to do well"*.

Lecturers benefit from constantly learning from each new cohort of students – this includes classroom feedback from enthusiastic and engaged student partners and from examples of current nursing practice. This spirit of partnership leads to improved engagement. Academic engagement is related to *"effective learning"* (Gibbs, 2010) and is necessary for deep (as opposed to surface) learning (Ramsden, 2003).

Another main emerging theme from the student evaluations was that the structure and range of teaching methods helped learning:

> *"Lecturers made it easier than normal to concentrate by involving the class and making the sessions enjoyable."*

> *"Lecturers would involve us which was fun and helped enhance the learning."*

Indeed, Thomas (2012) acknowledges this sense of students being accepted, valued and included by others in the academic classroom session increases a sense of belonging and improves engagement and Neary (2009) argues that students become active engagers rather than passive receptors within the partnership process. Although partnership working is generally regarded as a good thing (Ball *et al.*, 2010), there are some barriers to its effectiveness, for example, it cannot be assumed that all partners will understand their role within the partnership, leading to a lack of commitment and understanding of the benefits from working in this way. Huxham and Vangen (2005) suggest that unless clear benefits from partnership working are identified it should be best avoided because that way of working is highly resource consuming, in both time and personnel. Students expecting a didactic teaching approach (being 'spoon-fed') do not always appreciate the time invested in partnership working. Instead it is their perception that the use of time would be better utilised in a more conventional educative fashion.

There is inertia on the part of some students to move from the traditional model of teacher-directed learning to one that is more learner-managed within a partnership (Goodyear, 1999). In our experience some students perceive that learning only takes place within timetabled sessions and there is a decided lack of recognition that the module hours include extensive time for self-directed study despite the self-directed student hours are clearly identified in the students' module guide/handbooks. Students who have previous negative experiences of partnership working often demonstrate a reluctance to share information and knowledge. This is based on the belief that 'unstructured' sessions lead to their learning from each other's ignorance rather than appreciating the value of peer interaction and associated opportunities for enhanced individual performance (Dillenbourg *et al.*, 1996). The same authors confirm that partnership working recognises that the actual interaction of people is as important as the learning they are undertaking. In the evaluation data they offered, some students acknowledged the benefits of group interaction:

> "...lectures felt like having a chat with your friends, no holds barred, you could throw in ideas to explore, ask whatever you wanted or let others know what you had read about the subject, without fear. This improved confidence as you could engage with the subject and feel empowered and enthused to learn and find out more."

The value of group interaction is recognised in the ideas of socio-constructivism; in its most pure state, constructivism theory assumes that the students build up an understanding of a topic and then discover the principles of the topic for themselves (Schunk, 2011; Jackson *et al.*, 2006). Social constructivists see both the context in which the learning occurs and the social contexts learners bring to their learning environment as invaluable, with the teacher becoming a facilitator in the learning process as opposed to an expert (Jackson *et al.*, 2006).

Group working

The number of students involved in each of our module deliveries ranges from 70 to 100. The responsibility for student engagement is a joint one between the institution and the students themselves (Trowler, 2010) and so the lecturers deliberately attempt to involve and empower the students by breaking the large amorphous mass into smaller student-selected 'friendship groups'. The students then have the responsibility to engage purposefully in the educational activities creating a "*joint proposition*" (Coates, 2005). This empowerment is a necessity with any collaboration to ensure its success (Huxham &Vangen, 2005).

Students get the feeling of belonging and ownership by generating a team name, thus creating a positive student identity (Trowler & Trowler, 2010) and stimulating a creative process. Setting a creative task at the outset requires active thought which in itself stimulates engagement because creativity requires cognitive and explorative engagement, offering a focus for deeper learning (Davis *et al.*, 2000). Taking on a group identity also confers a modicum of anonymity, which increases student confidence. The opportunity for peer support is created within these smaller groups, along with the identification of any preferred group roles (Belbin, 2010). Social engagement creates a sense of belonging and offers informal support through interaction with friends and peers (Thomas, 2012) and learning partnerships encourage interaction within the groups and stimulate competition between the groups. This provides a dynamic and enjoyable learning environment for all learning partners, and is of particular value to those students least prepared for Higher Education (Trowler & Trowler, 2011).

Interpersonal ties within 'friendship groups' directly correlate to the attainment of team goals (Balkindi & Harrison, 2006); this type of working inspires students to engage and participate in group-activities and students, who are reluctant to speak out, find the confidence to do so within this safe environment. Our students mentioned how much they enjoyed the group work and in particular a quiz we organised and how the fun element encouraged participation;

"The group work technique was good and motivating."

"Having teams massively increased group participation compared to other modules where only the same few people would contribute."

The lecturers have noted an increase in students' participation as a result of group working and competition. The benefits of enhanced group-working skills to the employability of the individual should not be underestimated. One student commented that:

"Team working was especially memorable because, whilst we were given a task to complete as a team, it was the wider aspects of learning that came with this that were also beneficial to future working within a multidisciplinary team. It gave development of interpersonal skills and experience of working as a team with people of different ages and abilities. Through time orientated team tasks, experience and understanding of process/task development was gained in order to achieve an overall outcome. Time management skills were also developed due to having to plan and prioritise what needed to be done and by when in order to meet the delivery deadline. Delegation skills were practised as individual tasks needed to be allocated to those team members not putting themselves forward. As part of this module an assignment was allocated and the enthusiasm and motivation gained through lectures carried through to this self-learning; something that will be required during working life through Continued Professional Development."

This resonates with the educational ideology of enterprise that students need to be given the skills to thrive in their careers (Trowler & Wareham, 2008). Moreover, the time management (planning and prioritising) and delegation skills utilised through time-constrained team-tasks are also invaluable within the employment market (Rao, 2010).

Promoting student engagement through innovative delivery

The design of the module is cyclical and informed by student evaluations that take place at the end of each module. The module content varies in relation to the positive and negative feedback from previous groups. Any proposed timetable changes are then negotiated with the current students. In line with academic theory (Trowler & Trowler, 2011; Kuh, 2009; Janes, 2006; Merrill, 2001), the module employs a variety of teaching and learning methods, moving away from the more traditional teaching technique of 'lecturing'. The methods chosen are designed to promote self-directed learning and to stimulate and encourage active participation. Moodle, the institution's virtual learning environment, is central to the module and is presented in an eye-catching way. The Moodle site is structured to correspond with the module timetable and is easy to access and navigate. The interactive quality of Moodle allows for the use of videos, work books, quizzes and on-line forums which enable the students to acquire new knowledge as they interact with the environment, course activities and other learning partners. Embedding Moodle into the fabric of the module allows the students to revisit and re-engage with resources thus enriching and accelerating their learning process. Moodle is employed as part of an overall blended learning approach in conjunction with other learning opportunities (Janes, 2006). Other teaching and learning methods used include real-life examples in the form of applied vignettes, simulation and realistic role play, literature-led debates, quizzes, games (including turning point, an interactive quiz), work books and Virtual Case Creator (VCC), an online resource providing virtual interactive clinical scenarios. In their evaluation data, students commented on how the range of teaching methods helped their learning:

> "Liked the variety of teaching methods used, helped learning."

> "Liked that there were more tasks than presentations."

> "I liked the style of teaching – good that it was not all PowerPoint."

"VCC assisted in backing up what was learnt in lectures."

"Using real examples in VCC was very helpful."

Many of the students commented on the teaching delivery using words like 'enjoyed', 'good' and 'excellent' and that the lecturers made the module easy to follow/understand in a relaxed environment:

"Loved record keeping. The topic sounded dry but in fact the way it was delivered everyone went away thinking about it."

"The module co-ordinators explained everything clearly."

"Lecturers were able to keep the group engaged, this is quite rare for our group!"

"The diversity of teaching styles used, from role play to team working, meant that every lecture was different, refreshing, exciting and engaging. It enabled some of the messages to be 'seen' from different angles, reinforcing the message and making it more memorable. Recall of relevant events that had happened to the lecturers gave reality to the information that was being discussed, making it more engaging and fun."

"The series of lectures on healthcare record keeping were particularly memorable. The subject, whilst sounding quite dry, delivered some very crucial messages in several engaging ways. Firstly, we were shown a video of a mock legal trial where a nurse was being questioned by a barrister about an event that had happened several years earlier. The barrister's questions were related to the healthcare records that the nurse had written. The video delivered a serious message in a fun and engaging way, particularly because one of the lecturers was acting as the nurse in the video. Secondly, we partook in a mock trial where we had to answer barrister's questions relating to a set of healthcare records that we had written. Whilst the thought of partaking in the role play lecture caused some feelings of trepidation, the range of emotions elicited from participating was surprising and it reinforced understanding and provoked reflection. Had this message been delivered though overhead slides it would not have been so engaging and the message would most likely have been lost."

The lecturers are blended professionals by virtue of both their professional and academic expertise (Whitchurch, 2009) thus ensuring relevant and legitimate experience is shared. Several comments were made about how hearing the lecturers talk about real life experiences made the lecture enjoyable for example: *"Relevant experiential stories helped learning"*. Students also felt that they had learnt a lot: *"Have learnt so many new skills and techniques"*. Any group activities completed are awarded points and these are collated to identify the 'winning' groups and allow prizes to be awarded at the end of the module:

"It also made me work harder as I wanted to win!"

"Liked group work which helped me get more involved."

"Having the group competition really encouraged me to participate in the discussions and lectures."

Identifying the competitive element recognises that successfully formed groups have a need to succeed and the group dynamics play to individual strengths and assumed roles (Belbin, 2010) enhancing the overall success of the team (Bryson *et al.*, 2009). The use of gaming in education has been reported to benefit learning by encouraging engagement and participation and retention of knowledge (Whitton, 2011; Giddens *et al.*, 2010).

Evaluation of the partnership approach: conclusion and challenges

To complete the cycle the module is evaluated in a variety of ways. The culmination of the 'competition' involves a quiz to ascertain the knowledge acquired throughout the module and the acquisition of points stimulates competitiveness. Verbal feedback is elicited which enables all learning partners to be involved and captures a total picture of the module and its effectiveness. The feedback process is reciprocal and the students are given feedback as to their participation and adherence to the initially negotiated 'ground rules'. The written module evaluation form is completed by the students and used to develop an action plan for the next module delivery.

The effectiveness of the approach is demonstrable by the lecturers being the inaugural (2012) winners of the Faculty of Health student nominated 'Extra Mile Award for creative and engaging teaching'. Chapman, P. *et al.* (in this volume) talk about giving the students a voice with the 'Extra Mile' student led teaching awards. This facilitates active participation in recognising good and engaging teaching. The module also receives consistent positive evaluations from the student partners. The lecturers' approach to teaching record keeping (with their DVD 'Court Proof Records') was also endorsed through the award of first prize at the Royal College of Nursing Education Conference in Harrogate 2012.

It is acknowledged that the balance of power changes at the point of student assessment (Bryson *et al.*, 2009), when it moves towards the lecturers; however, assessment is of course integral to the module structure and much is completed collaboratively through team working.

We have shown through the sharing of students' evaluation narratives the importance partnership working and a variety of teaching methods have on student engagement. The use of an engaging, partnership approach to teaching benefits all learning partners and has a powerful impact on learning.

As we conclude this chapter, we reflect what our key messages would be for those who would seek to replicate our approach. Our advice is summarised below:

+ Allow yourself time to plan innovative ways to deliver your key messages;

+ Be enthusiastic, humorous and lively when presenting your sessions;

+ No 'them and us' – genuine partnership working – verbalise this, it needs to be said and heard;

+ Establish and agree 'ground rules' for partnership working throughout the teaching experience;

+ Recognise that the actual interaction of people is as important as the learning being undertaken (Communication skills, manners, courtesy, respect for everyone).

By implementing such advice, we believe that the success we have had we our approaches will be easily attained by others.

About the authors

Amanda Andrews is a senior lecturer within the Community Health Department, School of Nursing and Midwifery, Faculty of Health at Birmingham City University. She can be contacted at **amanda.andrews@bcu.ac.uk**

Jo Jeffries is a student on the Graduate Diploma in Adult Nursing course at Birmingham City University. She can be contacted at **jo.jeffries@mail.bcu.ac.uk**

Bernie St Aubyn is a senior lecturer within the Community Health Department, School of Nursing and Midwifery, Faculty of Health at Birmingham City University. She can be contacted at **bernie.st.aubyn@bcu.ac.uk**

Chapter 13

Social Media: An Effective Way to Build a Community and Develop Partnerships to Promote Student Engagement?

Emma Flint and James Roden

Introduction

Our chapter primarily demonstrates how fostering a community through the use of social media can help to support student engagement. We critically analyse the extent to which the community so formed can be used to develop partnerships between students and staff, in some cases even before a student formally embarks on undergraduate study at university. In the first part of the chapter, we examine our case study, namely the creation of an open student and staff Facebook group (the 'Group') to support the induction of our new students to the School of Law at Birmingham City University (BCU). The rationale behind the creation of the Group and an evaluation of its impact is offered. Personal reflective narratives from both staff and student participants highlight the student engagement processes emergent from the Group.

We go on to examine the benefits of the community formed by the Group, centred on the empowerment of students through an investment in their learning experience. Our findings show that there are challenges surrounding the changing identity and roles of students and staff in supporting the academic processes underpinning the community. Quantitative data taken from surveys with students who engaged with the Group, discussing the positive and negative aspects of the project is presented and evaluated. Our chapter ends with a critical examination of key lessons learnt from this student/academic partnership and presents recommendations for the way forward.

Context and motivations

The undergraduate law programme (or 'LL.B' as it is more commonly known in the UK) at BCU has over 750 students enrolled on a full and part time basis across its three years of study. Each year, between 200-250 new first year students (or 'Freshers' as they are commonly known) choose to study the LL.B at BCU. As well as being accredited by the UK professional legal bodies, the LL.B aims to help students to develop problem solving, research and personal skills; thus equipping BCU law students with the academic knowledge and key employability competences that are in demand by employers.

In common with any other undergraduate programme in the UK, the LL.B is operating in a higher education sector that has recently undergone radical change. As recognised by Lefever *et al.* (2010:2), today's student body is a more diverse group than ever before in terms of approaches to study, ages of students, and their motivations for pursuing higher education. This diversity of students results in a diversity of expectation, which, if not met, can easily lead to disengagement. This view is reflected in the findings of the *What Works? Building student engagement and belonging in Higher Education at a time of change* publication (Thomas, 2012).

Much of this expectation formation takes place in the period immediately before and during a student's first year of undergraduate study, a process that becomes even more challenging when dealing with the student numbers enrolled on the LL.B. Academic staff teaching on the LL.B face challenges in ensuring its students are retained each year and that they progress successfully through their studies. Early transition into university life is acknowledged by Lefever *et al.* (2010:2) as being one of the crucial phases in a student lifecycle in terms of future retention and progression, but perhaps, more importantly, in terms of promoting active student engagement during their studies.

There are a number of definitions of 'student engagement' but, for the purposes of our chapter, the definition of student engagement that is best aligned with the aims and purpose of the Group is that of Trowler (2010:3): *"Student engagement is concerned with the interaction between the time, effort and other relevant resources invested by both students and their institutions intended to optimise the student experience and enhance learning outcomes and development of students and the performance and reputation of the institution."* Thomas (2012) acknowledges that nurturing participation is key to student engagement and our chapter examines the extent to which social media contributes in assisting students and institutions alike in the development of a community to assist that process.

Use of social media by students in Higher Education

Social media networks are a well-recognised aspect of everyday student life. A report by the JISC (the UK's lead agency for information on and research into digital technologies in Higher Education) commissioned in 2007 entitled 'Great expectations of ICT' showed that 73% of first year undergraduates made use of social media networking sites (Page, 2009). A further JISC-commissioned report conducted by Ipsos Mori suggested an ever-higher rate of usage by British undergraduate students of social media networking sites – well over 95% (Madge *et al.*, 2009). This was corroborated by feedback from students involved with the Group, which showed that, 90% of the BCU law undergraduates use social media on a daily basis. This suggests our law students are *"Digital Natives"*, an illustrative term originating from the work of Prensky (2001:1) and explored further by Ashfield *et al.* (in this volume) who offer a discourse on social media and the promotion of employability.

Facebook is the favoured social media network amongst BCU law students. Feedback from our questionnaires shows that, out of those law students who use social media, 73% identify Facebook as their preferred social media network. Twitter was another popular social media network, with 22% of law students using it in preference to Facebook. The remaining 5% use other alternatives such as Google+, Tumblr and Ning. Interestingly, whilst 10% of law students use LinkedIn, they did not view it as social media in the same vein as Facebook or Twitter. Yet, as evidenced in the wider work of Harte and Jackson (2011:3), those platforms are used interchangeably by media students when creating new social media resources to promote their employability.

As Page (2009:22) summarises, Facebook allows participants to: *"Interact through a constantly evolving set of networks based on college or university, friendships, interest groups, favourite movies, and other criteria. The site allows its users to create a profile page and forge online links with friends and acquaintances. Many use it to stay in touch after finishing school, and as a way to share their life publicly."*

Research by Madge *et al.* (2009) concluded that Facebook is an important social tool used by the majority of students to aid their settling-in process at university. It was with this in mind that the Group was initially created. However, an examination of additional motivations, both extrinsic and intrinsic, for the creation and engagement with the Group is explored in the personal reflective accounts of the student and academic partners later in our chapter.

Formation and recruitment

During the summer of 2009, an 'open' group was created which allowed any Facebook user to add themselves to this nascent community. Facebook was chosen to host the Group over alternatives largely due to the functionality of the 'group' option that other social media platforms did not have. It was hoped that a Facebook 'group' page would promote more of a sense of cohesion than a Facebook 'like' page. Keeping the Group 'open' instead of 'closed' or 'secret' promoted inclusion and meant that the pre-induction support aims of the Group would be maximised. Whilst an academic was required to moderate usage of the Group, existing law students were recruited to act as student advisors. Our hope was that this would encourage prospective students not to feel embarrassed or shy and to reveal 'real' answers as opposed to any official 'party line' responses from academics. Six students were selected to act as the formal 'student advisors'. As in the SAP project evaluated by Hutchings *et al.* (in this volume), those six students were selected as student partners based on personal tutor recommendations as opposed to a selection based on formal criteria; although those unselected were still encouraged to engage with the project and ended up posting regularly in the Group.

In subsequent iterations of the Group, outgoing student advisors have helped to select the new student advisors. The academic partner met with the student advisors to discuss how the Group should be run and give guidance on how to deal with questions posted by prospective students. The student advisors posted profiles of themselves and highlighted aspects of the School of Law that they thought noteworthy (such as results from recent mooting or 'mock trial' competitions that law students had participated in, trips to Parliament and pictures from the Law Ball).

Information about the Group was included within the joining instruction letter sent out to those students who had a confirmed place on the LL.B programme to start in September 2009. The academic partner also sent an email to the same students containing a direct hyperlink to the Group. Due to the open nature of Facebook, students could easily access the Group prior to being allocated official BCU login details. Links to the Group were also provided on the BCU home web page and included within the main BCU Facebook group and Twitter feed. In subsequent years, the BCU Students' Union also put a link to the Group on their own general Fresher Facebook group. By including information on the Group in this way, it was hoped that students would appreciate that the Group was an officially sanctioned one and that they could rely on the advice posted in it. It also made the purpose of the Group clear, in that it was a community space designed to help students to adjust to university life by getting to know their fellow prospective students and by asking questions of current students. Participant numbers for the Group, generally show a yearly increase in participants, as shown in Table 1 below:

Year	Number of LL.B 1st year enrolled students	Number who joined the Group	% take up	Number of LL.B 2nd & 3rd year enrolled students	Number who joined the Group	% take up
2009/10	201	51	25%	411	16	4%
2010/11	204	65	22%	407	24	6%
2011/12	253	98	39%	406	73	18%
2012/13*	308	143	46%	404	48	12%

Table 1: Breakdown of student participant numbers each year

* (Note: These figures only represent four months usage (August – November) in comparison to the figures for previous years which reflect twelve months usage of the Group)

The student advisors also responded directly to any questions raised by the prospective students via messages on the group 'wall' or specific discussion threads. An examination of the number of wall posts and comments made in reply to such posts showing a significant increase each year gives an overview of how actively students engaged with the Group – see Table 2 below:

Year	Number of wall posts made	Number of comments made in respect of those posts
2009/10	488	105 (Note: these figures reflect that Facebook comment functionality was only enabled part way through this Group, resulting in a higher number of original wall posts as opposed to comments)
2010/11	131	386
2011/12	390	2225
2012/13	212	1163 (Note: These figures only represent four months usage (August – November) in comparison to the figures for previous years which reflect twelve months usage of the Group)

Table 2: Comparison of number of wall posts and comments made

The range of topics posted on the wall varied, although during August-October, the vast majority centred on typical pre-induction matters and what to expect from life studying as a law student. Other popular posts centred on the more social side of student life, such as finding out where other students were living and who was going to the various Fresher social events. Overall, the subject matter of these posts reflects both the community building objective of the Group and, as found by others who have run similar social media projects such as Page (2009) and Madge *et al.* (2009), the social dimension of Facebook itself.

Collection of feedback and surveying participants

Feedback of students' experiences of the group has been collected through completion of questionnaires (hard copy and online) along with student focus groups. In September 2010, a year after the first Group was first started, all of the LL.B students were asked to complete a written questionnaire. At that stage, the questionnaire was designed to capture basic information regarding the use of Facebook as a social networking tool as opposed to any distinct support for induction. The questionnaire evolved alongside the further iterations of the Group into its current online format, which students are invited to complete each year (stage one in early October at the end of the law school induction period and stage two at the end of the academic year in May/June, once students have had an opportunity to reflect upon their use of the Group across the year). The questionnaire utilises a combination of quantitative evaluation with open-ended questions to allow respondents to elaborate further on any point made. Evaluation of this feedback data shows a number of positive benefits flowing from the staff-student engagement processes underpinning the Group.

Student engagement processes

Building a community

The key theme that emerged from all of the feedback was the generation of student engagement emerging from the creation of a community by the Group. Other research has shown that the sense of belonging to a community is at the heart of successful retention for Higher Education students (Thomas, 2012:6). Most obviously, the Group acted as an information-sharing platform, ranging from dissemination of induction timetables, what books to buy, what pre-reading to do in advance and even how to get around campus. New students commented that they had made friends even before the course started:

> *"I thought it would be a great way to meet new people on my course and make friends before moving to Birmingham…I got a lot of help on the basic administration side of being a Fresher such as moving into halls of residence and getting help to understand my timetable too."* (Student 1)

The community formed by the Group resulted in a social cohesion that aligns with other descriptions of belonging, akin to student engagement, in educational environments (Goodenow, 1993:25). The students, through the Group, feel better prepared to deal with life at university:

> *"I certainly gained confidence for when I arrived and felt more comfortable with the whole new experience of uni. Knowing I could rely on [group participants] to quickly respond to any questions I had and help me out as much as possible made it less daunting."* (Student 2)

The cohesion and sense of community also extended beyond the new first year participants to those students acting as student advisors, reinforcing the concept that a student's sense of being accepted or valued also contributes to a sense of 'belonging' (Goodenow, 1993):

> *"The minute I got involved in the Facebook group, from 2009, through to the present day, I felt immediately accepted. However, the real feeling of involvement in a bigger community came, for me personally, with being an official advisor. People would ask for my advice and begin to take note of who I was. They would then feel happy enough to engage me in conversation if they saw me around University. This made me feel like I was part of something bigger, something that was more than just a casual 'meet and greet'. I felt like I was assisting people in making the most of their course."* (Student 3)

As noted by Page (2009:25), *"…the issues that underpin retention are too complex to be related simplistically to a single factor"* it is impossible to conclude directly whether any increases seen in retention rates of LL.B students are attributable to the Group. However, the outputs from the case studies detailed by Thomas (2012:12) make it clear that projects that engage students make them more effective learners and more likely to progress through continuation of their studies. Anecdotal evidence from the feedback on the Group substantiates this and shows that individual students did feel that the relationships/bonds created by the Group between staff and students helped with their own personal retention:

> "I developed a strong friendship with [the academic partner] through my involvement with the Group. She was the one lecturer I knew I could then turn to for support when I thought I could no longer carry on with university". (Student 4)

Finally, breaking down barriers and giving these "Digital Natives" the ability to ask any question in a familiar forum whilst realising that their peers probably wanted to ask the same, was greatly appreciated:

> "I was less worried about appearing like an idiot on Facebook than directly in front of my lecturers, so it made it easier for me to ask questions. I became fairly well known on the course through the page just because people saw me post and getting involved throughout the year." (Student 4)

Fostering a learning community

In the academic year 2011/12, instead of usage dropping off towards the end of the first term, which had occurred during the first two iterations of the Group and is something noted by other running similar groups (Page, 2009), the Group has taken on unexpected roles. As the year progressed, the Group was used for more highly developed communication activities, such as the formation of study groups online, with posts encouraging students to enter into debates on legal subjects outside scheduled teaching sessions. For example, the news story of the 2011 attacks in Norway perpetrated by Anders Breivik, led to extended discussions in the Group on the concept of diminished responsibility. Using Facebook to organise group meetings for project work and for revision purposes were other uses evident from the Group. This concept of Facebook becoming more than just a social network and rather a blossoming informal learning environment is supported in the work of other research projects concerning the use of Facebook in the higher education sector (Madge *et al.*, 2009).

However, for us, it has taken a number of re-iterations of the Group for this to occur, which reflects that it takes time for Groups of this nature to 'settle in' at departmental level and for students to both become accustomed to having a resource like the Group to utilise and being confident enough to use it in more than an information gathering manner:

> *"People would post links to news stories and talk about how it conflicts with or follows current legal practice. This was a huge benefit of the Group. It allows people to voice their opinion on a matter, show their interpretation and be corrected on black letter law if needed. It was also a good way of showing the first years how everything they are learning is not just an academic tool; it is used in everyday life...Many of the assessments used on the LL.B are 'problem questions', where a factual scenario is given and you have to apply the law to it. By placing real life contexts on the Group, this can only have benefited those joining and made them more prepared for the problem question assessments: they have firsthand knowledge of the way these scenarios are dealt with in reality."* (Student 5)

Student-centred approaches & 'expectation-setting'

Interestingly, feedback from the non-first year users of the Group shows that it empowered existing students by allowing them to feel part of the 'expectation-setting' process to enrich the student experience, both in terms of outlining what prospective students should expect from BCU and, equally importantly, what BCU should be expecting from students in return. These are key factors that promote student engagement and the sense of belonging, which in turn helps nurture success and retention in Higher Education students (Thomas, 2012).

Enhancing employability

One unexpected impact of the Group has been the way in which students actively use it to enhance employability by signposting job opportunities, training schemes, careers workshops or webinars with one another and using the community as a sharing forum prior to interviews or assessment days. One student reflected that:

> *"I think the group definitely encouraged me to apply for first year open days at law firms and I actually got a place on one so yes I think it was a great help…in terms of expanding my CV and legal experiences."*
> (Student 6)

By engaging with the Group in this way, students start to develop confidence from advising one another and develop the motivation to actively manage their career path from the outset of their studies. The Group also helps to promote other key employability skills such as team working, communication and networking; all skills stressed by the JISC (2009) as being of key importance in the 21st century for graduates (Lefever *et al.*, 2010).

Identifying 'at risk' students and offering student support

From a staff perspective, not only does the Group allow staff to get to know students prior to course commencement, providing support and guidance where necessary, it also allows for the identification of students who may need additional support, such as teaching adjustments or for working mothers/mature students. Formative assessment regimes that allow for timely and targeted academic interventions and pastoral care such as personal tutoring (both of which the LL.B programme utilises fully) are primary mechanisms for identifying 'at risk' students and providing student support. The flexibility of the Group helps to supplement such well-established support mechanisms and, as the reflective account of the academic partner demonstrates, the ability to help students prior to any primary support mechanism is a very powerful tool.

Impact on student learning outcomes

When asked to what extent (if any) the Group helped to make students feel part of a participative learning experience (one of the LL.B learning outcomes), student feedback was mixed:

"I think it helps to a certain extent but ultimately those that want to get involved will and the Facebook group helps those that would have done, do more." (Student 7)

Another learning outcome for the LL.B is to provide students with *"a range of transferable and marketable skills, leading to employment opportunities in the legal profession and in a range of other careers"* (programme documentation). As already noted above, the community sense of the Group helped students develop their employability skills:

"The Group had many people from different backgrounds, at different levels and with different careers aspirations contributing. As such, whenever someone had achieved something new which would help towards their career, such as gained work experience in a law firm or won a competition, it would generally get posted on the site...the Group was a great place to advertise careers events, ensuring that the maximum amount of people knew about it and had the opportunity to improve their prospects." (Student 8)

Challenges and unexpected outcomes

Social media fluidity and targeting the 'non-joiners'

Each year there are students who do not join the group. It may be because they do not use social networking sites, as reflected in the examination of the assumption that only young people are at ease with the use of social media by Ashfield *et al.* (in this volume). It may be that some students prefer to use social media other than Facebook (although this does not directly correlate with our aforementioned empirical data on social media usage by law students). It is perhaps more likely, as borne out by the reflections of Ashfield *et al* (*ibid*), that modern *"Digital Natives"* see social media as being a social space only and are therefore reluctant to use it in ways that are seen as being aligned to more academic purposes. However, the personal reflective account of the student partner clearly demonstrates a paradigm shift from an initial engagement with the Group, on a purely social basis, to a later engagement pattern that supported the academic processes that underpin formative education.

Some students do not join as they are unaware of the Group and these students have expressed a feeling of being left out or disadvantaged. To help combat this, for each iteration of the Group, the academic partner has ensured that it is advertised as widely as possible. With regards to access to the Internet, that issue is harder to address, with a report from the JISC, albeit in 2007, noting that some concerns over digital access still existed. Within the Law School, as part of its new eLearning strategy, a number of laptops are available for students to sign out and use as part of their studies, so it is hoped that this anticipatory action will help mitigate any manifestation of this problem in subsequent years.

Staff reservations on involvement

Some staff within the Law School have been reluctant to get actively involved due to having reservations of being 'friends' with students on Facebook. This is reflected in the literature on social networking groups, which highlights that academic staff from a variety of disciplines and institutions have concerns with the use of social networking or out-of-class interactions (Lefever *et al.*, 2010). Some academics are philosophically opposed to the use of Facebook, reflecting the tensions of using a commercial enterprise, where every like or dislike is recorded for generating advertising revenues, for more nurturing and community building purposes. In order to effectively support student engagement and encourage staff to get more involved, further training on the benefits of the Group is required. Some have even gone so far as to suggest that there should be a commitment by all institutions to ensure that staff related policies are developed that appropriately reward staff who improve learning and teaching to engage and retain more students in Higher Education (Thomas, 2012).

With research from LexisNexis in September 2012 revealing that one in five clients now find their legal representation via social media (TRiG 2012), the need for BCU Law students to use social media to promote their own employability becomes ever more pressing. Therefore, reluctance on the behalf of law academics to engage with social media from a philosophical perspective may no longer be an option if universities are to produce the 'blended professional' legal graduates, as explored by Gough *et al.* (in this volume), that modern graduate recruitment demands.

The role of the academic partner

In addition, the role of the academic partner as moderator is a difficult one – moderation is necessary to ensure inappropriate posts are not being made or bad advice is not being given, but over-moderation discourages student ownership of and participation in the project. Further insight into this role can be found in the personal account of the academic partner involved in the Group (later in the chapter).

Tendency to promote surface learning

The group has at times unfortunately influenced students to take a surface learning (as opposed to deeper) approach to their studies (Marton & Säljö, 2005; Biggs, 1987; Ramsden, 1992), especially around assessment deadlines/exam period, when students have posted strategic questions looking for quick answers rather than taking a more self-directed approach to their learning (Knowles, 1975). This was noted by student participants in the feedback on the Group – for example:

> "[The Group] does provide a quick fix for those that lack motivation or who don't listen or don't turn up but that's the only time you'll see or hear from those people." (Student 9)

Despite there being alternative sources of academic support at BCU such as the Centre for Academic Success as examined in the work of Warmington *et al.* (in this volume), students particularly turned to the Group for help and guidance around assessment time, again reflecting that they are *"Digital Natives"*. Although this was mainly a positive experience, it sometimes developed into activities that could be characterised as students looking for answers to summative assessments. This in turn led to the unexpected issue of confrontation between the student advisors and those seeking answers, with the latter disliking what they regard as being 'disciplined' by their peers:

> "[The Group] turned from useful tips to students asking full blown questions about coursework...When the students were reminded of the purpose of the group, mainly by other students, it became problematic and they did not like it. When it was used in the right way, [the Group]

was very helpful to all students, but as previously stated, it had its draw-backs." (Student 10)

Concerns about 'spoon feeding' online information to students have been raised by other academics (Blair, 2005) and using online resources to provide rapid or quick fire communication to students may well reduce a student's ability to be reflective and evaluative. This cannot be argued as applying across the board to all student participants but it certainly applies to some individuals. However, this potential negative effect needs to be offset against the clear benefits, such as developing key employability skills and the sense of community promoted by the informal academic learning spaces as discussed earlier in this chapter.

The problem can be managed by the setting of clear expectations, both at the outset and regularly throughout the life of the endeavour, concerning the use of and the purpose of the Group – a methodology supported by those who advocate peer mentoring and assessment such as Vickman (2012). In addition, clear correlations can be drawn with the difficulties often found by students when they first engage with a peer assessment task – provided clear guidelines are set, students often report high degrees of satisfaction from involvement with peer assessment opportunities (*ibid*). Having students involved in this expectation-setting process, combined with the message being promoted from their peers about avoiding plagiarism/collusion, is a strong tool in discouraging academic misconduct (Namwar and Rastgoo, 2008). It is the opinion of the academic partner that the opportunities that arise within the Group from student-led discussion outweigh these concerns.

Privacy and the importance of an online presence

Concerns have also been raised in questionnaires about the privacy settings of the group. Students have forgotten that the group is 'open' and could be accessed by prospective employers (and current members of staff) when making some of their more 'casual' observations regarding their time at BCU. This negative effect has been noted by other academics, such as Oliver (2008), who expresses concerns relating to online commu-nities and their potential to conflict with some of the aims of education provision. However, to counteract the effects of this, the academic partner regularly posts reminders about the public nature of the Group and has organised workshops on the importance of creating a strong online presence when making job applications within the legal professions. Whilst the results of the feedback from students outlined above offers some insight into the positive and negative aspects of the Group, the following reflective accounts from two participants, describing the different staff and student experiences, add the weight of narrative to this perspective.

A reflective account: the academic partner

"Having practised law as a qualified solicitor for over 10 years, starting teaching at BCU in September 2008 was an overwhelming experience for me, akin to starting as a new undergraduate student. Luckily, alongside my first year of teaching I also completed a Postgraduate Certificate in Learning and Teaching in Higher Education at BCU. This course introduced me to learning and teaching theories in higher education that encourage student engagement, which I was keen to implement in my own teaching. In addition, during my first year, I was introduced to a colleague in the School of English who had already run a Facebook group during 2008, from which the feedback had been positive. Therefore I decided to start a similar group within the Law School to help provide pre-induction support.

I sent out an email asking for student volunteers and received approximately thirty responses. Based on personal tutor recommendations, I picked six students to help with the initial group, who came from a range of backgrounds, ages and modes of study. After giving them some initial guidance on how to answer questions posted from students, I planned to leave the running of the Group to the student advisors, with me acting in a supervisory moderator role. However, this was the aspect I found most challenging – sometimes student advisors gave (unintentionally) misleading advice which needed to be corrected or enquiries went unanswered for long periods by student advisors (largely due to them being unsure on how to answer a specific query). Others have reflected on the difficulty of this role (Page, 2009; Madge et al., 2009) and feedback from the Group by students has expressed concerns about this "sometimes lecturers jumped straight in and made first year students conscious about asking questions". Having learnt from this early experience, students now 'tag' me (the Facebook equivalent to being 'copied' into an email) in those posts they specifically want me to comment upon. When that happens I try to keep my interaction with the site as minimal and as positive as possible.

My involvement with the Group has been rewarding on many levels. Firstly, it has specifically helped to identify students who need extra help or support. For example, in 2009/10, a student who was pregnant used the Group extensively – she went into labour the day before Freshers' week started and was posting in the Group whilst in labour as she was worried about missing her Law School induction! I'm pleased to report that the student concerned did not have to interrupt her studies, went on to be a formal student advisor for the Group in the next year and recently graduated with an upper second class honours degree.

As a result of the Group, I have forged a number of close bonds with students in a way that I would not have had an opportunity to do in formal teaching sessions. I respectfully disagree with the assertions of Hutchings et al. (in this volume) and believe that it is possible to maintain a professional distance and yet allow productive friendships and partnerships to develop between academic and student partners in SAP projects. Academics who have concerns regarding 'privacy' issues can be comforted by knowing that with the right Facebook privacy settings and by declining specific 'friend' requests from students or using alternative Facebook accounts, an academic can still post in the Group without fear of personal information being accessed by students. However, I think that students appreciate the humanisation or demystification of academics through reading Facebook posts that often resonate with the everyday features of their own lives. This in turn builds a rapport and trust that leads to an ethos of partnership, an aspect that is reflected upon by Jefferies et al. (in this volume) as being key to a successful learning environment.

Indeed, my involvement with the Group led to me receiving awards in the 2012 Birmingham City Student's Union Extra Mile Awards for providing extra support and employability sessions for students – see Chapman et al.(in this volume) for further explanation of these student led awards and how they prompt student engagement. Yes, it is a time-consuming process (my partner calls himself a Facebook widow during the Fresher period) but that is a small price to pay for the positive aspects flowing from the Group.

Each year, students involved have found new and more engaging ways to provide support to their fellow students. In 2012/13, the student advisors for the Group have used podcasts and recorded their own video introduction to life as a LL.B student, all of which have been very positively received by the student users.

Kuh (2003) concluded that what students do during their time as a student matters more to their success and development than anything else. This has been directly borne out by my experience of involvement with the Group, which I hope continues to evolve and grow during future iterations."

A reflective account: a student participant

"I was involved with the Group as a Fresher in 2009 and subsequently as an official student adviser thereafter. When I joined, the student advisers immediately made me feel welcome and I began to feel part of a community straightaway. Every query or problem I had was responded to in a way that made me feel included even before I had officially enrolled at BCU. Furthermore, it was refreshing to see that there were current students willing to engage with new students to give advice where needed. The Group definitely had a community feel to it because it was exclusively a group for the LL.B students. This meant that your posts weren't lost in the crowd or ignored whereas those in the generic main BCU Fresher's Facebook group for all new Freshers tended to get overlooked easily.

I wanted to become a student adviser with the subsequent Groups to give something back. I liked the community nature of the Group and that all three years socialised with each other and wanted that to continue. I also felt that my participation in the previous year's Group as a Fresher would assist new students to feel comfortable in the knowledge that all the questions they had were no different to the ones I had asked just twelve months previously. The retention of the advisors continuing to be part of the community formed by the Group despite having graduated from BCU demonstrates the pride that the BCU law students have in their Law School.

Hutchings et al. (in this volume) explore the intrinsic and extrinsic motivations for students in becoming involved with a SAP project. This exploration is equally relevant to my immediate case; I was not part of the original creation of the Group and arguably my first contributions as a student advisor were due to extrinsic motivations, such as the development of my employability skills and to 'look good on my CV'. However, as the Group has evolved as a community and my involvement with the Group has evolved, intrinsic motivations for my continued involvement have taken over. This is because I took a deep-seated interest in the success of the Group, as I felt part of a team of students who actually owned the project. On a personal level, I felt empowered by my position of responsibility and was determined to not let BCU or myself down.

When I first started using the Group, I viewed Facebook as a purely social space. Indeed, my first interactions with the Group were merely social in nature, to try to make friends prior to starting at BCU. I did not view Facebook as having any value as a learning environment. However, my views on this have shifted throughout the iterations of the Group. Using the Group to form study groups and for revision purposes made me realise that it can have an academic dimension. This realisation prompted me to start posting about news stories relevant to aspects of our degree to try to prompt my fellow students to appreciate the wider uses of the Group. These discussions with other students made for a dynamic and entertaining extension of the learning environment outside of structured teaching sessions.

There were challenges with regard to the discipline aspects of advisor role that I found challenging. Students would tend to forget that their peers moderated every post in the Group and reminders of this (by us) were not always looked upon favourably. Whilst it was awkward at first to have to remind students of academic misconduct regulations, sometimes causing confrontation, it has helped me develop personally in that I am now less reluctant to shy away from taking positions of authority.

Overall, I am proud to have played such a part within the evolution of the Group. Post-graduation, my role has changed again and I can see myself continuing to post and advise students going forwards following qualification as a solicitor."

Conclusion and recommendations

"There is no doubt about it, without the Facebook group, I would not have made many of the friends I now have. I would not have been as involved with the University as I am now and thus would have a worse CV and career prospects. The societies I have been involved in would not have won awards for fundraising as I would not have been able to raise much awareness. I would not have established the bond I have with the tutors, meaning that I wouldn't have felt like I could gain the extra help I needed when I needed it. In short, without the Facebook group, I would not be where I am today." (Student 11)

As this testimony from a student participant demonstrates, social media can be a powerful tool in promoting student engagement. Student and academic partnerships using social media can be formed even before a student formally enrols. A review of the data from this project demonstrates that not only does the Group promote social cohesion by the creation of a community, but that in turn it can empower student to lead in the expectation-setting process, creating opportunities for students to feel engaged as partners within their learning experience.

The Group clearly provides an opportunity for university students to become confident to develop peer networks with their fellow students and create links with academic members of staff. This in turn nurtures a real sense of community and 'belonging' at a pre-entry stage and beyond, recognised as being key to promoting student engagement. Participants in the Group develop *"knowledge, confidence and identity as successful Higher Education learners"* (Thomas, 2012:7). This was best evidenced by the additional unexpected benefits that arose during the project, such as the use of the Group as an informal learning space and the development of employability skills by participants. This is something that can be expanded in future iterations by working in conjunction with those other colleagues at BCU who use social media networks to help students develop employability skills. In addition, to further nurture the informal educational potential, the academic partner plans for a 'rebranding' of the Group to emphasise longevity beyond mere induction purposes and to encourage use of the Group by students in preparation for seminar sessions to discuss ideas. However, the success of these developments will be dependent on an increased participation from other academic members of staff.

In addition the limitations of Facebook itself need to be recognised – it is only one of many social media networks and so over-reliance on it should be avoided. There is also no simple fix for issues concerning surface learning and academic misconduct that arise from the use (or rather, perhaps 'misuse') of social media communities in the academic sphere. But a Group of this nature is definitely the *"social glue"* (Madge *et al.*, 2009:17) that can be used to build partnerships that support a student's happy transition into university life and promote ongoing active student engagement.

About the authors

Emma Flint is a Solicitor and Senior Lecturer in the School of Law at Birmingham City University. She can be contacted at **emma.flint@bcu.ac.uk**

James Roden is a recent graduate of the School of Law at Birmingham City University. He can be contacted at **jamesroden12@yahoo.com**

Chapter 14

Beyond the Curriculum: Deepening Reflective Practice and Widening Student Engagement

David Chapman and Atief Ishaq

Introduction

Our chapter explores the personal journeys of the authors and our changing identity and roles as student and academic. The evolution of our co-learning partnership and development as reflective practitioners reveals a diverse range of opportunities for personal development as well as wider social and institutional learning. We begin by proposing a conceptual framework of reflective practice and engagement, which extends beyond notions of formal curriculum into a wider process of co-learning, engagement and social learning. The framework is proposed as being dynamic and flexible in order to bring together and inter-relate *Educational Development, Professional Development, Personal Development, Lifelong Learning, Organisational Learning* as well as *Social Learning* and *Community Engagement* in ways that can be used together by fellow academics and students.

The chapter begins with our experiences in Higher Education and a large-scale public body describing the ways we have developed as a co-learning partnership over almost a decade. Through these accounts we illustrate how the conceptual framework can deepen reflective practice and deepen student engagement. Our key message is that student academic partnerships can develop from a starting point of individual and personal development into co-learning partnerships that are ultimately able to engage with wider communities of practice (Wenger, 1998) that enrich the experiences of all those involved. We believe that our framework can directly benefit the development of student academic partnerships across the wider community of institutions, academics, employers and professions but are mindful that effective utilisation of the model will require a shift to a 'mindset' in which partnerships extend well beyond concepts of formal curriculum and the traditional links across sectors that underpin such activity. Of course, we appreciate that most universities have a great many partnerships and links to support their work, but that many of these are based on research, consultancy and institutional initiatives, rather than in the type of student academic partnership we propose here.

Our framework is intended to enable those interested in developing student engagement to reflect upon, and map, the position of their own programmes in relation to their strategies for engagement within and beyond the curriculum. We conclude that student academic partnerships should be seen and developed as longer term, dynamic and interactive relationships that can be sustainable while building links between, students, institutions, academics, employers, professions and communities; and so fundamentally enriching the experience of learning as reflective practitioners and engagement for all.

Background

As authors we have both developed our interest in the subject of this book from our perspectives as practitioner and teacher in the subject domain of planning and regeneration where effective engagement is essential for success and where it results in more informed and responsive decision-making (Ishaq, 2007). While within the planning profession the term 'community' has been seen in many different ways, it is nonetheless vital to remember that communities are seldom of one mind but rather comprise a multitude of different interests, agendas and needs (Wilcox, 1994). Responding to these needs requires wide-scale interdisciplinary working – something that is not always easy to achieve in practice settings or in Higher Education (Chapman, 2009). Some of the lessons we identify in relation to student engagement owe much to our reflections upon the challenges facing planning practitioners in achieving effective community engagement and our framework attempts to contextualise these lessons for student engagement in various disciplines and to help to develop multidisciplinary reflective practitioners.

The chapter draws upon our experiences as we have progressed from a traditional student-academic relationship into a co-learning partnership in which we frequently interact as 'reflective practitioners'. Although we recognise that it is not unique and that many diverse partnerships, linkages and networks exist throughout Higher Education, we contend that such relationships are not as commonly found as perhaps they might be.

A framework for reflective practice

From our experience we have identified six key strands of activity that have developed in our reflective co-learning partnership, namely: *Educational Development, Personal Development, Professional Development, Lifelong*

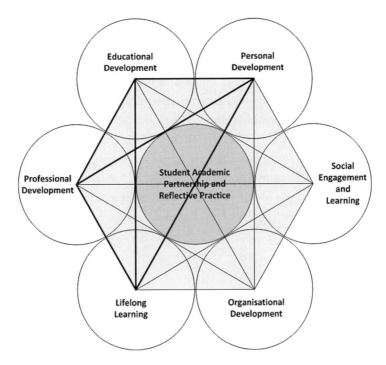

Figure 1: A framework for developing Student Academic Partners as reflective practitioners.

Learning, Organisational Development and *Social Learning and Engagement*; the relationships between these strands of activity are illustrated in Figure 1. Although in some ways it reflects the model offered by Thomas (2012), we believe that it nonetheless provides a useful framework for the mapping and development of engagement beyond the curriculum.

The framework we offer builds upon existing well-established areas of engagement, which are indicated in Figure 1 by stronger lines of linkage. It also suggests further areas of opportunity that as yet are not as widely used as they could be and these are shown in the framework as lighter lines of linkage.

Established areas of engagement

In the more established areas of engagement it is clear how *Educational Development,* through the award of academic credits and opportunities for progression, plays a vital part in establishing a basis for engagement; but it is also important to realise that such engagement may diminish or cease at the end of this educational development activity. Unless we engage with the developing needs of practice of both students and academics, so as to simultaneously engage them in a process of *Professional Development* within the course and beyond it, we run the risk of limiting opportunities for engagement that will have meaning beyond the lifetime of a programme of study.

Of course, it is hoped that through exposure to *Educational Development* and *Professional Development* activity learning habits and values are accrued that lead to continuing *Personal Development* and *Lifelong Learning.* While these four strands are to some extent pursued personally they can also become more widely shared as engagement and co-learning experiences develop.

Widening areas of engagement

Beyond these personal and interpersonal opportunities there are at least two further areas of potential. The first is the opportunity for student/academic partnerships to play a part in contributing to *Organisational Learning,* and the second to *Social Learning and Engagement.* For example, both of our (authors') experiences have included organisational changes and from time to time we have contributed to the process of change. This is never simple and it has been argued that many organisations are inhibited from effective 'learning' because the way they operate fails to allow for the possibility that its operation and practices are out of kilter with the aims and values that it espouses internally and professes publicly (Argyris and Schön, 1996). Co-learning partnerships, critical reflection and engagement can contribute significantly to effective organisational learning and they can also play a valuable role in engaging with wider communities of interest.

Personal reflection

As we have sought to conceptualise engagement as a development route, we have experimented with various metaphors – we began with the concept of a 'ladder' of development but on reflection we have concluded that the metaphor is too instrumental in that it implies a rigid route. We concluded that the notion of 'stepping-stones' conveys the much more diverse, flexible and heterogeneous learning process that can lead to development as much because of the choices and discoveries that are made by each individual student as from the structure of the curriculum. In the following pages we illustrate, through reflection upon our experiences, our development as co-learners along these 'stepping-stones' of education, personal development and professional development. We also reflect upon how the concept of co-learning partnerships might be promoted more widely throughout Higher Education and how they might engage with organisational and social learning activities more widely. As authors, we are aware that we have taken quite different paths to where we are today but believe our diverse experiences are valuable in the way we interact and work today. Given that our diverse paths define the context of our conception of co-learning partnerships, it may be helpful to briefly sketch out our backgrounds and personal narratives.

Personal narrative of the student partner

"As co-author and the 'student' in our partnership I came into education in the UK when I was 7 years old and struggled to make sense of how to learn. However from an early age I was involved in the family business

and this gave me a firm appreciation of the value and distinctiveness of learning by doing. My first entry into further education was to BTEC National Diploma, and then onto a four year Degree course. This path helped me to evaluate what I needed to achieve and why. I found myself receiving positive recognition and more importantly my first academic success in what was a positive working environment where lecturers and students worked together with real life work experience and support from professionals in the area. Encouragement of independent learning, the coursework style of assessment (with a small element of exam based learning), and group working allowed personal skills development to grow and my own management style to form. While my career in retailing was enjoyable I needed to search for a new challenge that would allow me to build on the personal skills and core interests.

I questioned myself rationally and emotionally and found that my natural interest in the built environment drew me towards subjects like surveying and planning and I spoke with practitioners and academics in the field to understand their journey into their respected areas, while trying to gain a glimpse of their personal motivation and desires of their expected professions. I researched the respected strands open to planners within their profession, and read the guidance provided by the key professional body, the Royal Town Planning Institute (RTPI, 2004) on how to enter the profession and develop into a reflective practitioner. I was fortunate to receive positive assurances that my transferable skills and desire to learn placed me in good standing. From this I decided that a first-hand perspective of what it required was needed in order to be a Planner would be useful and I found temporary work for a local authority in a support function for the Planning Department. There I gained hands-on knowledge of the work involved and was introduced to 'Planning Aid' (charitable organisation) as a volunteer. There I found the breadth of work and the joy of working with committed individuals refreshing, while also noting the positive responses of the public who welcomed the engagement with them to make 'planning' understandable.

The personal support, guidance and 'mentoring' I received from colleagues allowed me to share my experiences and more importantly learn from those around me who were able to crystallise what it was to be a Development Control Planner, an Enforcement Officer and forward Planner. However I was only able to fully appreciate the work I undertook with

Planning Aid and the work of people in the profession when I began to study and relate my experiences to the theoretical ideas that I was introduced to in my academic studies.

I entered a bridging programme that was designed to facilitate entry for mature students into postgraduate studies. That was where I first met David (co-author). This bridging programme (Diploma/Advanced Diploma in Professional Studies) proved valuable and as my interest, confidence and desire to learn grew, a chance presented itself via employment and traineeship at Birmingham City Council including employer support for further study at Master's level. I was fortunate to find an employer that believed in my ability and had a structured learning culture. The close working relationships and interactions between those at work and academic professionals was vital to me in drawing full value from the learning opportunities on offer. Andrews et al. (this volume) also point to trust and partnership as important factors in enhancing learning."

Personal narrative of the academic partner

"As co-author and the 'academic' in our partnership I (David) had spent some twenty years in architectural and planning practice before entry into Higher Education in the late 1980s, sponsored by the leading urban design practice. This transition as a blended professional (Whitchurch, 2009) proved challenging as I moved from a place where role and purpose were clear and defined into the different world of the academic, where the very diverse cocktail of potential roles and responsibilities are often comparatively ill-defined, called for significant adjustment. The contrast between practice, where projects were tackled instrumentally and entrepreneurially, and an academic life where engagement as a teacher, researcher, manager, practitioner, curriculum developer and quality enhancer are as much a matter of personal motivation as they are managed or directed, was stark. A number of experiences have shaped my personal approaches to teaching and learning, approaches to student academic relationships, and curriculum development, but the principal influence has undoubtedly been participation in the BCU postgraduate teaching programme, which culminated in the award of the MA in Education. This study stimulated continuing personal research and many of the theoretical ideas

introduced then have been influential in the development of my ideas and attitudes, in particular Schön's (1983) concept of the reflective practitioner. The earlier work of Dewey (1974) that Schön referred to, which suggested that students cannot simply be told what they need to know but must be enabled to see it themselves, was also highly influential. In this it is also important to appreciate that the disciplinary context (the field of planning) is contested, being simultaneously faced with considerable practical and philosophical challenges and being charged with a responsibility for action in response to those challenges. The necessity to prepare students for this context has real influence on the approaches adopted in curriculum design, pedagogy and engagement."

The development of planning education at BCU

Planning education was begun in Birmingham in the 1950s to equip people to undertake the reconstruction that was needed following World War II and to respond to new planning legislation. The courses were part-time and primarily for local authority staff and architects, but they evolved into a range of full and part-time courses at pre-degree, degree and postgraduate levels. They continue to respond to the changing needs of practice and the requirements for initial planning education established by the Royal Town Planning Institute as guided by learning outcomes (RTPI, 2004).

It is not necessary to explore the complex and changing context for the discipline of planning here, but it will be helpful to draw out a few key aspects of significance to our experiences and our argument. Firstly while for many the mention of planning conjures up the image of permits, bureaucracy and restrictions it is concerned with the very practical needs for sustainable development. For example the utopian visions of Ebenezer Howard in the late nineteenth century were not simply about effective or efficient development; they represented a social project concerned with humanity and social life. The perceived certainty that these ideas relied upon was questioned in the second half of the twentieth century when it became clear that reliance upon technical rationality was at least partly misplaced. As Schön recognised:

"...we have become aware of the importance to actual practice of phenomena – complexity, uncertainty, instability, uniqueness and value-conflict – which do not fit the model of Technical Rationality." (Schön, 1983:39).

Practitioners sought to engage with the complexities and uncertainties that Schön recognised and to focus much more upon questions of problem definition. Today a very heterogeneous postmodern picture has emerged in which the concerns are with spatial relationships, community engagement and governance. Clearly this has wider significance for partnership and civic engagement as a means of *"...collective deciding ..."* and as *"...an interactive and interpretive process..."* (Healy, 1992:247). Thus given the diversity of activities that the discipline of planning involves, it is not surprising that preparing students for this complex and contested field is challenging.

Importantly the challenge of engagement is directly relevant for planning where the importance of citizen participation and engagement in decision-making processes is of great importance. The 'ladder of citizen participation' developed by Arnstein (1969) and the critique of it by Collins and Ison (2006) has been conceptually important and these inform teaching and learning strategies in many ways. Examples in practice include the development of sustainability 'code books' through engagement in a process of social learning in Seattle (Holden, 2008) and the co-learning approaches inspired by Mee Kam Ng at the University of Hong Kong, where planning students undertake a range of interactive community workshops during the course of their studies.

Our reflections

It is not necessary to describe in detail the structure of all the planning related courses that have been offered by BCU but it will be helpful to briefly outline the route that I (Atief) took as this illustrates the value of linked 'ladders' of awards. In my case I took the Diploma/Advanced Diploma in Professional Studies in Planning and Environment and then the MA in Spatial Planning, which I completed in 2008. Figure 2 shows an outline of the structural relationships, which for me developed my personal approach to lifelong learning.

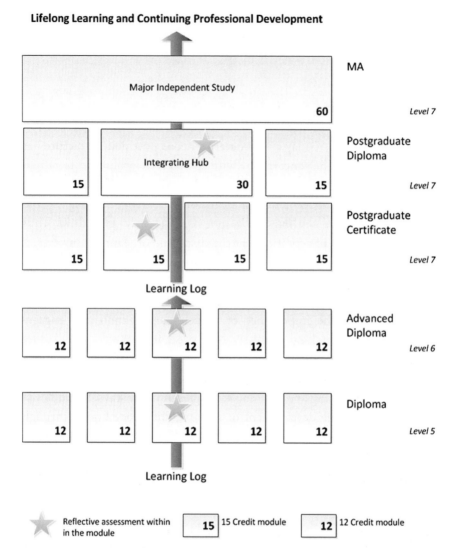

Figure 2: A 'Ladder' of awards and the Learning Log

Developing beyond graduation

After graduation from the MA in Spatial Planning I (Atief) moved from my initial trainee post into the position of a Senior Planning Officer and my co-learning partnership with David continued as I sought out opportunities of professional and personal development. I was increasingly seeking a learning culture, and developing a hunger to learn. Thus our relationship moved from mentee / mentor and student / academic towards one characterised by a sharing of working experiences and insights. This allowed me to continue to critically reflect on learning and organisational cultures, while still focusing on my personal development.

My experiences of planning have been extended by my long-standing voluntary work and engagement with Planning Aid, which is a charitable body that assists individuals, groups and communities less able to engage in planning processes to do so. Importantly this allowed me to bridge a number of knowledge gaps in practical ways and it really helped me to develop my transferrable skills to explain planning issues to stakeholders, such as on regeneration schemes and those objecting to planning applications. This invaluable hands-on exposure enabled me to appreciate much more deeply the thought process and skills needed to be successful in the field.

Influences upon pedagogy and curriculum design

From an academic point of view it is clear that, while students naturally aspire to achieve their target award and, where appropriate 'initial' professional qualification, it is lifelong learning and continuing professional development (CPD) that will play a vital continuing role in their future professional practice. Preparing students for this reality presents a key issue for curriculum design and development. The insights of Schön (1987) into professional education have always been influential and his research into teaching in design studios and conservatoire schools of music were especially relevant for planning and the built environment where support and guidance are far more effective than didactic instruction. The importance of learning through active engagement and the value of reflection in action as well as in retrospect were very influential insights as they help us to appreciate something of the complex ways that professionals often respond to the unexpected by making adjustments and corrections, frequently in ways that even they find difficult to explain (*ibid*). Similarly the importance of developing in students the capacity to frame problems was crucial to our understanding of the pedagogical challenges being faced. In this, the idea of the learning cycle (Kolb, 1984, Gibbs, 1988), with stages of conceptualisation, experimentation, experience, and reflection has also been influential. And, as most of the students concerned have been mature adults, Knowles' ideas (1984) of what he called andragogy (or educating adults) and the critical role of setting a climate of engagement has also been particularly influential in developing teaching and learning strategies.

A key ingredient of this at BCU has been the Learning Log, which was initially introduced to encourage students to engage more actively with their personal 'specialist' studies. However it soon became evident that it could really help students to take a reflective overview of their studies and personal experiences as a whole, and to make connections with their work or life experiences generally. Figure 2 shows a ladder of awards in which the Learning Log provides a thread that joins them and flows into lifelong learning and professional development. The Learning Log is not marked, but a bone fide submission is a requirement of the final award. Consequently, the quality of the submitted Learning Log relies on students being intrinsically motivated to draw full learning value from its completion. For further exploration of ways to promote intrinsic motivation see Hutchings *et al.* (in this volume)

Interestingly when the RTPI remodelled its approach to conferring full professional membership through the Assessment of Professional Competence (APC) it adopted a similar approach to the Learning Log by requiring applicants to submit a reflective report upon at least two years experience in practice. In devising their approach the RTPI explicitly recognised that planning practitioners: '...*rarely encounter standard problems needing standard solutions and it is thus the ability to learn in a reflective manner through taking action that is the hallmark of the true professional.*' (RTPI, 2012:5)

Developing beyond the curriculum

The concept of 'ladders of opportunity' in curriculum design has been influential in the development of planning education and related fields at BCU; and as our experiences have shown the diverse needs and capabilities of students are invariably well served if they have access to an integrated package of learning opportunities in which there are a number of recognised entry and exit points to meet each different students' individual needs. This is illustrated by the many students who have progressed from programmes designed to enable access from pre-degree through to gaining distinctions at Master's level. Also significant are those who have entered HE with professional qualifications who have subsequently undertaken the University's Postgraduate Programme in Education – each stage providing a new and formative experience. In this, while the Learning Log helps to develop links between academic awards it also helps to build a bridge from the academic awards into initial professional education and professional practice.

As an academic involved in shaping these ladders I had initially only partial appreciation that the formal elements of the curriculum actually form only a part of the learning experience and had little understanding of the value that extracurricular and interpersonal relationships can have. This is an important conceptual point for programme design in a much wider sense where the opportunities for engagement should be considered alongside the structure and content of the curriculum. While the curriculum presents a somewhat more rigid 'ladder' it does signpost direction and provide context and continuity of engagement. However, as we show in Figure 3, a much more diverse and flexible pattern of 'stepping-stones' can be conceived that can extend personal and collective learning and engagement, beyond the curriculum.

As I (Atief) reflect on my educational experiences I conclude that I have drawn great learning benefit from a number of interlinking opportunities for educational development. As illustrated above, the relations between the educational setting and its progressive role in the provision of initial professional education for the planning discipline also developed in me the desire to continue as a lifelong learner. For me the idea of stepping-stones is helpful as it captures the challenge of making sense of likely steps and directions; not necessarily with clear ideas of the end

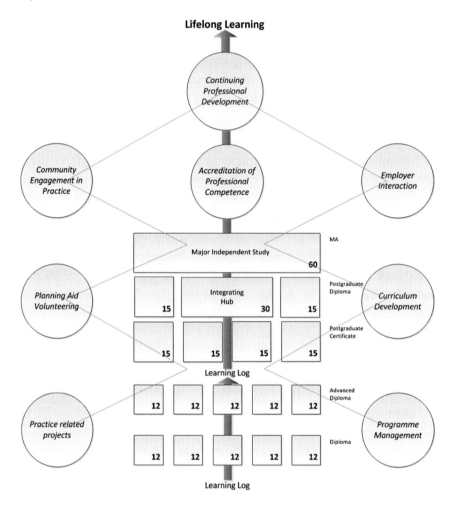

Figure 3: Stepping-stones to engagement beyond the curriculum

goal, but with a hope and expectation that it was a move towards a desired area of interest and personal development that would allow me to grow. These stepping-stones, which are not a rigid path, are sometimes walked and sometimes jumped! My increasing engagement with organisational change in my work has also been a key trigger for development as I recognised the need to challenge assumptions, perceived truths and to develop creative thinking and options.

Conclusions

The subject domain of Planning has much to offer by way of conceiving models of student engagement. Just as citizens have a vested interest in the planning decisions that affect the world around them, so students have a vested interest in their education and the curriculum they experience. We have drawn upon the inclusive culture and practice of Planning as a discipline to frame our conceptions of engagement, partnership and co-learning; furthermore, we have drawn upon our identities and associated expectations for continuing professional development to extend the notion of co-learning beyond the taught curriculum – outwards during the duration of programmes of study and onwards after conclusion of study. Through this extension, we contend that co-learning partnerships developed as a consequence of student engagement, can lead to sustainable learning relationships that continue to shape identities and practice throughout working lives.

Our story here illustrates something of the richness of relationships that we have enjoyed across academic, professional and social communities. It also shows how we continue to move from an original identity of 'individual learners' to identities of 'reflective practitioners' and 'co-learners'. In many ways the journey we are on mirrors the progression from first, second and third person action learning and research described by Reason & Bradbury (2001) and in writing this chapter we hope to disseminate the fruits of our thinking and experiences to encourage the development in others of a new mindset in which a wider perspective of academic student partnership is taken.

These reflections may be perceived as over-optimistic in an era of 'massified' higher education (Scott, 2011) where the logistics of timetables and room booking can constrain teaching and learning strategies and essential relationships between students, academics and support staff may be diminished by a 'roller shutter' mentality. But we argue that building long term positive relationships, in which students are seen as primary stakeholders (Harvey, 1996) is critical for the health and wellbeing of institutions as well as their many potential partners and that any barriers to this should be minimised.

The framework we propose suggests ways in which partnership opportunities can be nurtured and sustained more widely than tends to be the case when partnership is limited to just the delivered curriculum and we hope it will encourage universities to become even more significant contributors in building co-learning communities. Although our framework does advocate a new mindset, it also provides a practical tool for programme evaluation and development. The stepping-stones do not take the form of a preordained path, or the instrumental ladder that we originally envisaged, but rather a series of alternative routes and steps that could be taken in various ways, each one potentially deepening student academic partnership and engagement. Importantly we see those steps as not beginning with enrolment and ending with graduation, but rather beginning in recruitment and extending into lifelong learning, employment and practice. For us while curriculum design, content and organisation have certainly played a part in setting the scene for our engagement as co-learners, it is the values and attitudes that we have mutually developed that will be the key to its future sustainability.

About the authors

David Chapman is Professor of Planning and Development, Birmingham School of the Built Environment, Birmingham City University. He can be contacted at **david.chapman@bcu.ac.uk**

Atief Ishaq has completed an MA in Spatial Planning at Birmingham City University in a continuing series of part-time studies. He is now Senior Development Planning Officer, Birmingham City Council. He can be contacted at **atief.ishaq@gmail.com**

Chapter 15

Engaging Students as Practitioners through Experiential Learning

Hannah Phillips, Tom Craig and Christie Phillips

Introduction

This chapter explores the enhancement of learning and engagement of students by applying performance practice and theory to engage children, young people and often vulnerable adults in community and educational settings. We begin by exploring applied performance, what it is, where it came from, pedagogical influences and challenges for practice. We define and discuss the influence of transgressive pedagogy on both applied performance practice and our programme.

Supported by personal accounts and reflections of practice, responses from industry based partners and a student survey developed by students Tom Craig and Christie Phillips, using social networking, we advocate the value of experiential learning through community engagement and reflective practice. We discuss the learning community we have built within this programme and the innovative model we have developed of identifying and empowering the student as a 'practitioner' rather than a 'student' throughout their programme and how the tutor also changes their identity to that of director / performance maker / facilitator. This shift in individual identities is supported by a shift in collective identity as a professional theatre company and has a positive impact on their learning, engagement and practice. We refer to students as practitioners within the programme but for clarity we will use the term student within this chapter.

We demonstrate throughout the chapter how engagement is core to our practice through *"active and collaborative learning"* (Coates, 2007:122). Students are consistently involved with or are running community engagement projects so they are also responsible for the engagement of others, the participants. We conclude with recommendations made throughout the chapter for enhanced student learning and engagement.

Applied performance

Applied theatre is an umbrella term for alternative arts practice which has community, educational, social or political objectives. Arts work that aims to make a difference to lives, to raise awareness, inform, intervene, engage, change and transport. The work is often found *"in non – traditional settings and /or with marginalized communities"* (Thompson & Jackson, 2006:92).

Throughout history, the theatre has been a platform for playwrights to voice their political opinions, a space to tell stories and share experiences. The debate in theatre theory continues *"whether the theatre should be viewed primarily as an engaged social phenomenon or as a politically indifferent aesthetic artefact"* (Carlson, 1993:454). Applied practice was born out of the radical view of theatre as a political tool. The main theatre movements which have influenced applied practice are political/alternative theatre, theatre in education and community theatre. The term applied theatre and applied drama came into being in the 1990s, used predominantly by academics and practitioners embracing a wide range of practice outside of mainstream theatre such as prison theatre, theatre for development, museum theatre, theatre in health, reminiscence theatre, community theatre and drama and theatre in education. Each of these areas are specialist areas of practice which are very different from each other, contextually and theoretically drawing on a wide range of subject knowledge and research both within and outside of drama and performance. As Nicholson (2005:2) states, *"applied drama and theatre are hybrid practices."* Therefore how do we effectively inform the undergraduate student both in theory and practice in all these different areas? We believe the student has to be given autonomy over their own learning and practice. They have to be given the opportunity to select areas of interest and specialise.

Throughout this chapter, we will use the term applied performance as opposed to applied theatre or applied drama as which this form of work is more commonly known. Our programme is entitled BA (Hons) Applied Performance (Community and Education). We use the term 'performance' as we feel it better describes the hybrid of art forms used in our work such as acting/drama, dance, movement and physical theatre, singing, poetry and spoken word supported by visual arts. We as a course team also felt using the word 'theatre' was not very accessible and unsuitable for practice, which was often happening outside a theatre space in order to encourage interaction and participation.

Pedagogical influences on applied performance

Theatre in Education (TIE) and Drama in Education (DIE), strands of applied performance which emerged in the 1960s, were heavily influenced by and contributed to the progressive practices of child- centred, active learning which were happening at that time. TIE focused on active audience participation for change through which learning would occur. Forms used in DIE such as role play, improvisation, teacher in role work and drama games and exercises became familiar forms of learning and teaching in both formal and informal education.

Similarly, applied practice has also been influenced by the work of Brazilian educationalist, Paulo Freire (1970) who also placed the learner at the centre of the pedagogical process and argued for *praxis*, informed action to evoke social change. Freire's work and text, *Pedagogy of the Oppressed* had a significant influence on the work of Brazilian director, Augusto Boal (1979) and his book, *Theatre of the Oppressed*. Boal's methodologies such as forum theatre, image theatre and invisible theatre have been fundamental to the movement and greatly inspired practitioners and practice.

The concept of *"transgressive pedagogy"* (Hooks, 1994), which challenges teaching authority and requires students' knowledge to transcend the scholarly and make personal connections with the work, is fundamental to applied performance work and the learning community we have built within this programme for both students as learners and students as facilitators and practitioners. We focus on experiential learning, activism, critical thinking and reflection. Applied performance practice promotes innovative learning strategies and actively encourages engagement through interaction and participation, advocating change and commitment to identity and community and how they link with culture and the arts. As Nicholson (2005:38) states: *"Applied drama has strong ties to education. Advocates of applied drama in its different guises have regarded its participatory, dialogic and dialectic qualities as effective and democratic ways of learning in many formal and informal educational contexts."*

Challenges for practice and undergraduate problems

We will now consider the challenges for practice and consequently the implications for developing undergraduate programmes within this area. There is a lack of research written about the relatively new and consistently evolving subject of applied performance. An article written in July 2011 focusing on our programme and a performance project we were undertaking at the time in schools and at Heartlands Hospital became the first community arts project to receive any editorial space in *The Stage*, the newspaper for the performance arts industry which was founded in 1880. Within Industry and Education, applied theatre/community arts is often seen as 'less than' mainstream theatre, Nicholson (2005:5) makes an insightful point, *"I find it interesting that other academic disciplines that customarily use the preface 'applied' often contrast it with 'pure"*. How do we ensure the 'applied' performance student is empowered and doesn't feel less than their fellow 'pure' acting student?

The skills of the applied performance practitioner are not only artistic and aesthetic, but the practitioner also needs to be able to be sensitive to and engage with audiences and participants, teach unskilled participants performance skills whilst being aware of vulnerable adults and young people's social wellbeing and emotional and mental health. They need to focus on both the individual as well as the group dynamic. Unlike the skilled actor who can tell many a story with conviction and truth even if the content does not resonate with them, the applied practitioner must really care about the issues being presented and reflected upon. Prendergast & Saxton (2009:12) distinguish between the two types of theatre as *"Presentational* theatre" and *"Representational* theatre". The applied practitioner needs to be informed; they need to be politically and socially active, artistically campaigning for change. Can this level of engagement and commitment be taught?

There are also ethical challenges with any applied performance project relating to the professional conduct of a practitioner working within a community, similar to tutors working with students in educational contexts. Ethical partnerships have to be made between practitioners and participants and organisations. Both practitioners and participants need to be kept safe. Practitioners need to be fully engaged and empathetic but keep a professional distance. How do we monitor this? Should students be working with individuals and groups before they are fully trained? How do they train if they do not experience? In a recent student-led survey of current students and those just graduating, 95.7% of students from this course agreed they learnt more through experiential learning. Other ethical considerations include: how do we define a community? If you are not a member of the community you are working with, should you be doing the project? When doing a project, which objectives are you working to: the participants', the community's, the funder's, the service organisations' or your own artistic and learning objectives?

The assessment and evaluation of applied performance provides challenges for all practitioners and artists. As Prendergast & Saxton (2009:24) comment, *"a key question for any applied theatre company is how do we balance privacy and protection with the need to prove worth?"* There is also the question of how we evaluate the effectiveness of the work. What are we assessing and why? Who is the evaluation for: funders, service providers, practitioners or participants? Are we assessing the quality of the work, the content, how it is done, the value of the work, the impact made? How do we measure value and impact? How long do we wait to reflect and evaluate? Prendergast & Saxton, (2009:25), conclude: *"Qualitative approaches to assessing move away from measuring how a presentation has succeeded or failed and toward considering its broader effect and affect on individuals and communities."*

This leads us to question how we as a Higher Education Institution assess the practitioner's work. Should we be assessing the practitioner's work at all and whether instead we should be assessing their own assessment and reflection of their projects and their work?

Student as reflective practitioner

Practice and theory are interlinked and are reliant on each other to develop, *"theory and practice are not separate processes or modes of thought, with one based on action and another on reflection. They are interdependent and constantly in flux."* (Nicholson, 2005:14). Practice is consistently underpinned by modules which focus on the theory behind or in front of the ever shifting practice. We aim to *"create and maintain a stimulating intellectual environment"* and *"value academic work and high standards"* (Krause, 2005:12-14) to enhance student engagement. We have achieved this by developing academic standards through introducing academic workshops to the programme in partnership with the Centre for Academic Success at Birmingham City University. Authors Warmington *et al.*, in this volume, discuss these in more detail; in this way we have increased the amount of academic work within the programme.

Over the past three years, we have developed an innovative model of working which focuses on students shifting their identity from students to that of a practitioner throughout the programme. The emerging practitioner works in partnership with the tutor who also shifts their identity to a director/performance maker/facilitator. The practitioners collectively work as a professional company rather than a class or a group and are all empowered with individual roles and responsibilities within that company. In the recent student survey 73.9% agreed that identifying themselves as a 'practitioner' rather than a 'student' had had a positive impact on their learning and engagement in comparison to a 100% agreement that working within the model of a professional theatre company had not only aided the development of their individual skill bases but also supported their development and engagement through peer to peer learning.

We aim to provide practitioners opportunities to develop their own artistic practice and specialise in their own areas of interest throughout the programme. This is achieved by bringing in an eclectic range of artists and companies to deliver workshops and seminars to give students experiences in different styles and forms of work and practice. We encourage students to go and see work happening in the city, through ticket incentives or free performances through partnerships or arranging group bookings. We also offer students choice in terms of case studies, essays, presentations, work placements and projects so they have autonomy over in which areas of practice they decide to develop and deepen their knowledge and skills. It is very important to give these emerging practitioners space and opportunities to explore their own practice. We focus on making new work throughout the programme through predominantly devising and some new writing rather than using existing scripted performance; this is a much more beneficial way of engaging students, participants, audiences and communities. Making work requires collaboration and commitment; it demands research and thorough subject knowledge. It allows for a collaboration of art forms which can be selected from the skill bases of the practitioners and it encourages experimentation through a creative freedom. Andrews *et al.*, in this volume, make reference to Davis *et al.* (2000) and comment how *"creativity requires cognitive and explorative engagement, a focus of deeper learning."* Lamden (2000:2) suggests to students who are devising performance, *"You are in a position to control your own learning, and have freedom to produce a piece of theatre for an audience about a topic that concerns you."* When applying this practice the focus also needs to be on whom the work is for and its objectives.

We encourage students to make work which is both artistically and intellectually challenging yet accessible to for whom it is made. We actively encourage and support risk taking and pushing boundaries to make and create innovative work at the forefront of practice. The content and style of the work develops *"emotional engagement"* (Fredricks *et al.*, 2004: 62-63) from students and audiences/participants. This may be either through emotional responses to the contemporary, innovative style of work exemplified by our multi discipline, fast paced Theatre in Education performances or the numerous flash mobs and site specific work we have created. Alternatively, it may be an emotional connection to the issues explored within the work such as hate crime, identity, sexual exploitation and homelessness. As a company engagement is embedded within our practice and we look for new ways to encourage participation and interaction as opposed to the forum/workshop formulas that young people are expecting. Our Theatre in Education/Performance for Young People has a thirty strong ensemble cast to whom the young audiences can relate and are in role as peers creating a sense of peer to peer facilitation and learning encouraging engagement.

Craig's personal account of a tie project

"Hatin' On was a Theatre in Education piece commissioned by West Midlands Police to be performed in secondary schools in Great Barr and Handsworth to highlight the growing number of 'hate crimes' and the August 2011 Riots. In post-riot Birmingham and a heated political climate heavily influenced by social media, the need for outreach work and dialogue between adolescents and police was essential.

The process developed through discussion, research, devising and direction. This second year module required my entire year group to collaborate as a professional company, drawing upon the skill bases of individual practitioners to make work, inspire and encourage each other through peer to peer learning. My objectives as a learner within this module were to apply my skill bases to the devising process, be directed as an actor within a company and collaborate and contribute to both the process and the company. This was a tutor directed piece which emerged from student devised work. Devising was stimulated by research compiled by the company which we discussed & practically explored during sessions. Together we began to develop ideas and verbatim accounts which evolved into a montage of scenes which were directed and shaped. We used art forms relevant to the target audience; verbatim text expressed through poetry and spoken word and choreographed sequences of current dance styles. The performance was underscored by an arrangement of songs and tracks familiar to the young audiences throughout the tour who sang along or physically related to the mood of the music. In reflection, it is these elements that contributed to the success of the piece, the accessibility of the performances and consequently the engagement of the young people.

Opportunities for reflection came throughout the process. We were often encouraged to edit or develop our product, reconsider the choices we had made and given notes and feedback from the director. We focused on intent, reiterating meaning, questioning purpose and who this work was for. Through a pedagogy which is continuously nurturing a reflective practice I have developed not only as a practitioner but I have also strengthened my understanding of applied performance theory and my *academic work. As I progress through my degree I have discovered that the continuous engagement of practice followed by reflection has been fundamental in my development from a 'student' to a 'practitioner'."*

Reflection

As Craig states reflection is fundamental to the student's development of practice and transition into a practitioner and throughout we actively develop "the Reflective Practitioner" (Schön, 1983) through offering students the opportunity to reflect on their practice as part of our assessment strategy. We asked earlier in the chapter how we as a Higher Education Institution assess the practitioners' work: stating that we as a course team question whether we should be assessing the practitioners' work at all and whether instead we should be assessing their own assessment and reflection of their projects and their work. This is something we have introduced in the professional placement module where the practitioners are assessed not on what they do but how they reflect on their own practice and that of the company/organisation.

Neelands (2006:37) suggests that critical reflective practice is "*based on open dialogue, negotiation and the fostering of critical thinking and action amongst the community and learners and teachers*". As a course team, we would agree with this and this is the learning and teaching environment which we attempt to create. Both students and tutors are consistently reflecting on their own practice. In order to emphasise the importance of this reflective practice we have increased the amount of reflective writing throughout the course, we have introduced assessed individual oral reflective tutorials and are currently exploring different ways to assess reflection. In the student survey 69.6% of students agreed or strongly agreed the concentration on nurturing personal reflection by tutors had been imperative to their own personal development throughout their degree programme; however 21.7% remained neutral and 8.7% disagreed. We would be interested to conduct further more detailed research into this area looking at results from different years and if there was a noticeable difference in results from those practitioners who have graduated and using reflection within their professional practice including writing evaluative reports compared with those still studying.

The professional company

Collaboration is essential in this type of work and there is a strong focus throughout the programme to develop collaboration skills, team work and group dynamics. Practitioners concentrate on their collective identity as well as individual identities supported by staff who run practical sessions/workshops focused on collaboration, conflict resolution and theoretical sessions concentrating on the structure and running of a professional theatre company.

The model of a professional company is used for projects in years one and two. Practitioners learn through observation and experiential learning. They are given roles and responsibilities but the director/maker steers the company. This prepares them to run their own company, Cathouse Theatre Company, in their final year.

Cathouse Theatre Company was formed by practitioners three years ago as part of their final community arts project. The community company has a mission statement, a bank account and organisational structure. Projects have included a reminiscence and intergenerational project, a project working with homeless participants and two hospital based projects at the Queen Elizabeth Hospital, Birmingham, one with long term patients and one with military patients and their families.

C. Phillips' account of working with participants in a Cathouse Theatre Company project

> "Bored On the Ward (BOW) was a project created and carried out by our in-house student Company, Cathouse Theatre Company. The key aims of this project were to work with older patients at Queen Elizabeth Hospital, Birmingham to increase physical and mental stimulation through applied theatre and dance theatre. After five months of planning we began work with this community group. During our preparations we created a set of workshops that we thought would be appropriate for this community. However, when working with the group we knew instantly that we would have to adapt and change our approach. This realisation could only happen by practically realising the project and working with the client group."

"The participants responded very positively to our new set of workshops. Throughout the workshop process we adapted our approach to fit each patient's personal needs. This was a skill you could only learn whilst working hands-on with the community group. The more practical experience we obtained, the more our confidence grew which in turn developed our practice. We developed new skills and knowledge of how to interact with this client group and communicate with individual participants. We also developed our ability to liaise with the service providers and the organisation's management team who were assessing our productivity. The patients responded positively to our work by joining in and instigating the ideas behind our workshops. We began to have 'regulars' at our sessions and could observe and record their progression throughout the project."

"In this yearlong project, we collaborated and functioned as a professional company, fundraising, managing, developing and delivering workshops, devising and performing and evaluating our individual and company's work. This project and experience has equipped me for future employment. I would now feel confident to develop and run a community arts engagement project, I have developed my own skill base, my understanding of how a company runs and would now understand how to adapt and develop my own practice to fit with the needs of any client group I may work with."

Tutor evidence of engagement

During this final project and the students' final year, student retention and progression increases to 100%. There are no issues with attendance and punctuality and students select to work throughout their holiday between spring and summer terms, in the evenings and the weekends as they prioritise the availability of the client group/participants they are working with and the needs of the community based arts project. They develop strong working relationships with the participants, third sector organisations and each other. Students become extremely focused and positive about the work they are doing creating their own learning communities. They engage in large amounts of research, feasibility studies and engage with workshops or extracurricular classes outside of the

University to develop new skill bases to support the work they are doing. They become the applied performance experts with their participants but also within that area of practice sharing their work and knowledge with other students and staff not involved in the project. Assessment levels increase and student satisfaction for the final year and in particular this module/project increases to around 95%.

Student &participant partnership

We will now explore the students' relationship with participants; the term we use for those they are attempting to engage or work with. We will explore participation in terms of engagement and empowerment for both practitioner and participant.

In applied performance the audience is integral to the work. Whether as a participant in a workshop, participant in a project or making a performance where the audience member may physically interact or may emotionally connect with the piece because the issues being explored are relevant to them, either way they are an important, active participant.

Applied performance practitioners will often find themselves working with particularly vulnerable individuals or situations such as asylum seekers or refugees, children in hospital or young people in local authority care. Their role is to 'empower' individuals and communities. This brings about questions of power. Prendergast & Saxton (2009:25) ask *"How central are power relations to all participatory elements of an applied theatre process? How can these relations be made evident and kept in continuous negotiation?"* These questions of power relationships resonate with questions asked of the tutor/student relationship and students are required to ask these same questions around power relations when working with participants.

Setting up a project is complex and very time consuming. Who do you want to work with and why? Does a group already exist or do you need to set one up? How do you make contact with an existing group? How do you collaboratively decide on a community need? How do you fund the project? How do you artistically realise the community need / issues? This all has to be considered before a project begins. Students explore this process theoretically and practically throughout their programme.

The process of developing a community based project takes time, commitment and thorough research. How can students engage others and not be engaged themselves? Engagement is core to the work we do. Students are often working with communities to achieve some form of social change or intervention; they must be fully committed to the project. Every project is different; political and social objectives are constantly shifting, applied performance practice is always evolving. Practitioners are therefore consistently in the role of learner, throughout their training and careers. Prendergast & Saxton (2009:16) who refer to Practitioners as *"Facilitators"* suggest: *"The applied theatre facilitator is a multi-disciplinarian who must know about theatre and how it works as well as being equipped with an understanding of teaching and learning."*

During their programme, the student is in role as learner and teacher/facilitator as is any practitioner effectively engaging in applied performance projects including their tutors. They are going through a process of experiential learning and reflection but the participant also becomes learner so the student also needs to be able to shift their identity to teacher/facilitator to support the participant in this learner/participant centred process. The student now has to have a thorough understanding of engagement and deal with issues around engagement; ensuring participants attend their sessions, workshops or rehearsals, challenging any disruptive behaviour and encouraging active involvement, offering opportunities for participants to engage with projects at different levels and attempting to create a positive, creative environment where participants feel safe, feel a sense of community and belonging and can emotionally connect with the work and the issues being explored.

Participant becomes a student

The following is a quote from a participant of *Inside/Out*, a Higher Education Innovation Funded project we ran in 2009, working with issues and people affected by homelessness and displacement. This participant decided to apply two years later for the BA (Hons) Applied Performance programme, and has now completed year one as a student.

> *"I was part of a Youth Theatre Company called First Chance, a company developed by St Basils who work with young people, aged 16-25, who*

are homeless or at risk of homelessness and the Birmingham Repertory Theatre. First Chance helped me be more empathetic towards other peoples' circumstances especially when given the opportunity to work alongside a Birmingham School of Acting project Inside / Out about homelessness. Devising, improvising and working with new people and different cultures was a great experience. This inspired me to further my education into combining creative skills with teaching. The Applied Performance Degree is providing me with the right tools and awareness needed to travel round the world as a professional practitioner, having a positive impact on people's lives. I want to break negative cycles for young people today, in the local and wider community. I can't change the world but I now feel as if I can inspire and work with others to make small social changes."

Industry, third and public sector partnerships

We have a number of industry partners, such as, The Birmingham Repertory Theatre, mac Birmingham and the Play House/Language Alive. Industry and Industry Professionals significantly influence learning and development, through seminars, workshops, projects and placements. 96% of students in the recent survey agreed or strongly agreed that working alongside industry professionals and practitioners has had a positive impact on their learning and practice.

Throughout the programme we focus on pathways to employment, Industry needs and why practitioners need to develop in the model we are suggesting. Dr Steve Ball, Associate Director of the Birmingham Repertory Theatre who has been responsible for developing one of the largest Learning and Participation departments in a theatre in the UK and has made a significant contribution to the development of Drama and Theatre in Education, says of the course and the partnership:

"The theatre industry is dependent upon drama schools and universities to provide them with well-trained actors and theatre makers. The same is true of theatre education practitioners who deliver learning and participation programmes to schools and communities.

Our partnership with Birmingham School of Acting / Birmingham City University through the BA (Hons) Applied Performance programme ensures we are able to engage with emerging practitioners who have the knowledge, skills and values to succeed in the rapidly changing worlds of theatre and education."

The Play House, a Theatre and Drama in Education Company, currently offer graduates from our course two paid practitioner posts each year in collaboration with The Birmingham Repertory Theatre. We work with partners to offer paid and unpaid opportunities throughout the programme as youth theatre assistants and workshop leaders. In the recent survey 95.4% agreed that these extracurricular opportunities had developed their skill bases, experience and practice. Placements from Big Brum and mac Birmingham have also led to paid employment whilst practitioners are still studying. The placement is chosen and sourced by the practitioner, supported by staff; however, the placement is not assessed; the practitioner's reflection of their own practice and that of the organisation is what is assessed. 91.3% of students agreed and strongly agreed that their placement had proved fundamental to both their learning and practice. 100% agreed the opportunities presented to them on placement have enabled them to develop as a practitioner engaging effectively in professional practice.

Students are also offered professional opportunities outside of their modules, running youth theatres on Saturdays and during holidays, workshop assistants and running after school arts provisions in partner schools, some of which are voluntary opportunities and some are paid work. This is evidence of both behavioural and cognitive engagement; students want to be involved with extracurricular projects, demonstrating commitment to their learning and practice.

Throughout the programme students develop an eclectic practical skill base, they inform their practice through theory and are offered professional opportunities and a professional identity to support their transition into *"blended professionals"* which Whitchurch (2009:2) defines as *"individuals who draw their identity from both professional and academic domains."*

Craig's Placement Account

"*My most substantial benefit from the course has been my professional placement at the Play House. I was part of a schools tour of an interactive performance to primary schools in Birmingham and also developing and delivering a programme of in role workshops following the tour.*

I became a fully-fledged member of the company working with a director and two professional teacher actors and three other practitioners from our course. I felt able to contribute fully to the devising process feeling I was adequately equipped in terms of my skill base, my understanding of the devising process and knowledge of theatre and drama in education. My practice developed by being mentored by these professionals and working within their devising methodologies and rehearsal process. My repertoire of drama games and exercises increased, my facilitation skills developed, I learnt how to make drama more inclusive for those who English was an additional language or who had never experienced drama before.

During my placement we were invited back in to the School of Acting to perform the piece to second year students on our course and run the workshops with the first year students to enable us to share our work and receive tutor and peer feedback. The students were able to express artistic and pedagogical thoughts and opinions followed by a question and answer session regarding our professional placement process and experiences. Questions and discussion centred around the following topics, professionalism, devising performance for children and storytelling, interactive performance and participation, the application of performance for learning, engaging children through performance and project management.

Reflective note keeping was essential to my process, developing a process journal and writing an extensive reflection was fundamental to my development as a practitioner. Chapman & Ishaq, in this volume, echo the importance of keeping a journal when they discuss the use of what they refer to as a 'learning log', which they express to be imperative to the reflective progression of their students to professionals."

Third & public sector partnerships

We have also developed Third Sector and Public Sector Partnerships in response to community needs within Birmingham. We have been working with West Midlands Fire Service for the past three years developing an interactive life skills workshop programme at their Safety Centre, *Safeside*. Third year practitioners are in the Safety Centre for a full day a week working in role with young people in Key Stages 3 & 4 (11 -16 years) improving personal safety, decision making, managing risk and raising issues of behaviour, social or antisocial within the community. Rob Hattersley, Safeside's Education Co-ordinator feels this partnership is a valuable contribution to their work:

> *"Safeside's Lifeskills programme, which runs during term time for secondary pupils, is considerably enhanced by the involvement of Birmingham City University students who deliver interactive workshops in our realistic safety scenarios including a dark alleyway, a double decker bus and a court room. Our visitors learn a great deal about personal safety through engaging with the role play and discussion, delivered in such a professional and enjoyable way by the students."*

In 2011, we were funded by West Midlands Police to deliver a theatre in education project exploring hate crime and the August 2011 riots for a two week tour of schools in the Perry Barr Constituency in the West Midlands. This has led to us successfully applying for a larger funding bid in collaboration with Birmingham & Solihull's Women's Aid from Birmingham Community Safety Partnership to make and deliver a theatre in education piece, a film and workshops exploring girls' relationships to gangs. The new piece of work, 'She' will be performed to school audiences consisting of year ten girls (14-15 year olds) in Birmingham at The Drum Arts Centre over a period of three weeks, two performances a day. When delivering this work, practitioners not only engage in research but also receive specific training from the Third Sector partners; in this case Birmingham & Solihull's Women's Aid. This type of collaborative practice is essential for developing pedagogical content knowledge that enables practitioners *"to make ideas accessible to others."* (Shulman, 1987)

Recommendations

We have not answered all the questions posed in this chapter as they are presented to raise awareness and initiate further discussion and debate rather than to arrive at certainties in an ever evolving practice.

We will conclude by summarising the recommendations we have made within this chapter for enhanced student learning and engagement:

- The value of experiential learning through community engagement projects;

- Empowering the 'student' as a 'practitioner' and the 'class' as a 'professional company' has a positive impact on learning and engagement;

- The joint role of 'learner' and 'teacher / facilitator' gives the student the responsibility for the engagement of others;

- The importance of offering practitioners autonomy and choice over their learning and areas of specialism;

- The value of professional placements, extracurricular opportunities, and industry partners to provide practitioners with professional experience and pathways to employment;

- Students need to be supported to develop their practical skill base, academically stimulated with theory to inform their practice and offered professional opportunities and a professional identity to support their transition into blended professionals;

- The importance of offering emerging practitioners' space and opportunities to explore, develop and reflect on their own practice;

- The value of assessing the practitioner's own reflection and assessment of their project rather than assessing their actual work;

- An emphasis on making new work and innovative practice to engage students, audiences and participants.

Building learning communities and implementing innovative practice is essential to the development of higher education provision. This approach to learning and the development of the reflective applied performance practitioner is crucial to the development and the future of the relatively new and ever evolving applied performance practice.

About the authors

Hannah Phillips is the Programme Director of the BA (Hons) Applied Performance (Community and Education) programme at Birmingham City University and can be contacted at **Hannah.Phillips@bcu.ac.uk**

Tom Craig is in his final year of the BA (Hons) Applied Performance (Community and Education) programme at Birmingham City University and can be contacted at **tomcraigapplied@gmail.com**

Christie Phillips graduated from the BA (Hons) Community and Applied Dance Theatre programme at Birmingham City University in 2012 with a first class degree. Christie can be contacted at **christiephillips@live. co.uk**

Lightening Up the Dark Side: a Partnership Approach between a Students' Union and the University

Paul Chapman, Sarah Blatchford and Elgan Hughes

Introduction

Over the last decade the United Kingdom's (UK) Higher Education sector has witnessed an increased focus on student engagement and an emergent repositioning of student and staff relationships. This has resulted in substantial scrutiny of the complex nature of the student experience. As a consequence, a challenging dialogue was stimulated on the position of Birmingham City Students' Union (BCSU) within its changing university landscape. Alongside a series of student activities, which place students at the heart of the design and delivery of their education provision, BCSU and Birmingham City University (BCU) are on a journey of partnership development which mirrors the developing role of students within their own learning experience. The impact and benefits for all are substantial, characterised by an increased sense of engagement, a reinvigorated approach to staff and student involvement and new directions in the championing of the student voice within 'quality' systems (Brown, 2011). Through a reflective narrative account of the process, associated projects and the dialogue between parties, this chapter showcases the lessons learned from the generation of a learning community through partnership.

The relationship between a university and its students' union (SU) has always been an interesting dynamic but never before has the scrutiny been so widely debated and the potential for impact so great (Burns, 2012a). Embodied in the 1994 Education Act, the role of SUs in the United Kingdom (UK) is one of being the primary champion of the student voice and sole representative body of the student experience to their parent institution. This is a role that has long been held sacred by the SU movement. Over many years SUs have sought to protect and champion student interests, challenge policy and practice and hold universities to account, sometimes employing the tactics of student demonstrations, protests and campaigns (Grattan & Meakin, 2012). Back in the 1960s the National Union of Students (NUS) stated that involvement in student representation could make important contributions to not just a student's academic experience but also to wider society, an ethos that continues today.

In 2010 with a change of UK government, there was an increase in support for the political activity implied above, showing there is still a role for it at a national level. However in our more local context, the changing relationship between the Students' Union and the University has not been characterised by adversarial campaigning but has been one of action through partnership. We feel this form of change is synonymous with an evolution in the role of students themselves within universities, on campus and as part of their own learning experience within the learning community.

The definition of community takes many forms and is highly nuanced. Chapman and Ishaq (in this volume) offer definitions of communities which extend beyond the curriculum, engaging external stakeholders and when combined create a positive impact on the learning experience at a local level; Wenger (1994) describes communities of practice as 'social participation' with as wide a reach as possible.

For the purposes of this chapter we see the learning community as a development from a series of interventions including the changing nature of the role of the student, a closer relationship between staff and student (see Flint and Roden in this volume) and the increasing emphasis on students as producers of learning experiences as opposed to students as recipients of learning. We agree with Rush and Balamoutsou (2006) cited in Trowler (2010) who suggest that when students engage with a learning community, they are: "...*positive about their identity as a member of a group;*

focused on learning; ask questions in class; feel comfortable contributing to class discussions; spend time on campus; have made a few friends; and are motivated in some extra curricular activity".

Student engagement leading community development

The path to effective student engagement is not clear-cut (Solomonides *et al.*, 2012); in a period where student engagement can be said to be suddenly fashionable it can be argued that SUs have been engaging students proactively for decades to try to create positive change and foster values of democracy and leadership. Similarly, institutions would suggest that they too have been engaging students in a variety of ways to improve learning and enhance retention and progression through to graduation.

Defining student engagement is also, in itself, challenging. The Higher Education Academy (HEA 2012a) offers a model (Figure 1) of student engagement, showing individual dimensions within the overall spectrum of student engagement and thus demonstrating the difficulty in providing an absolute definition.

The UK's approach to student engagement has tended to be defined by projects localised in scope focusing on only certain dimensions within the learning experience, whereas the wider, international definition of student engagement is a theoretical concept in its own right, broad in scope and influencing of high-level strategy (Trowler, 2010). That said, student engagement, and thus the role of SUs, has become more prominent within the wider UK HE sector over the last few years. National bodies such as the Higher Education Funding Council for England

Figure 1: Dimensions of student engagement (taken from HEA, 2012a)

(HEFCE), the HEA, the Quality Assurance Agency (QAA) and the National Union of Students (NUS) have all instigated reports and projects on student engagement and have documented the move to more partnership working between SUs and universities.

This move has occurred against a backdrop of higher tuition fees suggesting an increase in personal financial investment and an increase in students' expectation of their university experience (Van der Velden, 2012). For the purpose of this chapter we use, as a frame of reference, three dimensions of student engagement: the impact on the individual learner; the design and delivery of the curriculum and student involvement in university quality systems. Buckley (2012) summarises the contrast between these dimensions of student engagement as being between pedagogy and politics. That is, the impact on the individual and learning development alongside a need for students to be empowered in the critique of the learning experience. In essence, a true community includes all facets of student engagement as both inputs and as outcomes (Trowler, 2010).

In 2009, the Centre for Higher Education Research and Information (CHERI) highlighted a difference in the approach to student engagement between universities and SUs. The report said that universities focused on the 'consumer' role of students – a view that contrasted with that of SUs who were more concerned with developing a community of learners (Little *et al.*, 2009). The report went further; stating that a defined 'model' of learning community was not evident. Nonetheless it supported a move away from the one way, transactional approach between students and their universities to ways of working that lead to the fostering of a fuller involvement in the wider learning experience.

Compared to the wider sector, the debate at BCU was less differentiated with both the SU and the University looking to broaden their student engagement activity. There was a deliberate approach by the institution's (then titled) Director of Learning and Teaching to the SU to discuss opportunities for collaboration. This approach led to the Student Academic Partners Scheme (SAPS). This was the catalyst for our ongoing approach and as a consequence of these conversations the then President of BCSU detailed the changing nature of the role of students and set out a strategic vision for the development of a learning community in an internal publication:

"[The] vision is to create a learning community at Birmingham City University, whereby students work in close collaboration with academic and support staff to enhance their learning experience…as well as providing new avenues of capturing student opinion and feedback." (BCU, 2009)

This change of direction with new emphasis on partnership, collaboration and mutual working was a strong public statement of intent. It has been expressed from some quarters, that moving closer to the university, from the perspective of the SU, is (in colloquial terms) a move to the 'dark side' and by association a negative move. Of course, this move impacted on BCSU through both practical and policy terms in ways that may challenge those who hold certain views but it has also afforded involvement in an arena in which students, and by association BCSU, are supported to become proactively involved in design and delivery of their own learning experience.

For many years SUs have been championing the quality of the academic experience of students via student representation and other quality assurance routes. They have also supported student involvement in wider learning opportunities that lay outside of the curriculum such as participation in sports, societies and volunteering programmes. However, a move to a role that proactively enhances the quality of learning and teaching through formal academic partnership projects with the university was innovative for BCSU and the sector. This created a significant strategic change for BCSU as historically, extracurricular activities within SUs have focussed on building social networks and have been located within a personal development agenda (Burns, 2012b). However, this shift towards being involved in the development of learning and teaching created a raft of new engagement opportunities for students This included the new academic manifesto (BCUSU, 2012) which built on the personal impact previously offered as well as enhancing the quality of the overall learning experience.

Narrowing the gap

Debates between unions and universities can result in a reaffirming of the traditional 'them and us' position (Grattan & Meakin, 2012), defended by structures and memorandums, which can often lead to stalemate and political 'toing and froing' (Bell *et al.*, 2006). The emergence of a collaborative approach, adopted by BCSU and BCU, is now becoming more common and seen in much more of a positive light (Greatrix, 2012). Despite this approach becoming perceived more widely as good practice, the debate continues within the SU movement itself as it looks at the implications of partnership and collaboration. What does an SU put at risk by working more closely with their institution? What does the SU potentially gain by so doing? Which paradigm offers more value?

Some resistance to a partnership model was encountered early on in our journey, both at an individual level and at an organisational level. Staff who were used to working at arm's length with the University were not necessarily resistant to change per se, yet concerns were raised that a closer working relationship with the University could result in the University attempting to dominate the relationship with its own agenda and unduly influence the SU to the detriment of the student experience. This would be particularly important if the SU felt pressure to frame future developments or strategic plans in such a way as to align itself with University priorities rather than its own or those of the students. Some queried whether there was a risk of loss of ability to be critical of the University or a lessening of an ability to oppose the University standpoint on issues. As most staff would not be involved in the strategic decision to work more closely with the University, crucial to gaining buy-in would be clarity as to how it would benefit students and effective dissemination of the rationale for the decision to change approach.

Whilst, the level of independence felt by a Union is not necessarily linked to formal governance structures and may be more determined by personalities and/or historical attitudes (Bell *et al.*, 2006); from an organisational perspective, a change in relationship may necessitate a re-examination of value sets or even a constitutional shift. For others, concern for the reputational impact brought about by such a move within the union sector may hamper closer working.

Concerns were also raised from the University's perspective from those staff whose only understanding of the SU was based on their own student experience, when the focus was more on cheap alcohol and social events, or through having had a poor experience with the SU previously, or judging the SU as not professional enough to be involved in academic issues.

Perhaps a more useful question to ask would be whether this is actually a new relationship or rather just a development of a relationship between individual unions and universities that was already there. By seeing it as merely a development of an existing relationship (to benefit students) a union could still place itself firmly within the traditions of the SU movement, whilst accepting that the narrowing of the gap between itself and the University should engender more opportunities to influence and effect change in a more coherent way and across a wider sphere. From BCSU's perspective it is still crucial that we are able to say no to the University, when necessary; when we think a decision the University has made is not in the best interests of our students. However, it could be that with the development of this relationship and a shared understanding of our objectives the need to say no won't arise as often. The approach taken by BCU and BCSU has been recognised as an example for others to follow evidenced by the HEA instigating the inaugural 'Students as Partners' Change Academy initiative following conversations with BCU, whose staff are incorporated into the initiative as external consultants (detailed below).

Building on the student voice

A key feature of this debate is the growing need to relax the previously commonly held view that SUs hold the monopoly on student engagement, the student community and thus the student voice. Recent work by the QAA and NUS states that the best results within the agenda of student engagement leading to a positive impact on students occur through collaboration to empower students to be shapers of their own learning experience (Flint & Roden in this volume; NUS & QAA, 2012a)

At the beginning of our partnership journey it was clear that local good practice in student engagement was commonplace outside of the boundaries of SU activity such as the Bartholomew *et al.* (2010). More telling was that this occurred outside of the core values and functions of the BCSU, namely: representation, democracy and the facilitations of student activities. The question therefore arises: Could BCSU be a credible student body if not involved in each and every one of these dialogues between staff and student cohorts and the institution?

The increased tuition fee structure recently put in place in England, places a new dynamic between students and universities, with a focus on students receiving a better experience from all aspects of their university life, including more transparent expectation-setting via student charters and agreements (Van der Velden, 2012). Although this notion is not uncontested (see Warmington *et al.* in this volume), an effective response to these new expectations may require an SU that is more accessible and more flexible in engaging with its students.

If this premise is correct it will create the need within SUs to be swifter and more responsive to the student voice. This suggests a need for new ways in which to capture, articulate and feed back on this voice at all times (see Rowe *et al.*, in this volume). The role of students in matters relating to academic quality is becoming more apparent (Brown, 2011) and student engagement in its own right is becoming a dimension of the quality process variable (Gibbs, 2010). Students offer a crucial role as a key participant in curriculum design, a resource for delivery, and as a source of feedback about academic quality along with a host of more defined roles specific to pedagogic development (Bovill *et al.*, 2011; Wilson, 2012). Ultimately students, whatever the role they adopt, become *"integral to the success of the higher education endeavour"* (Thomas, 2012:23).

Much of this activity sits outside the normal role of a SU whereby we have traditionally defined the student experience as being a combination of out of classroom activity alongside academic compliance. As the term 'enhancing the student experience' became commonplace, it was clear through our involvement in activities such as SAPS that the reach of the SU should extend into more specific activities. It was essential that these developed a student's learning experience by placing the students at the heart of their learning and within a learning community.

Furthermore, BCSU has continued to develop this line of thinking by instigating a major project as part of the HEA's Change Academy Initiative 'Students as Partners' (HEA, 2012b) mapping out the true extent of the student voice and the relationship and interactions between BCU/staff and BCSU/students and formulating new ways of maximising the student voice so as to influence change within the University. The Student Advisory Board employing students within the feedback process is an example of this new form of intervention (Rowe *et al.*, in this volume).

This shift to a strategic partnership with the university can be a challenging move for a SU to make as it implies a loosening of the strongly held values of independence and autonomy and a move away from the protected views on formal student representation and democracy based within the 1994 Education Act. A move towards partnership brings with it a fear of dilution of this strategic intent alongside traditional SU values. Van der Velden (2012:5) identifies this as a 'struggle' between the "*adversarial watchdog on behalf of students and a collaborative approach which involves taking a seat at the table where all future planning of the student experience will take place*". However, at BCU, this new partnership approach has brought benefits, both measurable and substantial through a variety of activities and projects summarised later in this chapter in Table 1.

Students as agents of change

BCSU's journey has created a change in approach to working alongside formal structures and by so doing has facilitated students as true agents of change, which in turn has led to a significant shift in culture. For the SU, when the influence and impact of students in the university processes became significant enough (for the institution) that involving them became the norm we realised that we would not wish to revert to a more 'traditional' working relationship.

This significant impact included projects instigated with students as co-creators and key members of project teams; for example, the University's approach to designing a Student Charter was to employ a student as project lead, based in the SU, with a team of students to develop it. Student and Graduate Interns were employed in both BCU and BCSU following a strategic initiative to employ students across the university whenever possible (see Chambers & Nagle in this volume). This fundamental shift in the role of the student within the SU and the University has resulted in a change in the mindset of staff and students as to the nature and function of the student in BCU life.

Our partnership approach

The students as partners approach to developing this new state of mind was founded upon a set of building blocks:

Shared vision

Based on findings from a variety of surveys and feedback tools it was clear that both the University and the SU needed to increase the sense of belonging and attachment by students towards both organisations. With the need by both parties to fare well in the national benchmarking tool, the National Student Survey (NSS), the concept of 'Generating the Learning Community' was employed. This vision aimed to create a learning community within the University where students were proud to study here and had an enhanced sense of belonging. This was to be achieved by greater student participation and employment in all aspects of the University and SU work.

Building on success

BCSU and BCU have worked together before on many initiatives such as the Student Learning and Teaching Network (SLTN, 2012) yet the extent to which the two parties are now designing and delivering projects together is unprecedented. Previously the Centre for Excellence in Teaching and Learning (CETL), a HEFCE funded initiative, resourced a staff member based in the SU as well funding other projects. Today's partnership is affirmed by the 50% secondment of a senior post within the SU's engagement team to work within both areas with a much greater level of resourcing and financial commitment towards joint projects.

Planning for success

Naturally, as the range of activity has widened and the notion of partnership increased, the need for a more robust planning model has been necessary. Agreeing shared benefits and risks of projects, often through contractual arrangements, has been useful in ensuring parity and transparency in approach as well as creating buy in by others; and maintaining effective open dialogues between senior management within both BCU and BCUSU and student executive officer positions within BCUSU has been essential.

A blueprint for the future

These steps to working in partnership have created a blueprint for development of a broader range of activities, jointly designed and often co-delivered by students. This has the potential for students to maximise their experience at BCU. The partnership provides a framework in which discussions; pilot projects and initiatives can be fostered and developed by both parties. From this approach, an umbrella brand has been developed called 'OpportUNIty' which places students at the heart of the University in many areas through direct employment, academic partnership projects, academic mentoring programmes and student representative roles.

OpportUNIty was born from the same fundamental principles the partnership initially wanted to create within the learning community: students and staff working together, students benefiting by being involved in their learning experience and students becoming more involved within the structures of the university.

What works?

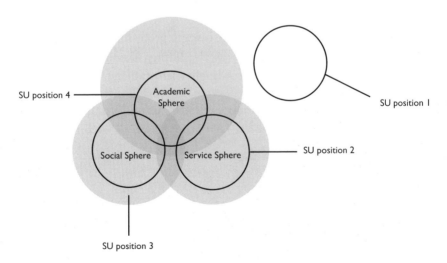

Figure 2: Adapted from the 'What Works' spheres supporting student engagement (taken from Thomas, 2012:15)

Our approach resonates with recent work by the HEA around student 'belonging' and its relationship to retention and progression that suggests there are three spheres that underpin a move towards effective student engagement. One of these, the academic sphere, fosters deeper, more effective interventions with the university. Traditionally the SU's role in this sphere may only have stretched to student representation on committees or via specific one-off projects or campaigns. By default, the SU has a major role within the other, social building and service, spheres yet having a deeper role within the academic sphere affords the students' union a greater range of meaningful engagement with students and vice-versa as a by-product of their attachment to the university. Figure 2 demonstrates the four positions that SUs may adopt within this model and from each position the ability to engage with the university community is different. We believe that BCSU is moving to establish a strong foothold in position 4 through our partnership activity with both students and the University.

SU position 1 – The SU is completely separate from the university as a truly independent organisation and acts alone with a 'watchdog' oversight role, instigating engagement with staff and students from outside in.

SU position 2 – The SU is within the central, professional service sphere alongside other departments such as the library, student services and academic support and engages accordingly with students.

SU position 3 – The SU solely support social networks and community building outside of the classroom regulating academic quality through student representation structures

SU position 4 – The SU engages at the heart of the university and learning experience, forging links with every aspect of the university in particular, at school, faculty and academic level through partnership activity

As cited as a case study in the recent report on understanding the barriers to student engagement (NUS & QAA 2012b:11), our partnership can be explained in three statements;

1. Equal partnership and collaboration between students and staff members contributing to the 'learning experience';

2. Students being integral to the design and delivery of learning interventions, pedagogic projects and student involvement opportunities;

3. The intended and unintended outcomes of student and staff interactions support and develop a holistic learning community.

Partnership into practice: the changing role of the student

Trowler (2010) together with reports from the NUS and QAA all show the range of roles and the great impact students now have within their learning experience. Research by the NUS and the QAA states that nearly 60% of students want to be more involved in the design of their own education compared with less than 30% of students who feel as if they are engaged in this process (Burns, 2012c). At Birmingham City we have been explicit in the planning and involvement of students, adopting several different roles within student engagement activity. The benefit of engaging students in a wider variety of educational roles and opportunities has both personal academic impacts on the individual as well as supporting the broader development of the learning community.

The continuing growth in student activity and the emerging role of students can be seen in Table 1 and how this links with the 'Students As Change Agents' model (Dunne and Zandstra, 2011) is demonstrated in Figure 3.

Traditional Role of Student	New Engagement Activity	Emergent Role of Student
Recipient of knowledge	Student Academic Partner in a SAPS project	Co-creator of learning experience alongside staff partner
Passive role in understanding good teaching	'Extra Mile' Student Led Teaching Awards See Andrews *et al.* & Flint and Rodin (in this volume)	Active participation in recognising good teaching and helping to shape it

Traditional Role of Student	New Engagement Activity	Emergent Role of Student
Student engagement through employment is defined, structured and happens at set points throughout the year	OpportUNIty: Student Jobs on Campus including Student and Graduate interns and Student Liaison Officers	Student engagement through employment occurs constantly and is organic

See Chambers & Nagle and Rowe *et al.* (in this volume) |
| Are part of an formal, structured and inflexible representative process | Student & Faculty Representatives | Are integral to the representative scheme, which is flexible, fit for purpose. Students interact with the university at all levels

See Rowe *et al.* (in this volume) |
Students raise issues to the SU who has a monopoly on the student voice and student feedback	Higher Education Academy Students as Partners Team looking at the student voice	SUs no longer have that monopoly but facilitate and support a fuller range of consultations with students at the heart
Student involvement is supported by the SU; 'we don't trust' the University working with students like this	Student Partnership Agreement (Student Charter) developed by staff and students	The university needs to work with students in this way within the modern HE landscape alongside the SU
Students have enough to do with their 'learning' hat on never mind their 'partner' or 'employee' hat	Student Academic Mentors	Students always have and will need to demonstrate an ability to wear different hats in the future, why shouldn't they practise now?
The SU has mainly represented what students feel is wrong with the university and the teaching / experience they receive	Students' Union Academic Manifesto	The SU is now opening up conversations with the university to develop specific aspects of learning and teaching by putting students as part if the solution
Student engagement happens within specific disciplines and set by teachers	OpportUNIty: cross faculty Collaborative Projects	Students can engage with activities and learning from multiple disciplines and design their own learning experience outside of their normal sphere of university life

Table 1: The role of the student within student engagement activity

This development of the roles available to students within a variety of contexts can be further developed as shown in figure 3 which illustrates how students are integrated into change processes at the University of Exeter in their 'Students as Change Agents' programme (Kay *et al.*, 2012). This details the opportunities for students to move from a 'passive' role within their learning experience into a much more proactive leadership role, of which they can design and deliver change within the institution.

Furthermore, the role of the student is evolving from low impact involvement through to becoming fully in control (Bovill & Bulley, 2011, Bovill et al., 2011) and by doing so, both BCSU and BCU have benefited along with the student. By practising what we preach, through collaboration, BCU has engaged students in quality enhancement activity, pedagogic design and delivery as well as increasing the interaction and relationships between staff and students. BCSU has widened its involvement and association with activities not fully explored before, as well as diversifying the range of ways to capture the student voice and enhance student representation - again exemplified in the HEA Change Academy, Students as Partners initiative (HEA 2012b). Through this process we have identified what we think are the key areas we need to focus on to give the range of students as partners activity the best chance of permeating through the whole of the University and through this, we have adopted a framework of the 5Ps:

+ **Philosophy** – can we create an ethos to share and influence others?

+ **People** – who are the key stakeholders in this process?

+ **Policy/Processes** – What policies and processes are supportive / prohibitive or need to be created or change?

+ **Pilots** – what are our key priorities to address and trial?

+ **Plan** – how are we going to do this?

In an approach to weave students and by association the SU, into the fabric of the university, our location within the academic sphere within Figure 1 is becoming cemented further through a broader range of student activity with a more diverse range of student roles (Figure 3); this is done with a view to create the community of learners we originally intended, together with all the direct and indirect benefits this brings.

The benefit to the Students' Union and University

The wider benefits of a partnership approach have been detailed in the recent NUS manifesto for partnership (Wenstone, 2012). Mirroring this, we feel the impact on students, staff and the university life at BCU is dramatic as a result of the partnership approach we have adopted and the relationships we endeavour to foster between staff and students. The most recent survey undertaken with students involved in the third iteration of our flagship Student Academic Partners scheme shows that nearly 90% of students had a positive response when asked if they felt part of a partnership with their staff counterparts and nearly 90% of students had a positive response in relation to feeling part of the learning community, with 60% of students saying they felt closer to the University. One student summed their experience up as;

> *"[it] felt good to actually be part of the university, not just as a student. Being involved in trying to improve things for students (best methods of assessment, improving employment focus). Very rewarding to be able to discuss issues with lecturers and staff as an equal - both trying to improve things."*

The impact of this new student engagement agenda has influenced key policy and strategic documents within both BCU and BCSU. The BCU corporate plan 2011-16 now includes references to the partnership and states as a key driver to continue the 'engagement of students as active partners in the development of their learning experience'. It also documents the goal 'to be an exemplar for student engagement, working in partnership with students to create and deliver an excellent university experience and achieve high levels of student satisfaction and graduate employment'. At the time of writing, and before the conclusion of the application process, the (2012) SAP Scheme had received over 70 project applications for funding as well as 29 applications under the Student Academic Mentoring Programme and 29 applications for Collaborative Projects with a combined value of over £250,000.

The BCSU new strategic plan 2012-15 includes themes of becoming more relevant and easier to engage with by removing barriers for

EMPHASIS ON THE STUDENT VOICE

STUDENTS AS EVALUATORS OF THEIR EXPERIENCE (THE STUDENT VOICE)

Students off feedback, views and opinions and are listened to on an institutional basis, in order to build an evidence-base as a basis for enhancement and change. Decisions for action tend to be taken at subject and/or institutional level.

BCSU Examples:

- Extra Mile Teaching Awards
- Formal and Informal Student Voice Activity
- Students engaged in 'Quality systems
- Academic Manifesto

STUDENTS AS PARTICIPANTS IN DECISION MAKING PROCESSES

Students engage in institutional decision-making, in order to influence enhancement and change. Decisions for action tend to be taken collaboratively with staff and students.

BCSU Examples:

- Student Representatives
- Student Advisory Boards
- Student Councils
- Student Partnership Agreement

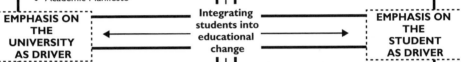

EMPHASIS ON THE UNIVERSITY AS DRIVER

Integrating students into educational change

EMPHASIS ON THE STUDENT AS DRIVER

STUDENTS AS PARTNERS, CO-CREATORS AND EXPERTS

Students are collaborative partners in curriculum provision and professiona development, in order to enhance staff and student learning. Decisions for action tend to be taken at subject and/or institutional level.

BCSU Examples:

- Student Academic Partner Projects
- Opportunity Collaborative Projects
- Student and Graduate Interns
- Student Academic Mentors

STUDENTS AS AGENTS FOR CHANGE

Students are collaborative partners in pedagogic knowledge aquisition and professional development, with the purpose of bringing about change. Decisions for action tend to be promoted by students and engaged with at subject and/or institutional level.

BCSU Examples:

- Student Academic Partner Projects
- Opportunity Collaborative Projects
- Academic Manifesto

EMPHASIS ON STUDENT ENGAGEMENT

Figure 3: BCSU Activities mapped against a theoretical model for students as change agents (taken from Dunne & Zandstra 2011:17)

involvement as well as creating a greater sense of belonging. BCSU also aims to diversify its menu of opportunity for students. It has an aim to become involved in their university life away from traditional sports and societies; looking at new engagements through volunteering, in the curricula and beyond.

BCSU also aims to impact on every student at BCU. With the challenge of having an impact in relation to over 24,000 individual definitions and expectations of a positive student experience, our approach of partnership and collaboration can help to ensure that these experiences are real, relevant and personal. At its best, it is the feeling that what we are doing actually is playing an important part in a student's time at university, the fact that people in the University contact us to get involved in things; they see us as integral to the whole student experience, or at least able to have an impact on it.

Conclusion

The full extent of the relationship between BCSU and the BCU is hard to define within the confines of this chapter. In the realities of a busy world many of these interactions and developments were both strategic and opportunistic, as leaders in both organisations saw the chance for projects and alliances that could benefit the student experience at that time within a changing HE landscape. Through our initial success, this has been built upon with new ideas and initiatives that have been instrumental in changing the culture of both organisations and as such, have impacted on both students and staff.

The creation of shared understandings and a common language between the different organisations was a significant step in the development of this collaboration and through it, a wider selection of staff members have been brought on board. This vision gained further recognition and momentum through winning the Times Higher Education (THE) Award in 2010 for 'Outstanding Support for Students' for the work undertaken through the Student Academic Partners scheme. The philosophy of partnership between staff and students as well as BCU and BCSU were significant within the award nomination and this provided a key springboard for further activity. The success of that first project and the THE award demonstrated that the partnership worked.

This recognition also demonstrated that BCSU was a key partner on campus and able to deliver within areas previously seemed to be on the periphery or within heavily prescribed parameters. Walls that had traditionally prohibited activity through separatism are being removed and doors that had previously been shut or only open at clearly defined points in the year are becoming increasingly irrelevant. Of course, our approach isn't perfect and obstacles do arise and with it the need to revisit the guiding roles and remit of each organisation. Yet, through a very recent history of shared understanding, success and on-going communication, the starting point of working together to a solution is quicker to instigate, easier to find and will, in the main, include students.

In defining our journey it is useful to ask 'what came first?' Was it the changing role of the student, around which we simply evolved? Was it the discussion and application of the learning community? Was it the concept of working closely together with students and staff, through which projects that simply fell into place within the opportunities created? Both parties were very clear that in the beginning we wanted to create a learning community and what followed is an organic process towards embedding effective and meaningful student engagement.

Student engagement at BCU encourages students to be partners and proactive change agents, to share their ideas of learning and teaching as they seek to enhance learning opportunities that are supported throughout the whole student journey. We believe student engagement is a mindset, a culture that is adopted through collaboration rather than merely a series of projects, initiatives or piecemeal reactions to poor satisfaction scores in surveys. This partnership, and the benefits it brings, is demonstrable in the relationship between BCU and BCSU.

About the authors

Paul Chapman is the Head of Engagement at Birmingham City Students' Union. He is partly seconded to the University's Centre for Enhancement of Learning and Teaching. He can be contacted at **paul.chapman@bcu.ac.uk**

Sarah Blatchford is the Representation Coordinator at Birmingham City Students' Union. She can be contacted at **sarah.blatchford@bcu.ac.uk**

Elgan Hughes is the current President of Birmingham City Students' Union 2012/13 and was Vice President Campus Engagement 2011/12 He can be contacted at **union.president@bcu.ac.uk**

Collected Bibliography

1994 Group (2009). *Beyond the Curriculum: Opportunities to Enhance Employability and Future Life Choices.* Policy Report. November 2009. London: 1994 Group.

Ahfeldt, S., S. Mehta & T. Sellnow (2005). Measurement and analysis of students' engagement in university classes where varying levels of PBL methods of instruction are in use. *Higher Education Research and Development,* Vol. 24, No. 1, pp. 5-20.

Allan, J. (1996). Learning outcomes in higher education. *Studies in Higher Education,* Vol. 21, No. 1, pp. 93-108.

Allen, D. E., R. S. Donham & S. A. Bernhardt (2011). Problem-based learning. *New Directions for Teaching and Learning,* Vol. 2011, No. 128, pp. 21-29.

Argyris, C. & D. A. Schön (1996). *Organisational Learning 11: Theory, Method, and Practice.* Massachusetts: Addison Wesley.

Arnstein, S. (1969). A ladder of citizen participation in the USA. *Journal of the American Institute of Planners,* Vol. 35, No. 4, pp. 216-224.

Ashton, D. (2010). 'You just end up feeling more professional': Media production and industry-ready personhood. *Networks,* Vol. 10, pp. 14-19.

Ashton, D. (2011). Media work and the creative industries: Identity work, professionalism and employability. *Education and Training,* Vol. 53, No. 6, pp. 546–560.

Audit Commission (1998). *A fruitful partnership: effective partnership working.* Oxfordshire: Audit Commission.

AUSSE (2009). *Engaging Students for Success, Australasian Student Engagement Report.* Australasian Survey of Student Engagement, Australian Council for Educational Research.

Austin, M. & S. Hatt (2005). The Messengers are the Message: A Study of the Effects of Employing Higher Education Student Ambassadors to Work with School Students. *Journal of Widening Participation and Lifelong Learning*, Vol. 7, No. 1, pp. 1-8.

Balkindi, P. & D. A. Harrison (2006). "Ties, leaders and time in teams": Strong inference about network structure's effects on team viability. *Academy of Management Journal*, Vol. 49, pp. 49-68.

Ball, R., T. Forbes, M. Parris & L. Forsyth (2010). The evaluation of partnership working in the delivery of health and social care. *Public Policy and Administration*, Vol. 23, No. 3, pp. 387- 407.

Bartholomew, P. & N. Bartholomew (2011). Learning through Innovation. In Nygaard, C., N. Courtney & C. Holtham (Eds.) *Beyond Transmission: Innovations in University Teaching*. Faringdon, Oxfordshire: Libri Publishing Ltd., pp. 99-116.

Bartholomew P., S. Brand, & D. Cassidy (2010). Distributed Approaches to Promote Stakeholder Ownership of Postgraduate Programme Design. In Nygaard, C., L. Frick & N. Courtney (Eds.) *Postgraduate Education – Form and Function*. Faringdon, Oxfordshire: Libri Publishing Ltd., pp. 59-76.

Bartholomew, P., S. Brand & L. Millard (2009). Developing a Coordinated Strategy to both Encourage Innovation and Improve Students' Learning Outcomes. *Improving Students' Learning Outcomes*. Frederiksberg: Copenhagen Business School Press, pp. 81-96.

Baumeister, R. F. & M. R. Leary (1995). The need to belong: Desire for interpersonal attachments as a fundamental human motivation. *Psychological Bulletin*, Vol. 117, pp. 497–529.

BCU (2009). *Connect: June*. Internal communication publication. Birmingham City University.

BCUSU (2011). Twelve Points to Improve Your Course. *Spotlight on Students' Union Excellence – The Campaigns Edition*. October, pp. 41-42 National Union of Students.

Beard, R. M. & I. J. Senior (1980). *Motivating Students*. Boston, MA: Routledge and Kegan Paul.

Belbin, R. (2010). *Team Roles at Work*. Oxford: Butterworth-Heinemann.

Bell, T., P. Greatrix & C. Horton (2006). Universities and their Unions, The Future Relationship between Universities and Students' Unions. The University of Warwick. http://oxcheps.new.ox.ac.uk/MainSite%20pages/Resources/OxCHEPS_OP28.pdf [Accessed 12 February 2013].

Belluigi, D. (2010). Creating the Conditions for Creativity: Looking at Assessment in Fine Art Studio Practice. In Nygaard, C., N. Courtney

& C. Holtham (Eds.) (2010) *Teaching Creativity – Creativity in Teaching.* Faringdon, Oxfordshire: Libri Publishing Ltd., pp. 47-64.

Bembenutty, H. (2011). New directions for self-regulation of Learning in postsecondary education. *New Directions for Teaching and Learning*, Vol. 126, pp. 117-124.

Biggs, J. (1987). *Student Approaches to Learning and Studying.* Hawthorne: Australian Council for Educational Research.

Biggs, J. & C. Tang (2007). *Teaching for Quality Learning at University.* Maidenhead: Open University Press.

Birmingham City University (2010b). Graduate Destinations Summary Report 2009/10 – For students who left the university in the 2009/10 academic period Birmingham. http://www.bcu.ac.uk/student-info/careers-and-job-prospects/graduate-destinations [Accessed 13 February 2013].

Birmingham City University & Birmingham City Students Union (2010a). Creating the Learning Community through Student Academic Partners. http://www2.bcu.ac.uk/docs/media/celt/SAP_Brochure_Spreads.pdf [Accessed 13 February 2013].

Birmingham City Students' Union (2012). *Student Academic Partners* http://www.bcusu.com/learning/saps/ [Accessed 20 October 2012].

Bishop, D., K. Crawford, N. Liddle, E. Russell & N. Jenner (2012). *Engaging academics and students within subject committee meetings.* Presentation at RAISE Conference, Southampton, September 14. http://raise-network.ning.com/page/resources-from-2012 [Accessed 15 October 2012].

Black, G. (2005). *The Engaging Museum: Developing Museums for Visitor Involvement.* London: Routledge.

Blair, A. (2005). Online learning: its implications for deep learning, assessment and retention, Coventry University. http://www.heacademy.ac.uk/assets/documents/subjects/csap/Online_learning_its_implications_for_deep_learning_assessment_and_retention.pdf [Accessed 28 August 2012].

Blease-Dudley, J. (2011). Liverpool Students' Union Teaching Awards. *Is there a public interest in higher education? QAA Annual Conference.* University of Nottingham. 30 June 2011.

Boal, A. (1979, 2000, 2008). *Theatre of the Oppressed.* London: Pluto Press.

Bovill, C. & C. J. Bulley (2011). A model of active student participation in curriculum design: exploring desirability and possibility. In Rust, C. *Improving Student Learning (18) Global theories and local practices: institutional, disciplinary and cultural variations.* Oxford: The Oxford Centre for Staff and Educational Development, pp. 176- 188.

Bovill, C., A. Cook-Sather & P. Felton (2011). Students as co-creators of teaching approaches, course design, and curricula: implications for academic developers. *International Journal for Academic Development*, Vol. 16, No. 2, pp. 133-145.

Boyd, D. M. & N. B. Ellison (2007). Social Network Sites: Definition, History, and Scholarship. *Journal of Computer-Mediated Communication*, Vol. 13, No. 1, pp. 210-230.

Brennan, J. & T. Shah (2011). *Higher education and society in changing times: Looking back and looking forward*. Centre for Higher Education Research and Information. Milton Keynes: Open University Press.

Brown, S. (2011). Foreword. In Nygaard, C., N. Courtney & C. Holtham (Eds.) *Beyond Transmission-Innovations in University Teaching*. Faringdon, Oxfordshire: Libri Publishing Ltd., pp. ix-x.

Brown, S., S. Armstrong & G. Thompson (Eds.) (1998). *Motivating Students – Staff and Educational Development Series*. London: Kogan Page.

Bryson, C. & C. Hardy (2010). *Why does student engagement matter?* London: National Union of Students.

Bryson, C., C. Hardy & L. Hand (2009). *An in-depth investigation of students' engagement throughout their first year in university*. The UK national Transition Conference April 2009. Permission sought from author 28th Aug 2012.

Buckley, A. (2012). Pedagogy or Politics Conference presentation at RAISE Conference September 2012 http://raise-network.ning.com/page/resources-from-2012 [Accessed 18 October 2012].

Burns, L. (2012a). Real power for students. *Spotlight on Students' Union Excellence*. January, pp. 7 National Union of Students.

Burns, L. (2012b). Creating opportunities for all students. *Spotlight on Students' Union Excellence - Employability*. March, pp. 7 National Union of Students.

Burns, L. (2012c). Working together to drive change. *Spotlight on Students' Union Excellence*. April, pp. 7 National Union of Students.

Carini, R. M., G. D. Kuh & S. P. Klein (2006). Student engagement and student learning: Testing the linkages. *Research in Higher Education*, Vol. 47, No. 1, pp. 1-32.

Carlson, M. (1993). *Theories of the Theatre: A historical and critical survey, from the Greeks to the present*. London: Cornell University Press.

Carroll, J. (2005). Strategies for becoming more explicit. In: Carroll, J. & J. Ryan (Eds.) *Teaching International Students*. Abingdon: Routledge, pp. 26-34.

Chapman, D. (2009). Knowing our Places? Contexts and Edges in Integrating Disciplines in Built Environment Education. *Journal for Education in the Built Environment*, Vol. 4, No. 2, pp. 9-28. ISSN: 1747-4205 (Online).

Chickering, A. W. & Z. F. Gamson (1987). Seven principles for good practice in undergraduate education. *American Association of Higher Education Bulletin*, Vol. 39, No. 7, pp. 3-7.

Coates, H. (2005). The Value of Student Engagement for Higher Education Quality Assurance. *Quality in Higher Education*, Vol. 11, No. 1, pp. 25-36.

Coates, H. (2007). A Model of Online and General Campus-Based Student Engagement. *Assessment and Evaluation in Higher Education*, Vol. 32, No. 2, pp. 121-141.

Coates, H. (2010). Development of the Australasian Survey of Student Engagement (AUSSE). *Higher Education*, Vol. 60, No. 1, pp. 1-17.

Collins, K. & R. Ison (2006). Dare we jump off Arnstein's Ladder? Social learning as a new policy paradigm. In: *Proceedings of PATH (Participatory Approaches in Science & Technology) Conference*, 4-7 June 2006, Edinburgh.

Copper, A. (2012). Enhancing Employability through Media Industry Outreach and Knowledge Transfer. *Bridging the Gap*. Conference. Bournemouth: Executive Business Centre. 12-13 September 2012.

Corfield, T. (2011). The Best of Bristol. *Is there a public interest in higher education? QAA Annual Conference.* University of Nottingham. 30 June 2011.

Costa, A. & B. Kallick (1993). Through the Lens of a Critical Friend. *Educational Leadership*, Vol. 51, No. 2, pp. 49-51.

Cottrell, S. (2010). Personal Records: Recording Reflection and Achievement. In Cottrell S. *Skills for Success: The Personal Development Planning Handbook*. York: The Higher Education Academy, pp. 217-228.

Cranton, P. (2006). *Understanding and Promoting Transformative Learning*. San Francisco: Jossey-Bass.

Davis, B., D. Sumara & R. Luce-Capler (2000). *Engaging Minds – Learning and Teaching in a Complex World*. New Jersey: Lawrence Erlbaum Associates.

Dewey, J. (1974). *John Dewey on Education: Selected Writings*. Archambault, R. D. (Ed.) Chicago: University of Chicago Press.

Dillenbourg, P. (Ed.) (1999). *Collaborative-learning: Cognitive and Computational Approaches*. Oxford: Elsevier.

Dillenbourg, P., M. Baker, A. Blaye & C. O'Malley (1996). The evolution of research on collaborative learning. In Spada, P. & P. Reiman (Eds.)

Learning in Humans and machines: Towards an interdisciplinary learning science. Oxford: Elsevier, pp. 189-211.

Dineen, R., E. Samuel & K. Livesey (2005). The promotion of creativity in learners: theory and practice. *Art, Design & Communication in Higher Education*, Vol. 4, No. 3, pp. 155-72.

Dobozy, E. (2011). Resisting Student Consumers and Assisting Student Producers. In Nygaard, C., N. Courtney & C. Holtham (Eds.) *Beyond Transmission-Innovations in University Teaching.* Faringdon, Oxfordshire: Libri Publishing Ltd., pp. 11-25.

Duch, B. J., D. E. Allen & H. B. White (1997-1998). Problem-based learning: Preparing students to succeed in the 21st century. *Essays on Teaching Excellence: Toward the Best in the Academy*, Vol. 9, No. 5. http://www.podnetwork.org/publications/teachingexcellence/97-98/V9,%20N5%20Duch.pdf [Accessed 10 February 2013].

Dunne, E. & R. Zandstra (2011). *Students as change agents - new ways of engaging with learning and teaching in higher education.* Bristol: A joint University of Exeter/ESCalate/Higher Education Academy Publication. http://escalate.ac.uk/8064 [Accessed 3 September 2012].

Elliot, A. J., & M. A. Church (1997). A hierarchical model of approach and avoidance achievement motivation. *Journal of Personality and Social Psychology*, Vol. 72, pp. 218-232.

Fielding, M. (2011). Student Voice and the Possibility of Radical Democratic Education: Re-Narrating Forgotten Histories, Developing Alternative Futures. In Czerniawski, G. & W. Kidd. (Eds.). *The Student Voice Handbook: Bridging the Academic/Practitioner Divide.* Bingley: Emerald Group Publishing, pp. 3-17.

Foster, H. (2004). An Archival Impulse. *October*, Vol. 110, pp. 3-22.

Foucault, M. (2000). Truth and Power. In P. Rabinow (Ed.) *Essential Works of Foucault 1954–1984.* New York: The New Press.

Fredricks, J. A., P. C. Blumenfeld, & A. H. Paris (2004). School Engagement: Potential of the Concept, State of the Evidence. *Review of Educational Research Journal*, Vol. 29, No. 2, pp. 59-109.

Freire, P. (1970, 1993, 1996). *Pedagogy of the Oppressed.* London: Penguin.

French, J. R. P. & B. Raven (1959). Sources of Social Power. Reproduced in: Asherman, I. G. & S. V. Asherman (2001). *The Negotiation Sourcebook.* (2nd Ed.). Amherst, MA: Human Resource Development Press.

Gatfield, T. (2005). An investigation into PhD supervisory management styles: Development of a dynamic conceptual model and its management. *Journal of Higher Education Policy and Management*, Vol. 27, No. 3, pp. 311-325.

Gerosa, M. A., M. G. Pimentel, H. Fuks & C. J. P. Lucena (2005). *No need to read messages right now: helping mediators to steer educational forums using statistical and visual information.* In Stahl, G. & D. Suthers (Eds.). *Proceedings of computer supported collabative learning.* New Jersey: Lawrence Erlbaum Associates, pp. 160-169.

Gibbs, G. (1988). *Learning by Doing: A guide to teaching and learning methods.* Oxford: Oxford Polytechnic Further Education Unit.

Gibbs, G. (1992). *Improving the quality of student learning.* Bristol: Technical and Educational Services Ltd.

Gibbs, G. (2010). Dimensions of quality. York: The Higher Education Academy http://www.heacademy.ac.uk/assets/documents/evidence_informed_practice/Dimensions_of_Quality.pdf [Accessed 18 October 2012].

Gibbs, G. (2012). *Implications of 'Dimensions of quality' in a market environment.* York: The Higher Education Academy.

Giddens, J., L. Fogg, & L. Carlson-Sabelli (2010). Learning and engagement with a virtual community by undergraduate nursing students. *Nursing Outlook,* Vol. 58, No. 5, pp. 261 – 267.

Goodenow, C. (1993). Classroom belonging among early adolescent students; Relationships to motivation and achievement. *Journal of Early Adolescence,* Vol. 13, No. 1, pp. 21-43.

Goodyear, P. (1999). Pedagogical frameworks and action research in open and distance learning. *European Journal of Open and Distance Learning.* http://www.eurodl.org/materials/contrib/1999/goodyear/ [Accessed 14 February 2013].

Graduate Employability (2012). *Graduate Employability 2012: Improving Understanding amongst Students, Institutions, Business; Avoiding 'Generation Crunch.'* Conference. Westminster Studio: London. 29 February 2012.

Grattan, J., & B. Meakin (2012). University View 11th October 2012. http://www.walesonline.co.uk/news/education-news/2012/10/11/as-much-as-a-good-library-is-at-the-core-of-a-university-a-vibrant-students-union-is-at-the-heart-of-an-excellent-student-experience-91466-32008378/ [Accessed online 25 October 2012].

Gray, C. & J. Marlins (2004). *Visualizing Research: a guide to the research process in Art and Design.* Aldershot: Ashgate.

Greatrix, P. (2012). Working with, not against. *Times Higher Education* 15th March. http://www.timeshighereducation.co.uk/story.asp?storycode=419348 [Accessed 3 September 2012].

Grosjean, G. (2012). Still Active after All These Years: Lifelong Engagement with Learning. In Solomonides, I., A. Reid & P. Petocz (Eds.). *Engaging with Learning in Higher Education*. Faringdon, Oxfordshire: Libri Publishing Ltd., pp. 279-296.

Guardian, The (2012). University Guide 2013: League Table for Media Studies, Communications and Librarianship. http://www.guardian.co.uk/education/table/2012/may/22/university-guide-media-studies-communications-librarianship [Accessed 14 August 2012].

Hardy, C. & C. Bryson (2010). Student Engagement: Paradigm Change or Political Expediency? http://www.adm.heacademy.ac.uk/resources/features/student-engagement-paradigm-change-or-political-expediency [Accessed 18 October 2012].

Harper, S. (2006). *Principles for good practice in graduate and professional student engagement*. Pennsylvania: Selected Works.

Harper, S. R. & A. L. Antonio (2008). Not by Accident: Intentionality in Diversity, Learning and Engagement. In Harper, S.R. (Ed.) *Creating Inclusive Environments for Cross-Cultural Learning and Student Engagement*. Washington DC: NASPA, pp. 1-18.

Harper, S. R. & S. J. Quaye (2009). Beyond Sameness, with Engagement and Outcomes for All. In *Student Engagement in Higher Education. Theoretical perspectives and Practical Approaches for Diverse Populations*. New York and London: Routledge, pp. 1-15.

Harrison, A, (2012). University tuition fees 'affecting applications' says panel. *BBC News Online*. http://www.bbc.co.uk/news/education-19182000 [Accessed 9 August 2012].

Harte, D. & V. Jackson (2011). Media Employability 2.0. *Media Education Research Journal*, Vol. 2, No. 2, pp. 42-56.

Harvey, L. (1996). Transforming Higher Education: Students as key stakeholders. *Conference 'Quality Assurance as a Support for Processes of Innovation, Castle of Lejondal, Sweden, 10-11 September 1996*. http://www0.bcu.ac.uk/crq/publications/leondahl.pdf [Accessed 15 February 2013].

Hawk, T. F., & P. R. Lyons (2008). Please don't give up on me: when faculty fail to care. *Journal of Management Education*, Vol. 32, No. 3, pp. 316-338.

Hay, J. (2009). *Transactional Analysis for Trainers*. Watford: Sherwood Publishing.

HEA (2012a). Student Engagement Dimensions http://www.heacademy.ac.uk/resources/detail/studentengagement/Dimensions_student_engagement [Accessed 18th October 2012].

HEA (2012b). Students as partners: http://www.heacademy.ac.uk/resources/detail/change/SAP_CP [Accessed 18th October 2012].

Healy, P. (1992). Planning Through Debate: The Communicative Turn in Planning Theory. *Town Planning Review*, Vol. 63, No. 2, pp. 143-162.

Higher Education Funding Council for England (HEFCE) (2008). *Tender for a Study into Student Engagement*. Bristol: HEFCE.

Hobbs, R. & A. Jensen (2009). The past, present, and future of media literacy education. *Journal of Media Literary Education*, Vol. 1, pp. 1-11.

Holden, M. (2008). Social learning in planning: Seattle's sustainable development codebooks. *Progress in Planning*, Vol. 69, No. 1, pp. 1–40.

Hooks, B. (1994). *Teaching to Transgress: Education as the Practice of Freedom*. New York: Routledge.

Huxham, C. & S. Vangen (2005). *Managing to collaborate: The theory and practice of collaborative advantage*. London: Routledge.

Ipsos Mori (2007). Student Expectations Study, Joint Information Systems Committee (JISC). http://www.jisc.ac.uk/publications/research/2008/greatexpectations.aspx [Accessed 28 August 2012].

Ishaq, A. (2007). *Have accepted methods of community participation been effective in the delivery of area based regeneration initiatives?* Unpublished dissertation submitted for the MA in Spatial Planning, Birmingham City University.

Jackson, R., J. Karp, E. Patrick & A. Thrower (2006). Social Constructivism Vignette. http://projects.coe.uga.edu/epltt/index.php?title=Social_Constructivism [Accessed 14 February 2103].

Janes, G. (2006). Addressing the learning needs of multidisciplinary students at a distance using a virtual learning experience (VLE): A novice teacher reflects. *Nurse Education in Practice*, Vol. 6, No. 2, pp. 87-97.

Jessop, A. (2011). Student Academic Partners Programme. *Is there a public interest in higher education? QAA Annual Conference*. University of Nottingham. 30 June 2011.

JISC (2009). Higher education in a web 2.0 world: Report of an independent committee of Inquiry into the impact on higher education of students' widespread use of web 2.0 technologies. http://www.jisc.ac.uk/publications/generalpublications/2009/heweb2.aspx [Accessed 28 August 2012].

Johansen, R. (2007). *Get There Early: Sensing the Future to Compete in the Present*. San Francisco: Berrett-Koehler Publishers Inc.

Kantek, F. & N. Gezer (2008). Faculty members' use of power: midwifery students' perceptions and expectations. *Midwifery*, Vol. 26, pp. 475-479.

Karman, T. A. & M. D. Weber (1991). Student group approach to teaching using Tuckman model of group development. *American Journal of Physiology*, Vol. 261, pp. S12-S16.

Kay, J., E. Dunne & J. Hutchinson (2010). Rethinking the values of higher education - students as change agents? http://www.qaa.ac.uk/Publications/InformationAndGuidance/Documents/StudentsChangeAgents.pdf [Accessed 13 February 2013].

Kay, J., D. Owen & E. Dunne (2012). Students as change agents; student engagement with quality enhancement of learning and teaching In Solomonides, I., A. Reid, P. Petocz *Engaging with learning in Higher Education*. Faringdon, Oxfordshire: Libri Publishing Ltd., pp. 359-380.

Kember, D. (2001). *Reflective Teaching and Learning in the Health Professions*. Oxford: Blackwell Science.

Kirkpatrick, D. (1983). Four Steps to Measuring Training Effectiveness. *Personal Administrator*, Vol. 28, No. 11, pp. 19-25.

Knowles, M. (1975). *Self-directed Learning: A Guide for Learners and Teachers*. New York: Cambridge Book Co.

Knowles, M. (1984). *Andragogy in Action: Applying Modern Principles of Adult Learning*. San Francisco: Jossey-Bass.

Kolb, D. A. (1984). *Experiential learning: experience as the source of learning and development*. New Jersey: Prentice Hall.

Krapp, A., S. Hidi & K. A. Renninger (1992). Interest, learning and development. In Linnenbrink, E. A. & P. R. Pintrich (2002). Motivation as an Enabler for Academic Success. *School Psychology Review*, Vol. 31, No. 3, pp. 313-327.

Krause, K. (2005). Understanding and Promoting Student Engagement in University Learning Communities. *Paper presented as keynote address: Engaged, Inert or Otherwise Occupied? Deconstructing the 21st Century Undergraduate Student. James Cook University Symposium 'Sharing Scholarship in Learning and Teaching: Engaging Students'. James Cook University, Townsville, Cairns, Queensland, Australia, 21-22 September 2005.* http://learningspaces.edu.au/herg/assets/resources/StudengKrause.pdf [Accessed 16 February 2013].

Krause, K. & L. Coates (2008). Students' Engagement in First Year University. *Assessment and Evaluation in Higher Education*, Vol. 33, No. 5, pp. 493-505.

Kuh, G. D. (2003). What we're learning about student engagement from NSSE: Benchmarks for effective educational practices. *Change*, Vol. 35, No. 2, pp. 24-32.

Kuh, G. D. (2007). How to Help Students Achieve. *The Chronicle of Higher Education*, Vol. 53, No. 41, pp. 12-13.

Kuh, G. D. (2009). What Student Affairs Professionals need to know about Student Engagement. *Journal of College Student Development*, Vol. 50, No. 6, pp. 683-706.

Kuh, G. D. & S.Hu (2001). The Effects of Student-Faculty Interaction in the 1990s. *Review of Higher Education. Association for the Study of Higher Education*, Vol. 23, No. 3, pp. 309-332.

Kumar, A. (2009). Using Assessment Centre Approaches to Improve Student Learning. In Nygaard, C., C. Holtham & N. Courtney (Eds.) *Improving Students' Learning Outcomes*, Frederiksberg: Copenhagen Business School Press, pp. 205-224.

Lange, S. (2010). Learning through Creative Conversations. In Nygaard, C., N. Courtney & C. Holtham (Eds.) *Teaching Creativity – Creativity in Teaching*. Faringdon, Oxfordshire: Libri Publishing Ltd., pp. 173-188.

Leadbeater, C. (2008). *We-Think*. London: Profile Books.

Lefever, R. & B. Currant (2010). How can technology be used to improve the learner experience at points of transition? University of Bradford: http://technologyenhancedlearning.net/files/2010/04/ELESIGliteraturereviewFINAL240210.pdf [Accessed 30 April 2012].

Levesque, C., K. Copeland, M. Pattie & E. Deci (2011). In Jarvela, S (Ed.), *Social and Emotional Aspects of Learning*. Amsterdam: Elsevier, pp. 15-21.

Linnenbrink, E. A. & P. R. Pintrich (2002). Motivation as an Enabler for Academic Success. *School Psychology Review*, Vol. 31, No. 3, pp. 313-327.

Little, B., W. Locke, A. Scesa & R. Williams (2009). *Report to HEFCE on student engagement*. Centre for Higher Education Research and Information (CHERI), The Open University. http://oro.open.ac.uk/15281/1/Report_to_HEFCE_on_student_engagement.pdf [Accessed 11 February 2013].

Lizzio, A. & K. Wilson (2009). Student participation in university governance: the role conceptions and sense of efficacy of student representatives on departmental committees. *Studies in Higher Education*, Vol. 34, No.1, pp. 69-84.

Löfvall, S. & C. Nygaard (2012). Interrelationships between student culture, teaching and learning in higher education. In Nygaard, C., J. D. Branch & C. Holtham (2012), *Learning in Higher Education – contemporary standpoints*. Faringdon, Oxfordshire: Libri Publishing Ltd.

Lowden, K., S. Hall, D. Elliot & J. Lewin (2011). *Employers' perceptions of the employability skills of new graduates*, London: Edge Foundation.

Luescher-Mamashela, T. M. (2011). Student involvement in university decision-making: Good reasons, a new lens. *International Journal of Leadership in Education*, Emerging Scholar Manuscript Competition – Finalist Award Paper.

Madge, C., J. Meek, J. Wellens & T. Hooley (2009). Facebook social integration and informal learning at university: 'It is more for socialising and talking to friends than for actually doing work'. *Learning, Media and Technology*, Vol. 34, No. 2, pp. 141-155.

Markham, L. & J. Chui (2011). Exposing operations of power in supervisory relationships. *Family process*, Vol. 20, No. 4, pp. 503-515.

Markwell, D. (2007). The Challenge of Student Engagement. *Keynote address at the Teaching and Learning Forum. University of Western Australia, 30-31 January.*

Martin, A. J. (2006). Enhancing student motivation and engagement: The effects of a multidimensional intervention. *Contemporary Educational Psychology*, Vol. 33, No. 2, pp. 239-269.

Marton, F. & R. Säljö (2005). Approaches to learning. In Marton, F., D. Hounsell & N. Entwistle (Eds.). *The experience of learning.* Edinburgh: University of Edinburgh, Centre for Teaching, Learning and Assessment, pp. 39-58.

Mathiasen, H. (2008). Is there a Nexus between Learning and Teaching? – Communication as a Facilitator of Students' Knowledge Construction. In Nygaard, C. & C. Holtham. (Eds.). *Understanding Learning-Centred Higher Education.* Frederiksberg: Copenhagen Business School Press, pp. 111-129.

May, H. & K. Bridger (2010). *Developing and embedding inclusive policy and practice in higher education.* York: Higher Education Academy.

McAllister, L. (1997). An adult learning framework for clinical education. In: McAllister, L., M. Lincoln, S. McLeod & D. Maloney, (Eds.) *Facilitating learning in clinical settings.* Cheltenham: Nelson Thomas, pp. 1-26.

McAllister, L. (2001). The experience of being a clinical educator. Unpublished PhD thesis, University of Sydney. Cited in: McAllister, L. & M. Lincoln (2004). *Clinical Education in Speech and Language Pathology. Methods in Speech and Language Pathology Series.* London: Whurr Publishers Ltd.

McAllister, L. & M. Lincoln (2004). *Clinical Education in Speech and Language Pathology. Methods in Speech and Language Pathology Series.* London: Whurr Publishers Ltd.

McAndrew, P. (2010). Defining openness: updating the concept of "open" for a connected world. *Journal of Interactive Media in Education*, Vol. 2010, No. 10, pp. 1-13.

McCulloch, A. (2009). The student as co-producer: learning from public administration about the student university relationship, *Studies in Higher Education*, Vol. 34, No. 2, pp. 171-183.

Merewether, C. (Ed.) (2006). *The Archive: Documents of contemporary art.* London: Whitechapel.

Merrill, B. (2001). Learning and Teaching in Universities: Perspectives from adult learners and lecturers. *Teaching in Higher Education*, Vol. 6, No. 1, pp. 5-17.

Mezirow, J. (1997). Transformative Learning: Theory to Practice. *New Directions for Adult and Continuing Education*, Vol. 74, pp. 5-12.

Mezirow, J. & E. Taylor (2009). *Transformative Learning in Practice – Insights from Community, Workplace and Higher Education.* San Francisco: Jossey–Bass.

Miltiadou, M. & W. Savenye (2003). Applying Social Cognitive Constructs of Motivation to Enhance Student Success in Online Education. *Association for the Advancement of Computing in Education*, Vol. 11, No. 1, pp. 78-95. http://aace.org/pubs/etr/issue4/militadou.cfm/ [Accessed 10 July 2012].

Moreau, M-P. & C. Leathwood (2007). Balancing paid work and studies: working (-class) students in higher education. *Studies in Higher Education*, Vol. 31, No. 1, pp. 23-42.

Morgan, M. (2012). *Improving the Student Experience: a Practical Guide for Universities and Colleges.* London: Routledge.

Mortiboys, A. (2010). *How to Be an Effective Teacher in Higher Education.* Maidenhead: Open University Press.

Mortiboys, A. (2011). *Teaching with Emotional Intelligence.* London: Routledge.

Moxley, D., A. Najor-Durack & C. Dumbrigue (2001). *Keeping Students in Higher Education.* London: Kogan Page.

Namwar, Y. & A. Rastgoo (2008). Weblog as a Learning Tool in Higher Education. *Turkish Online Journal of Distance Education*, Vol. 9, No. 3, pp. 176-185.

Neary, M. (2009). *Student as producer: Risk, responsibility and rich learning environments.* Proceedings of the Centre for Learning and Teaching Conference 2008. www.brighton.ac.uk/clt/index.php/download_file/view/107/179/ [Accessed 14 February 2013].

Neelands, J. (2006). Re-imaging the Reflective Practitioner: towards a philosophy of critical praxis. In Ackroyd, J. (Ed.) *Research methodologies for drama education*, pp. 15-39. Stoke on Trent, UK: Trentham Books.

Nicholson, H. (2005). *Applied drama: the gift of theatre*. New York: Palgrave Macmillan.

NSSE. National Survey of Student Engagement (2009). *Assessment for improvement: Tracking student engagement over time—annual results 2009*. Bloomington: Indiana University Center for Postsecondary Research.

NUS (2012). A Manifesto for Partnership. http://www.nusconnect.org.uk/resourcehandler/0a02e2e5-197e-4bd3-b7ed-e8ceff3dc0e4/ [Accessed February 11 2013].

NUS & QAA (2012a). *Student Experience Research 2012. Part 1: Teaching and Learning*. National Union of Students and the Quality Assurance Agency.

NUS & QAA (2012b). *Understanding the barriers to student engagement, pp. 11*. National Union of Students and the Quality Assurance Agency.

Nygaard, C. & D. Z. Belluigi (2011). A proposed methodology for contextualised evaluation in higher education. *Assessment & Evaluation in Higher Education*, Vol. 36 No. 6, pp. 657-671.

Nygaard, C., N. Courtney & C. Holtham (Eds.) (2010). *Teaching Creativity – Creativity in Teaching*. Faringdon, Oxfordshire: Libri Publishing Ltd.

Nygaard, C., N. Courtney & C. Holtham (Eds.) (2011). *Beyond Transmission: Innovations in University Teaching*. Faringdon, Oxfordshire: Libri Publishing Ltd.

Oliver, J. (2011). Sheffield University's Student-Led Academic Awards. *Is there a public interest in higher education? QAA Annual Conference*. University of Nottingham. 30 June 2011.

Oliver, M. (2008). e-Learning Engagement and Student Retention. *Proceedings from the Making Connections Conference 2008*. http://mancons2.middlesex.wikispaces.net/Conference+Schedule [Accessed 28 August 2012].

Ostergren, J. A. (2011). The first year of professional service in Speech-Language Pathology: Supervisory role, working relationships and satisfaction with supervision. *Contemporary issues in Communication Science and Disorders*, Vol. 38, pp. 61-75.

Otter, S. (1992). *Learning Outcomes in Higher Education. A Development Project Report*. London: Unit for the Development of Adult Continuing Education.

Page, R. (2009). Facebook as a Pre-Induction Support Tool. In: *Effective use of Social Software in UK Further and Higher Education: Case Studies (JISC Paper)*. http://tinyurl.com/5a8zu31 [Accessed 30 April 2012].

Palmer, E. (2009). Using appreciative advising with international students. *The Mentor*. http://dus.psu.edu/mentor/old/articles/090909ep.htm [Accessed 10 July 2012].

Papadimitriou, A. (2009). Improving Students' Learning Outcomes via Teamwork & Portfolios. In Nygaard, C., C. Holtham & N. Courtney (Eds.) *Improving Students' Learning Outcomes*, Frederiksberg: Copenhagen Business School Press, pp. 191-203.

Pintrich, R. R. & E. V. DeGroot (1990). Motivational and self-regulated learning components of classroom academic performance. *Journal of Educational Psychology*, Vol. 82, pp. 33-40.

Prendergast, M. & J. Saxton (2009). *Applied Theatre: International Case Studies and Challenges for Practice*. Bristol: Intellect.

Prensky, M. (2001). Digital Natives, Digital Immigrants Part 1. *On the Horizon*, Vol. 9, No. 5, pp. 1-6.

Prensky, M. (2011). Digital Wisdom and Homo Sapiens Digital. In: Thomas, M. (Ed.) *Deconstructing Digital Natives: Young People, Technology, and the New Literacies*. New York: Routledge, pp. 15-27.

QAA (2009). Rethinking the values of higher education – consumption, partnership, community? http://www.qaa.ac.uk/Publications/InformationAndGuidance/Documents/Rethinking.pdf [Accessed 11 February 2013].

QAA (2011). Is there a public interest in higher education? *QAA Annual Conference*. http://www.qaa.ac.uk/Newsroom/Events/Pages/annual-conference-2011.aspx [Accessed 14 February 2013].

Quality Assurance Agency for Higher Education (2012). UK Quality Code for Higher Education, Part B: Assuring and enhancing academic quality. Chapter B5: *Student Engagement*. http://www.qaa.ac.uk/publications/informationandguidance/pages/quality-code-B5.aspx [Accessed 18 November 2012].

Räihä, P., M. Mäenisvu, M. Rautiainen & T. Nikkola (2011). The Sequence of Educational Innovation from University to Working Life. In Nygaard, C., N. Courtney & C. Holtham (Eds.) *Beyond Transmission-Innovations in University Teaching*. Faringdon, Oxfordshire: Libri Publishing Ltd., pp. 63-76.

Ramsden, P. (1992). *Learning to Teach in Higher Education*. London: Routledge.

Ramsden, P. (2003). *Learning to teach in higher education*. London: Routledge Falmer.

Ramsden, P. & D. Beswick & J. Bowden (1989). Effects of Learning Skills Intervention on First Year Students' Learning. *Human Learning*, Vol. 5, pp. 151-164.

Rao, M. S. (2010). *Soft Skill Enhancing Employability – Connecting Campus with Corporate*. New Delhi: I K International Publishing House.

Reason, P. & H. Bradbury (Eds.) (2008). *The SAGE Handbook of Action Research: Participative Inquiry and Practice*. [2nd Ed]. London: Sage.

Reid, A. & P. Petocz (2008). A Tertiary Curriculum for Future Professionals. In Nygaard, C. & C. Holtham. (Eds.). *Understanding Learning-Centred Higher Education*. Frederiksberg: Copenhagen Business School Press, pp. 31-49.

Reid, E. & I. Solomonides (2012). Student Engagement with Capability Development. In Solomonides, I., A. Reid & P. Petocz (Eds.). *Engaging with Learning in Higher Education*. Faringdon, Oxfordshire: Libri Publishing Ltd., pp. 145-166.

Rice, C. J. (2001). Teacher's level of care. *Education*, Vol. 122, No. 1, pp. 102-106.

Riley, T. & P. Hawe (2004). Researching Practice: the methodological case for narrative enquiry. *Health Education Research*, Vol. 2, No. 2, pp. 226-236.

Robinson, C. (2012). Student engagement: What does this mean in practice in the context of Higher Education Institutions? *Journal of Applied Research in Higher Education*, Vol. 4, No. 2, pp. 1-15.

Rowley, J. (2011). Innovation and Student Learning: ePortfolios for Music Education. In Nygaard, C., N. Courtney & C. Holtham (Eds.) *Beyond Transmission-Innovations in University Teaching*. Faringdon, Oxfordshire: Libri Publishing Ltd., pp. 45-61.

RTPI (2004). *Policy Statement on Initial Planning Education*. London: Royal Town Planning Institute.

RTPI (2012). *Preparing your APC submission*. London: Royal Town Planning Institute.

Rush, L. & S. Balamoutsou (2006). Dominant Voices, Silent Voices and the Use of Action Learning Groups in HE: A Social Constructionist Perspective. Paper presented at the British Educational Research Association Annual Conference, University of Warwick, 6–9 September In Trowler, V. (2010) *Student Engagement Literature Review*. York: The Higher Education Academy.

Samways, A. & C. Seal (2011). From Ethos to Practice – Pupil Voice at the Sweyne Park School. In Czerniawski, G. & W. Kidd. (Eds.). *The Student Voice Handbook: Bridging the Academic/Practitioner Divide*. Bingley: Emerald Group Publishing, pp. 133-141.

Schlechty, P. (2011). *Engaging students: The next level of working on the work.* San Francisco, CA: Jossey-Bass.

Schön, D. (1983). *The Reflective Practitioner: How Professionals Think in Action.* New York: Basic Books.

Schön, D. A. (1987). *Educating the reflective practitioner.* San Francisco: Jossey-Bass.

Schratz, M. & U. Blossing (2005). Big Change Question: Should pupils be able to make decisions about school change? *Journal of Educational Change,* Vol. 6, pp. 381-393.

Schunk, D. H. (2011). *Learning Theories: An Educational Perspective.* London: Pearson.

Scott, P. (2011). 'A Double Paradigm Shift? Transforming higher education systems – and research practices'. *Keynote presented at the 4th UK and Ireland Institutional Research Conference. Kingston University, 16-17 June, 2011.* http://www.heir2011.org.uk/programme/keynotes/peter_scott.php [Accessed 13 February 2013].

Seaford, C., L. Stoll & L. Coffait (2011). What should higher education be for? In Coffait, L. (Ed.) *Blue Skies; new thinking about the future of higher education.* London: Pearson Centre for Policy and Learning.

Shulman, L. (1987). Knowledge and teaching: Foundations of the new reform. *Harvard Educational Review,* Vol. 57, No. 1, pp. 1-22.

Skillset (2009). *2008 Creative Media Workforce Survey.* London: Creative Skillset.

Skinner, E. J. & M. J. Belmont (1993). Motivation in the Classroom: Reciprocal Effects of Teacher Behaviour and Student Engagement across the School Year. *Journal of Educational Psychology,* Vol. 85, No. 4, pp. 571-581.

SLTN (2012). http://studentlandtnetwork.ning.com/ [Accessed 18th October 2012].

Smith, K. A., S. D. Sheppard, D. W. Johnson & R. T. Johnson (2005). Pedagogies of engagement: Classroom-based practices. *Journal of Engineering Education,* Vol. 94, No. 1, pp. 87-101.

Smith, H. & R. T. Dean (2009). *Practice-led Research, Research-led Practice in the Creative Arts.* Edinburgh: Edinburgh University Press.

Solomonides, I., A. Reid & P. Petocz (Eds.) (2012). *Engaging with Learning in Higher Education.* Faringdon, Oxfordshire: Libri Publishing Ltd.

Streeting, W. & G. Wise (2009). *Rethinking the values of higher education - consumption, partnership, community?* Gloucester: Quality Assurance Agency for Higher Education.

Stuart, M. (2011). Responding to the Public Interest; are we doing enough? Is there a public interest in higher education? http://www.qaa.ac.uk/Newsroom/Events/Pages/annual-conference-2011.aspx [Accessed 14 February 2013].

Sullivan, G. (2009). *Art Practice as Research – Inquiry in the Visual Arts.* California: Sage Publications Ltd.

Tapscott, D. (1998). *Growing up digital: the rise of the Net generation,* New York, London: McGraw-Hill.

Taylor, P. & D. Wilding (2009). *Rethinking the values of higher education – the student as collaborator and producer? Undergraduate research as a case study.* Gloucester: Quality Assurance Agency for Higher Education, pp. 1-8.

The Research Intelligence Group (TRiG) (2012). Attorney Selection Research Study. http://press-room.lawyers.com/LexisNexis-Consumer-Focused-Attorney-Selection-Research-Study.html [Accessed 13 February 2013].

Thomas, H. (2012). Enhancing the Student Learning Experience. *Spotlight on Students' Union Excellence – The Collaboration Edition. April, pp. 23.* http://www.nusconnect.org.uk/news/article/nus/Helen-Thomas-column-enhancing-the-student-learning-experience/ [Accessed 16 February 2013].

Thomas, L. (2012). Building student and engagement and belonging in higher education at a time of change: final report from the What Works? Student Retention and Success programme. www.heacademy.ac.uk/assets/documents/retention/What_works_final_report.pdf [Accessed 18 October 2012].

Thompson, J. & A. Jackson (2006). Applied theatre/Drama: An e-debate in 2004: Viewpoints. RIDE: *Research in Drama and Education,* Vol. 11, No. 1, pp. 90-95.

Toker, A., J. Urkin & Y. Bloch (2002). Role of a medical students' association in improving the curriculum at a faculty of health sciences. *Medical Teacher,* Vol. 24, No. 6, pp. 634-636.

Trowler, V. (2010). Student Engagement Literature Review. York: The Higher Education Academy. http://www.heacademy.ac.uk/assets/documents/studentengagement/StudentEngagementLiteratureReview.pdf [Accessed 13 February 2013].

Trowler, V. & P. Trowler (2010a). *Student engagement evidence summary.* York: The Higher Education Academy.

Trowler, V. & P. Trowler (2010b). *Framework for Action: Enhancing Student Engagement at Intuitional Level.* York: The Higher Education Academy.

Trowler, V. & P. Trowler (2011). *Student Engagement Toolkit for Leaders.* Leadership Foundation for Higher Education. http://eprints.lancs.

ac.uk/61685/1/Deliverable_3_Student_Engagement_toolkit_for_leaders. pdf [Accessed 14 February 2013].

Trowler, P. & T. Wareham (2008). *Tribes, Territories, Research and Teaching: Enhancing the Teaching-Research Nexus.* York: Higher Education Academy.

Tunnard, P. (1991). *The learning, teaching and assessment of partnership working in social work education.* http://www.scie.org.uk/publications/ guides/guide23/files/guide23.pdf [Accessed 13 February 2013].

Unistats. (2012). Media Studies. *Unistats: From Universities and Colleges in the UK:* http://unistats.direct.gov.uk/Subjects/ Overview/10007140-US0051-06/ReturnTo/Search [Accessed 14 August 2012].

Universities UK (2012). *Bringing it all Together: Introducing the HEAR.*

Van der Velden, G. (2012). Student engagement: whose education is it anyway? *Talking about quality,* Issue 3. Gloucester: Quality Assurance Agency for Higher Education.

Vickman, P. (2012). Engaging Students in Peer Assessment. *Liverpool John Moores University.* http://www.heacademy.ac.uk/assets/hlst/documents/ case_studies/engaging_students_in_peer_assessment.pdf [Accessed 28 August 2012].

Waite, S., R. Cutting, R. Cook, J. Barnett & M. Opie (2009). Learning Outside the Classroom: Environments for Experiential Enrichment. In Nygaard, C., C. Holtham & N. Courtney (Eds.) *Improving Students' Learning Outcomes,* Frederiksberg: Copenhagen Business School Press, pp. 239-256.

Wenger, E. (1998). *Communities of Practice: Learning, Meaning, and Identity.* Cambridge: Cambridge University Press.

Wenstone, R. (2012). *A Manifesto for Partnership.* National Union of Students. http://www.nusconnect.org.uk/resourcehandler/0a02e2e5-197e-4bd3-b7ed-e8ceff3dc0e4/ [Accessed 12 February 2013].

Whitchurch, C. (2009). The rise of the blended professional in higher education: a comparison between the United Kingdom, Australia and the United States. *Higher Education: the international journal of higher education and education planning,* Vol. 58, No. 3, pp. 407-418.

Whitton, N. (2011). Game engagement theory and adult learning. *Simulation and Gaming,* Vol. 42, No. 5, pp. 596-609.

Wilcox, D. (1994). *The Guide to Effective Participation.* Brighton: Partnership Books.

Wilson, G. (2012). In the hot seat. *Spotlight on Students' Union Excellence – The Collaboration Edition.* April, pp. 25 London: National Union of Students.

Winchester-Seeto, T., A. Bosanquet & A. Rowe (2012). Smoke and Mirrors: Graduate Attributes and the Implications for Student Engagement in Higher Education. In Solomonides, I., A. Reid & P. Petocz (Eds.). *Engaging with Learning in Higher Education.* Faringdon, Oxfordshire: Libri Publishing Ltd., pp. 413-456.

Wisby, E. (2011). Student Voice and New Models of Teacher Professionalism. In Czerniawski, G. & W. Kidd. (Eds.). *The Student Voice Handbook: Bridging the Academic/Practitioner Divide.* Bingley: Emerald Group Publishing, pp. 31-44.